CW00550137

LONDON

A Fourteenth-Century
City and Its People

This book is dedicated with sincere love and affection to my dear friends Dave and Lainey Simpson, two of the bravest and most awesome people I know.

LONDON

A Fourteenth-Century City and Its People

Kathryn Warner

PEN & SWORD
HISTORY

AN IMPRINT OF PEN & SWORD BOOKS LTD.
YORKSHIRE – PHILADELPHIA

First published in Great Britain in 2022 by
PEN AND SWORD HISTORY
An imprint of
Pen & Sword Books Ltd
Yorkshire – Philadelphia

ISBN 978 1 52677 637 2

Typeset in Times New Roman 11.5/14 by
SJmagic DESIGN SERVICES, India.

Printed and bound by CPI Group (UK) Ltd, Croydon, CR0 4YY

Pen & Sword Books Limited incorporates the imprints of Atlas, Archaeology,
Aviation, Discovery, Family History, Fiction, History, Maritime, Military, Military
Classics, Politics, Select, Transport, True Crime, Air World, Frontline Publishing,
Leo Cooper, Remember When, Seaforth Publishing, The Praetorian Press,
Wharncliffe Local History, Wharncliffe Transport, Wharncliffe True Crime and
White Owl.

For a complete list of Pen & Sword titles please contact
PEN & SWORD BOOKS LIMITED
47 Church Street, Barnsley, South Yorkshire, S70 2AS, England
E-mail: enquiries@pen-and-sword.co.uk
Website: www.pen-and-sword.co.uk

Or
PEN AND SWORD BOOKS
1950 Lawrence Rd, Havertown, PA 19083, USA
E-mail: Uspen-and-sword@casematepublishers.com
Website: www.penandswordbooks.com

Contents

Glossary

Al(e)may(g)ne: Germany (modern French *Allemagne*).

Alemaund: German (modern French *Allemand*).

Bakstere: female baker (modern surname 'Baxter').

Bedel: beadle, an official responsible for keeping order.

Belringere: bell-ringer.

Blader: cornmonger (modern French *blé*, 'corn').

Boteler/botiller: butler, i.e. cup-bearer or bottle-maker.

Botoner: maker or seller of buttons; also used more generally for a person in the cloth trade.

Bowyer(e): maker or seller of archers' bows.

Bredmongestere: female bread-seller.

Brewstere, brewyfe: female brewer of ale.

Bureller: maker of burel, a coarse woollen cloth.

Callere: maker or seller of head-dresses.

Callestere: female *callere*.

Cambestere: either a female maker or seller of combs, or a woman who disentangled wool or flax with a comb.

Capper(e): maker or seller of caps.

Cardemakere: maker of toothed instruments for carding wool.

Ceynturer: belt-maker (modern French *ceinture*, 'belt').

Chapeler: hat-maker (modern French *chapeau*, 'hat').

Chaucer/chausier: shoe-maker (modern French *chaussures*, 'shoes').

Chandler/chaundel(l)er: candle-maker.

Coff(e)rer: maker or seller of coffers or chests.

Corder: maker of cord or string.

Cordwainer: maker of leather shoes.

Coster: seller of costard apples, which are the second-oldest known English apple after pearmains, first mentioned in 1292.

Cotel(l)er/cotiller: cutler, i.e. maker, seller or repairer of knives and blades.

Cotellerie: the trade of a cutler.

Coupere/coupper: cooper, i.e. maker, seller or repairer of wooden casks and barrels.

Cu/keu: a cook (modern French *cuire*, 'to cook').

Currier: person who prepared tanned leather for saddles, gloves etc.

Cutpurse: thief.

Deodand: Latin for 'gift to God'. In cases of death by misadventure, it was a fine paid to the king, to the value of the object which caused the accident.

Diere/dieghere: dyer.

Draper: seller of cloth.

Fannere: perhaps a maker or seller of fans.

Faytour: cheat, impostor, conman.

Felmongere: seller of hides or skins.

Fletcher: person who attached feathers ('fletches') to arrows.

Fruter(e): fruit-seller.

Frutestere: female fruit-seller.

Fuller(e): person who fulled cloth, i.e. cleaned, shrunk and thickened it.

F(o)urbour: furbisher, person who finished or polished bladed weapons.

(le) Fraunceys: Frenchman; *Français* in modern French.

(la) Fraunceyse: Frenchwoman; *Française* in modern French.

Fuster: saddle-frame maker.

Gaunter: glover (modern French *gants*, 'gloves').

Girdler: maker of girdles.

Glaswreghte: glass-maker.

Goldbetere: person who beat gold into gold leaf for gilding.

Heaumer: helmet-maker.

Ho(d)der(e): hood-maker.

Hokester(e)/hukstere: pedlar or hawker, usually female.

Holer: adulterer.

Hosier: maker or seller of hose or stockings.

Hostelere: hosteller, innkeeper; also called *haubergere* (modern French *auberge*, 'hostel').

Hue and cry: Anyone who saw that a crime had been or was being committed had to make a noise to alert anyone in the vicinity.

Ismongere: ironmonger.

Kisser(e): Possibly a maker of armour for the thighs (modern French *cuisse*, 'thigh'), or a leather-dealer.

Lacer: lace-maker.

Latimer: interpreter; person who understood Latin.

Latoner: person who worked with laton or latten, an alloy similar to brass.

Lavendere: laundress.

Lorimer: maker of small metal objects, e.g. for horses' harnesses; divided into *copresmythes* (coppersmiths) and *irensmythes* (ironsmiths).

Luter: lute-player.

Marberer: person who worked with marble.

Mazer: drinking vessel made of wood, usually maple-wood.

Mazerer/mazeliner: person who carved mazers.

Mercer: dealer in textile fabrics, especially expensive ones.

Mistery: guild of craftsmen or tradesmen; from the Italian *mestiere*, 'trade'.

Nakerer: minstrel who played a naker, i.e. a kettle-drum.

Nedelere: maker or seller of needles.

Neylere: maker or seller of nails.

Nightwalker: someone who was outside after curfew.

None: the ninth hour; roughly 3.00pm or mid-afternoon.

Oistremongere: oyster-seller.

Pain demaign: the finest and most expensive white bread (*pain* means 'bread' in French).

Palmer(e)/paumer: pilgrim; person who had travelled to the Holy Land.

Paternostrer: person who made rosaries and paternosters, i.e. strings of prayer beads.

Peautrer: person who made objects of pewter.

Pepperer: person who imported and sold spices.

Peyntour: painter.

Pheliper: fripperer, i.e. dealer in old clothes.

Pikere: pickpocket.

Plastrer: plasterer.

Poscenet: cooking-pot.

Prime: the first hour, about 6.00am.

Pulfrour: pilferer.

Pursere: maker or seller of purses.

Quernbetere: probably someone who carved millstones.

Rakiere: (muck-)raker, person who raked streets or latrines.

Rifflere: robber, plunderer.

Ropere: rope-maker.

Rorere: roarer; a disorderly, often drunk, person.

Salter(e): salt-seller.

Sawiere: sawyer, person who sawed timber.

Selkwyf: 'silk-wife', a seamstress.

Sext: the sixth hour, about midday.

Skinner: person who prepared and sold animal skins.

Solar: upper room of a house reached by ladder or narrow staircase.

Sopere: maker or seller of soap.

Spurrier: maker or seller of spurs for boots.

Stokfisshmongere: seller of dried, unsalted fish.

Tapicer: upholsterer or tapestry-maker.

Tap(pe)stere: female tavern-keeper.

Terce: the third hour, about 9.00am.

Thredwomman: 'thread-woman', seller of thread and yarn.

Tourte: rough brown bread.

Vespers: sunset.

Wagabund: vagabond.

Wastel: the second best kind of white bread.

Webbe: weaver.

Webster(e): female weaver.

Wirdrawere: wire-drawer; person who drew metal out into wire.

Wodemongere: seller of wood.

Wollemongere: seller of wool.

Ymager/ymaginour: image-maker, sculptor.

Money

The silver penny could be cut in half, or in quarters to make a farthing, and was written *d* for *denarius*. Twelve pennies made one shilling (*s*), and 20 shillings made one pound (£), i.e. 240*d*. Another unit of accounting was the mark, which was two-thirds of a pound and consisted of 160*d*, or 13*s* and 4*d*. The average wage for an unskilled male labourer in the early 1300s was around 2*d* a day or about £3 a year, and around 6*d* a day for master craftsmen. The richest man in England until his death in 1322 was Edward I's nephew Thomas, Earl of Lancaster and Leicester, who had a gross income of around £11,000 a year, and Thomas's nephew Henry, Earl of Derby, Lincoln and Leicester and Duke of Lancaster (d. 1361), was even wealthier.

Kings

The kings of England in the relevant period were:

Edward I, reigned 1272 –1307, married Leonor of Castile (d. 1290) then Marguerite of France (d. 1318);

Edward II, son of Edward I and Leonor, r. 1307–27, married Isabella of France (d. 1358);

Edward III, son of Edward II and Isabella, r. 1327–77, married Philippa of Hainault (d. 1369).

Introduction

In 1300, London had a population estimated at around 80,000 people, perhaps 100,000, a number which fell precipitously in the terrible year of 1348/49, when the first pandemic of the Black Death reached the city.[1] In the twenty-first century, its population is approximately 100 times larger. Although tiny by modern standards, London was vastly larger than any other fourteenth-century English town: York and Bristol came next on the list with around 10,000 or 12,000 inhabitants each. London's special place as the largest and richest city in the kingdom was widely recognised. Edward III called it the 'mirror and exemplar of the whole realm' in 1339, and in 1338, the mayor and bailiffs of Oxford wrote to the mayor and sheriffs of London 'offering them the honour and reverence due from a daughter to a mother'.[2] It is interesting to note that both Oxford and London were deemed female; the officials did not write 'from a son to a father'.

We are lucky that numerous sources survive from fourteenth-century London: wills, letter-books, coroners' rolls, records of the Assize of Nuisance, court rolls, plea rolls, royal writs, chancery rolls, and so on. Drawing on these sources and others, this book is a social history focusing on the people of London between 1300 and 1350, and various aspects of their lives. I have used the fourteenth-century spelling of given names and surnames; see Appendix 1 for a list of first names and diminutives. I have also used the original, and frequently inconsistent, spelling of London streets, wards, churches, etc; for a list, see Appendix 2. A list of the mayors of London from 1300 to 1350 can be found in Appendix 3.

Health

William, rector of the church of Seinte Margarete Lotheburi on the boundary of Bradstrete and Colemanestrete wards, evinced an insatiable curiosity about a disease he called *Le Lou*. This means 'The Wolf' in medieval French, and probably referred to the condition we now know as lupus, meaning 'wolf' in Latin. In the belief that wolf flesh could cure the disease, William ordered a cask of four dead wolves from abroad (where abroad was not specified) to be sent to his church. By the time the dead animals arrived in London, their corpses had become 'putrid', and William was hauled before the court of the mayor, Elias Russel, on Tuesday, 5 January 1300. Elias requested the advice of the physicians and surgeons of the city on the matter, and they informed him that they 'could not find in any of their medical or surgical writings any disease against which the flesh of wolves could be used'. When questioned further, William admitted that he did not in fact suffer from the disease called Wolf, nor did he know anyone who did.[1]

William's contemporaries were capable of recognising various ailments and afflictions, though usually not of curing them. The London coroners' rolls survive for a number of years in the fourteenth century (1300–01, 1321–26, 1336–40, and a handful of cases from 1367 to 1378) and illuminate some contemporary beliefs about diseases. One malady was called a *quinsy* and meant an inflammation or swelling of the throat.[2] Richard St Albans died around midday on 7 June 1301 in his workplace, a stable belonging to Reynald Woleward in the parish of Seinte Athelburga without Bisshopesgate. While 'grievously suffering from a *quinsy*', Richard 'fell down and suddenly died of that malady'. The jurors who investigated his death noted that his neck and throat 'appeared large and swollen'. On 3 April 1339 around Vespers, Johan Lynche was walking along the high street of Estsmethefeld 'when by reason of a *quinsy* from which he had long suffered, he fell to the ground and died'. Another disease was known as quartan fever, and William Otford died of it in

1

the house of William Molekyn in the parish of Seint Esmon the King on 27 June 1301. Overcome with weakness, Otford asked if he might rest in Molekyn's house, lay down on the ground, and died sometime later. Quartan fever, where the fever returned every fourth day, or tertian fever, every third day, meant malaria, then endemic in the low-lying, marshy areas of eastern England.[3]

Johan of Bristol was overcome by *morbum caducum*, 'falling sickness' or what we call epilepsy, early in the morning of Monday, 7 November 1300 as he was praying in St Paul's. He lay by a pillar until about midday, when he died 'through weakness and infirmity'. Although many people went into the church to pray, no one went to his aid. Another long-term sufferer of 'falling sickness' was Emme atte Grove of Guildford in Surrey, a beggar. Emme died in the Tower of London around None on 2 February 1337; while carrying a large earthen pot full of water, she fell headfirst into the Tower ditch. Another disease, known as *tisik* in the fourteenth century and later as *phthisis*, was pulmonary tuberculosis or a similar progressive wasting disease. Roger Brewere visited his friend Adam Ely in Walebrok ward on 29 July 1301, and about the ninth hour, left Adam's kitchen and found his wife Anneis in the hall. He complained to her that he was suffering from *tisik* and begged her to run and fetch a chaplain. Before Anneis could return, however, Roger fell down dead.[4]

Breaking a bone was often fatal. Seven-year-old Robert Seint Botulph was playing with three friends in Kyrounelane on Sunday, 16 May 1322 when a large piece of timber fell on his leg and broke it. Robert's mother Johane found him, rolled away the timber and carried him home, but he died two months later on 16 July. William Proudfot fell and 'broke his right thigh' while descending a flight of stairs in his home in Brigge ward in the evening of 30 November 1338, and died three days later. Johane Cotekyn, while going down the stairs from the solar in the house she rented from Hugh Waltham in Brigge ward one Saturday evening in August 1324, slipped and fell, and 'fatally crushed her body'. She died early on Tuesday morning. On Saturday, 6 May 1301, two friends named Peres of Huntingdon and Andrew Prille were drunk, and around Vespers decided to have a wrestling match in the home of another friend, Wauter Vigerous, in Douegate ward. Unfortunately, while they were wrestling Andrew broke Peres' right leg, and he died on 1 June; the jurors investigating for the coroner stated that the leg 'appeared fractured and gangrened', being capable of recognising gangrene. Death often came slowly to those who broke a bone, and also to the fuster Nichol Ruffyn of Walebrok ward in 1337. Guyot Rumbys severed one of the fingers on Nichol's left hand with his knife on 26 April (apparently deliberately, though the reason for the attack was not given), and Nichol died four weeks later on 22 May. Wauter Hodesdone was stabbed in the head in his home in the parish of Seinte Mildred at daybreak on 24 June 1326, and died around the third hour on 18 July.[5]

Robert Brewere was inebriated one Sunday evening in June 1301. When he saw an acquaintance named Robert Amyas (who was French and worked as a girdler, and died in London in 1342) in Wodestrete, he picked a quarrel with him which resulted in Amyas hitting him repeatedly with an oak stick. Brewere wandered off and spent the night lying by a tree in the churchyard of Seint Bertelmew the Litel. When he reported for work on Monday morning at the home of his master, fishmonger Henry Poteman, Henry reprimanded him for leaving his house without permission, gave him his wages, and ordered him to leave. Robert died in the home of Johan Butcher, a friend or relative, three days later. The jurors who investigated his death for the coroner, none of whom seemed to have any medical training whatsoever, declared, despite noting that Robert's body was bruised all over, that 'he was not nearer death nor farther from life by reason of the beating, but died from the illness he contracted from spending the night in the street'. They did not explain which illness would be contracted by spending a night outside in summer. Edward I pardoned Henry Poteman in 1304 for any involvement in Robert's death, though apparently disagreed with the coroner's findings, stating that Robert was 'lately killed in the city of London'.[6]

Isabel Pampesworth lived in a tenement in Quenehithe ward owned by the dean and chapter of St Paul's, was married to Robert, and had a son named Johan. Around Prime on Sunday, 29 November 1321, Isabel was left alone in her chamber in the solar while her son's servant, Cristine Iseldone, went down to the kitchen to fetch her some food. Isabel hanged herself from a beam with a piece of cord. Cristine found her and raised the alarm, and neighbour William Scot rushed upstairs and cut her down with his knife. He was too late and Isabel died fifteen minutes later, and in the ensuing investigation was said to have suffered from *frensy* for two years. 'Frenzy' was a word often applied to those who committed suicide and those who killed members of their families. In such cases, an inquest was held to determine whether the person had murdered their relative 'in a frenzy or feloniously'. If the killing was found to be felonious, the person was executed, but if the act was committed in a frenzy, s/he was imprisoned and released some months or years later, once believed to be restored to sanity.[7] Alis, married to the skinner Henry Warewyk and resident in the parish of Seint Benet Fink, also committed suicide when she drowned in the Thames in the evening of 5 February 1339. The jurors learned that she had been *non compos mentis* for half a year, and that she ran out of her home 'in a wild state' to the port of Douuegate a few hundred yards away and threw herself into the river.[8]

William Hampme died in the house of his employer, Richard Sawiere, in the parish of Seinte Marie Abbecherche in Kandelwikstrate ward on Sunday, 13 December 1300. William had suffered from 'a certain malady in his leg called a *festre*' for three years, and around Vespers a vein in his leg burst and he was unable to staunch the flow, and slowly bled to death. A *festre* meant a fistula, ulcer or festering wound. On 9 March 1339, Alisandre Hadleye died of a *posteme* or *postume*, an abscess or inflammation, in the house he rented in Douuegate ward from the Minoresses.[9] Henry Callere passed away in the ward of Crepelgate on 6 June 1340, in a house he rented from Wauter Blechyngleye, a cheesemonger. The investigating jurors determined, not entirely helpfully, that 'after the hour of curfew, the said Henry was going upstairs alone, when he fell down and died'. This is not untypical of the kind of medical detail one finds in the thirteenth and fourteenth centuries, and to give another example, when the sailor Henry Ambelcowe died near the Tower in August 1278, the jurors declared that he 'was suddenly struck by death'.[10] Robert Balsham, a cordwainer, died in his home in Billingesgate ward in the middle of the night on 10 February 1301, and the jurors stated that he had been 'afflicted with a grievous infirmity' for three weeks, rose from his bed, lay on the floor, and 'immediately died'. The infirmity was left unexplained.[11] It is often impossible to ascertain what ailments contemporaries were attempting to describe, and another example is the *French Chronicle of London*'s mysterious statement that in 1308 'there was a great malady of the eyes, whereby many persons lost their sight' in the city.[12]

The case of Rector William and the dead wolves indicates that there were a number of physicians and surgeons working in London whom the mayor consulted, and that the men themselves had 'medical or surgical writings' to consult. Only two surgeons are named in a 1319 tax assessment in London: Master William Surigien or Surrigicus ('surgeon' in medieval French and Latin) of the parish of Aldermariecherch, who died in 1322, and Master William Oteswiche, who lived in Bradestrate ward and died *c.* 1331. Master Gilbert the Surgeon was active in 1307 and made his will in 1312, Godfrey Ware, surgeon of Cornhulle, made his in 1319, Peres of Newcastle worked as a surgeon on Brettonestrete and died in 1329, and another Cornhulle surgeon appears in 1320; see below. The surgeon Henry of Rochester lived without Crepelgate and owned a brewery in Barbecanestret, and died in the plague year of 1349.[13] Robert Newcomen, whose name means that he was a newcomer to London, finished a ten-year apprenticeship with 'Henry the Surgeon and Katerine, wife of the same' in early 1310.[14] Remarkably, it seems that a London woman of the early 1300s was medically trained.

It is unfortunately impossible to ascertain how many physicians lived and worked in London, as they are not specifically identified in the tax assessment of 1319, and none of the many hundreds of extant London wills between 1300 and 1350 mentions that the will-maker or anyone in his or her family was a physician. Master William Medicus lived in a tenement in Basingestrete with his wife Margerie in 1303, and another physician was Master Gylard Galaron, associate of a family from Florence who settled in London (see 'Foreigners'). Master Lodowyk Arecia worked as a physician in London in 1345, and sold a medicine called *allumine de tysik* as a remedy for *tisik*.[15]

There is evidence that Cornhulle was the centre of medical treatment, such as it was, in early fourteenth-century London. Godfrey Ware the surgeon lived and worked there, and in July 1324 the goldsmith Nichol Walsh was attacked in the Tower of London by a man wielding a sword and was carried 800 yards to the Cornhulle house of Robert le Leche to be 'medically treated' for his head injury. Robert's name means 'the leech', which indicates what kind of treatment the unfortunate Nichol was subjected to.[16] Long on enthusiasm but short on ability, the surgeon Johan of Cornhulle promised in June 1320 to cure Alis Stockyngge of her 'infirmity of the feet' within two weeks, on payment of half a mark (80*d*). Johan went to Alis's home a mile away in Fletestrete and 'applied diverse medicaments against the said infirmity'. Unfortunately, not only did Johan's treatment not work, Alis 'was within six days unable to put her feet to the ground and her malady became completely incurable'.[17]

Alis's case shows that surgeons and physicians made house calls, at least to patients unable to walk. Some Londoners who were infirm and who could afford to do so employed a carer: in 1331, Richard Wyrhale left a shop on Alegatestrete to Idania, his 'body servant' (*corprancilla*).[18]

Roger Brewere asked his wife to fetch a chaplain, not a physician, when he was seriously ill with *tisik* in 1301, and this was an instinct shared by many of his contemporaries. It is apparent, however, that people travelled to London specifically to seek medical advice or treatment. William Wattepas from Essex walked to the city sometime before October 1300 'to be cured of a wound in his arm'. He died in London on 10 October, though not, the jurors declared, as a result of the wound. On 3 April 1325, Thomas Hodesdone quarrelled with his neighbour Thomas Brid in their native Hoddesdon, Hertfordshire, and Brid hit him on the top of his head with a weapon and inflicted a wound 'penetrating to the brain'. Thomas's friends took him to London for treatment, presumably on a cart – it seems most unlikely that he was able to walk or ride 20 miles with such a serious head injury – but he died six days later. Sir Robert Wateville, a knight in Edward II's retinue, fell ill while the royal household was near Guildford in Surrey in July 1326, and the king sent him to London with 40 marks (6,400*d*) to 'take cures there'.[19]

As well as being a hub for those seeking medical treatment, London was a place where numerous medicines could be purchased. Edward II's physician Master Étienne of Paris bought *drogeries* in London in July 1322 for the king to take on a military expedition to Scotland, including 'Apostle's ointment', an antiseptic; *saunguys draconis* or 'dragon's blood', a resin for healing wounds; 'God's grace', which was another ointment, and 'white' and 'dark' ointments; and calamine, ragwort, fenugreek, linseed, frankincense and myrrh.[20] A few London apothecaries, or spicers as they were often called, are mentioned between 1300 and 1350, including Simond Arcubus, who owned houses and shops in Grascherche, Honilane and Grobstrete, and his relatives Roger, Osbert and Thomas Arcubus; Johan Dachet (d. 1317); Johan Tiffeld, who owned tenements in Eldefisshstrete in the 1330s; David Tillebury of Wolchirchehawe, who died in November 1338; the Italian Nichol Guillim from Lucca in Tuscany, mentioned in 1332 and 1347; and Thomas Maryns, who qualified in 1310 after a seven-year apprenticeship with Roger Arcubus, and died in 1349.[21] There are no references in the coroners' rolls to apothecaries going to the aid of the many Londoners who were stabbed or bludgeoned, or suffered an accident.

Johan Spicer was active in the early 1350s on Cornhulle, more evidence that the area was the medical centre of fourteenth-century London. The mayor, aldermen and sheriffs asked four surgeons, the prior of 'Hogges' (who was probably French), Master Paschal, Master Adam Poletrie and Master David Westmerland, to examine a 'certain enormous and horrible hurt' – typical fourteenth-century medical language – which had appeared on the right side of Thomas Shene's jaw and which Johan Spicer had attempted to treat. The four men stated that 'if he had been expert in his craft' and had asked for aid and counsel, he might have cured the injury, but 'through want of skill' Johan had probably made the unfortunate Thomas's injury incurable.[22]

Foreigners

Modern London is one of the most multicultural and multiethnic cities in the world, and in the first half of the fourteenth century there was already a huge population from Italy, France, Portugal, Germany and the Low Countries, some of whom reached high positions in the city. Thomas Romeyn or Romayn, whose name sometimes appears as 'le Romeyn', meaning 'the Roman', was elected sheriff of London in 1291 and mayor in 1309, and the sheriffs and aldermen in the early 1300s included Simond of Paris and Roger of Paris.[1] It should be noted, however, that people often kept their father's name even when they themselves were English-born, so it is impossible to be certain whether Thomas, Simond and Roger had emigrated to London from Rome and Paris or whether one of their ancestors had. Thomas Romeyn's granddaughter Johane Burford married into the Betoyne family sometime before March 1329; all three families, the Romeyns, Burfords and Betoynes, were prominent London pepperers, and the Romeyns were partly Italian and the Betoynes partly French. One of the sheriffs of London in 1336/37 was Johan Northall, and in his will of May 1349 he mentioned his grandson Johan, son of his late daughter Wymarca and her late husband Bonaventure Bonentente of Florence. The half-English, half-Italian Johan Bonaventure was also mentioned in his grandmother Alis Northall's will of May 1361.[2]

English scribes often anglicised non-English names, which had the unfortunate effect of concealing the true number of foreign residents in London. Sometime in 1307, a man who bore the English-sounding name of Johan Nute made his will in London. Johan in fact was Italian, and left 'all his lands and tenements' in London, and all his lands in Florence, to his uncle Burgensis Fulberti, a horse dealer. Burgensis himself dictated his will in 1309, leaving the tenements in London and the lands in their native Florence bequeathed to him by his nephew, whom he called 'Johan Nute Fulberti', to three other nephews, William (or rather, Guglielmo), Simond and Cambin Fulberti. Cambin made his own will in London on

25 April 1346, calling himself 'of Florence'. He owned property near the monastery of San Donato in Polverosa just north-west of Florence, and named his brother as Guittus and his English-born son as James. His wife Cristine was probably English, as she was the executor of her uncle, a chaplain called William Thurnestone, in 1350. Cambin was named in 1333 as the tutor and guardian of the London-born two sons and five daughters of the late Cambin Fantini of Florence, and Fantini also had an older daughter, Johane, who married the London fishmonger Robert Freshfish. Gylard Galaron, physician, often appears on record with the Fulbertis and was probably a relative, or at least a close associate from their native Florence.[3] 'Johan Vanne' of the Ballardi, a merchant society from Lombardy, made his will in London in or shortly before October 1316, and it mentioned his wife Dame Jachelyn, his sister Dame Sita and Sita's husband Mayhew Guiscardinii. As well as owning tenements in London, 'Johan' or Giovanni owned lands and tenements in France. After his death, custody of his children Johan, Peres, Isabel, Nichol, Mayhew, Thomas, Johane and Idonea was given to his widow, their mother, now called Dame Jakelyne.[4]

An enormous number of Italians lived and worked in London in the thirteenth and fourteenth centuries. Orlandino Podeo from Lucca had lived in the city since at least 1275 and worked as the 'keeper of the Exchange', and was still resident in London in 1309. His brother Enrico also lived in the city from 1279 or earlier until 1289 or later.[5] Tommaso, son of Guidicio, still resident in the city in 1301, had lived in England since at least 1290.[6] The successful merchant Bankin Bromlesk from Florence lived in Candelwykstrete ward from at least 1319 to 1329 and owned a house in the parish of Seinte Marie Abbecherche, and the brothers Frisot and Totte Montclar, wine merchants from Lucca, moved to London in 1294 or earlier, and were still in England well into the 1320s. Edward I gave some houses near Ismongerelane to Frisot in February 1302.[7] Guydo Bonaventure lived in Langbourne ward in 1303, and was summoned to the mayor's court after assaulting Thomas atte Welle, a serjeant of the sheriffs.[8] Some of the numerous other Italians in London in the first half of the fourteenth century included, in 1310, the vintner Duchio Sak of Florence, and in 1338, the Genoese merchants Francekyn Bachoun, Bronnette Guilliam, Juste Chaucer, Antoigne Chetron and Pieres Jacoby.[9] One night at the end of 1337, eleven English sailors brawled in Tour ward with fourteen sailors who were, judging by their names, Italian; they included Antoninus Castayn, Aubretynus Ouraz, Gillelmus Venire, Cros Danevyl and Eularius Dambros.[10]

For 300 years from the middle of the twelfth century to the middle of the fifteenth, the kings of England ruled a large area of south-west France called Gascony. Many Gascons made their way to England during this period, and in the fourteenth century wine-sellers from Gascony lived and worked on the street called La Ryole, La Riole or La Reol in Vinetrye ward. An inhabitant of La Ryole in 1301 was Katerine la Frraunceyse, and she had lived in London since at least 1292.[11] England and France often went to war against each other, including between 1294 and 1299 and from 1324 to 1326, and the long series of conflicts between the two kingdoms which much later became known as the Hundred Years' War began in 1337. Perhaps for this reason, the number of French residents of London was far lower than the number of Italians, though even so, a few French people made their home in the city and some reached high positions. Guillaume Servat from Cahors moved to London in or before 1272 and served as alderman from 1309 to 1319, and Guillaume Trente, a wine merchant from Bergerac, was an alderman from 1309 to 1316. Trente left his house at the *Wynwharf* to his nephew William Noeyl.[12]

Two merchants from Montpellier, Étienne Soret and Étienne Cyvade, took part in an inquisition in March 1320 chaired by the mayor of London, Hamo Chigwelle, regarding the seizure of goods belonging to three German merchants whose names were recorded as Herman Swart of Sussalt, Conrad Broke and Tideman ate Way, both of 'Grippeswold'.[13] A man who drowned in the Thames in 1312 was named as Jean Pikard, servant of Jacques Roysi of *Reyns*, either Rheims or Rennes.[14] On 27 October 1323, a Frenchman called Jean de Chartres de Montlhéry (in the Île de France, 16 miles from Paris) died in the London home of an Italian, Master Pandulf of Lucca. Jean and two accomplices, William Wodeford and his wife Johane, broke into 'chambers, coffers and chests' in Pandulf's home in Melkstrete in the middle of the night, but when Jean expressed doubt and regret over their robbery, William and Johane hit him hard over the head with an axe. Astonishingly, they tried to burn his body in the fire in Pandulf's kitchen. Another criminal French resident of London was the goldsmith Adam Freynssh, who in April 1345 tried to kill Giovanni Poket of Lombardy near the house of the Austin Friars. Adam had two accomplices, Lazarin and Raginald Gargoyl of 'Geen', perhaps Genoa.[15]

The many deaths in the city during the terrible plague year of 1349 reveal other French inhabitants. Richard Alwy, resident in London and originally from Toulouse (he referred to himself as *Toulousere*), made his will on 3 February 1349, mentioning his wife Alis and his children Thomas, Richard, Isabel, Alis and Katerine, presumably all English-born. Richard left his tenements in All Hallows near London Wall to his two sons, his tenements in Morestret to his three daughters, and his tenements in the fields of Iseledon to all his children. His wife Alis received their house and garden in the parish of All Hallows. Richard's fellow Frenchman, Étienne Fraunsard from Amiens, died soon afterwards, and his will shows that both of his late wives and his mother were all named Juliane. One of Étienne's wives was a cousin of the girdler Robert Amyas (d. 1342), who beat Robert Brewere with a stick in Wodestrete in June 1301. Yet another French resident of London, Jean of Paris, wrote his will on 5 March 1349, and left his tenement without Crepelgate to the church of St Giles and shops and a garden in Fynesbery to his niece Cristine.[16]

Another Londoner whose family came originally from Toulouse was Michael Tholesan, though he himself was English-born, and his grandfather Johan Tholesan (d. 1259) was sheriff of London in 1249/50 and mayor in 1252/53. Michael was married to Juliane, and they had sons Johan, Robert, Reynald, Anketil and Michael and daughters Sabine and Johane.[17] Important fourteenth-century London inhabitants who were of French origin, though all of English birth, were the mayors Simond Fraunceys, Richard Betoyne and Johan Gisors, and the latter's brothers Anketin and Henry Gisors, both aldermen.

What is now Belgium, the Netherlands, northern France and western Germany consisted of a patchwork of small, independent counties and duchies in the fourteenth century. One of them was Flanders, now an area of Belgium, ruled from 1305 to 1322 by Robert of Béthune (b. 1249) and from 1322 to 1346 by his grandson Louis. Two sailors from Flanders, Johan Palling and Nichol Crabbe, had a bad quarrel on Wullewarf in Tower ward on Monday, 9 September 1325, which resulted in each man stabbing the other and in Nichol's death. Johan fled into sanctuary in All Hallows Berkyngecherch nearby. The medieval duchy of Brabant also lies in modern Belgium, and its capital was Brussels; its duke from 1312 to 1355 was Jan III (b. 1300), a grandson of Edward I of England. On 28 August 1340, two merchants from Brabant, Godekyn and Henryk Houndesbergh, who were cousins, had a furious row with the Englishman Wauter Waldeshey in the high street of Lumbardestrete opposite the church of Seint Esmon the King, which resulted in the Brabanters wounding Wauter 'in many places' with their swords. He died soon afterwards, and Godekyn and Henryk fled.[18]

A proclamation of April 1300 prohibited eight Portuguese and ten German vintners and taverners who lived in London from keeping hostels 'for eating and sleeping'. Some of the Germans were named as Thetardo Estreys, Arnado Wassemod, Godescalcus Hudendal and Tydeman Swarte. One of the Portuguese men was Gerard Dorgoil, still resident in London on 1 December 1312, when he appeared before the mayor and aldermen, accused of selling the wine of 'merchant strangers' at a higher price than the merchants themselves charged, and of 'selling the said wines to strangers without the intervention of a broker'. He was also said to have hidden the wines in a wharf enclosed with a fence, for selling wine after it had become 'unwholesome', and for taking it to the hostel of the bishop of Winchester 'to avoid discovery by the scrutineers in their annual search'. The freedom of the city was taken from him as a punishment. Another taverner of London in June 1350 was named as Johan (or Juan) of Navarre, a small kingdom in northern Spain.[19] There were far fewer Spanish residents and visitors to London than Italians, though the cloth merchants Benedict Ferrandes of Aragon, Albert Ferre of Barcelona and Juan Moles of Majorca came to trade in the late 1330s. English scribes recorded the name of one Spanish merchant as 'William Mountagu', an example of how the true number of foreign residents and visitors is easily obscured by the anglicising of names.[20]

In 1339/40, a resident of Farndone ward, trusted enough to be appointed one of the jurors who investigated suspicious deaths, was Gilbert of Alemaygne. The names of the jurors who investigated the drowning of Henry Overestolte in the Thames in June 1340, and those of the witnesses they questioned, also reveal the large number of foreign residents of London: Thomas of Spain, Herman Skyppere (who was German and whose name means 'skipper'), Johan Henaud (which means 'Hainaut', now in Belgium), and Johan Freynsshe or 'French'.[21] One German wool merchant active in London in 1301 was Johan Echelkerke of 'Thorpmond in Almaine', which perhaps means Dortmund, and in 1302 another German resident was Egbrith Werpe, also called Egbrytht Estreys.[22] The will of London resident Johan Triple in December 1324 names his wife as Alemanna; presumably she had German connections.[23] Rather curiously, 'German' was sometimes used as a given name for Englishmen in the fourteenth century, and German Brid was a fishmonger of the parish of St Olave towards the Tower who died before 1305.[24]

As well as the societies of Italian merchants, traders of the 'Hanse of Almaine', i.e. the Hanseatic League – a confederation of towns in northern Germany established in the 1100s to facilitate trade – often appear in fourteenth-century London records. A 'Guildhall of the Teutonic merchants' in London is mentioned in 1317 and 1344, and was granted to them during Henry III's reign (1216–72). A reference in May 1308 to 'the hall of the Danes' probably means this building. In 1342, the Hanse merchants pointed out that they had been 'charged with the repair and defence' of Bisshopesgate since 1282, and some of the Germans living and working in London at the time were named as Engelbert Colon, Sifrid Mayembergh and Rudeker Lymbergh.[25] Marion of Hongereye, i.e. Hungary, left a house near Aldresgate and rents in Eldefisshestrete in her will of February 1348, and Peres of Hungrie was another London resident of Hungarian origin.[26]

A man stabbed to death in the high street of Alegate ward in September 1339, though specifically stated to come from Twycross in Leicestershire, bore the name Rauf Sarasyn. The word *Sarasyn* or 'Saracen' was often used in fourteenth-century England and meant a Muslim, or a person of Arab or North African origin more generally. In 1305, Rauf Hardel leased three cellars in Vinetrye ward to men named as Bidan (or Bidau) of Arabi and Arnaud of Araby, a silver merchant. A coffrer working in London in 1310 was Adam of Antioch.[27] There is little evidence for other non-Europeans living in London in this period, though there was an awareness of the world far beyond western Europe: Edward II corresponded in 1307 with Oshin, king of Armenia, and Oljeitu, ruler of part of the Mongol Empire covering much of modern-day Iran, Iraq, Azerbaijan, Georgia, Turkey, Pakistan and Afghanistan. Edward also sent letters in 1312/13 to the king of Georgia and the emperor of Cathay, i.e. China.[28]

As well as all the foreign residents of London, people from other parts of England, and also from Wales and Ireland, moved there in numbers far beyond counting, to the point where immigrants outnumbered those born in the city. Seven hundred years ago, as now, London drew in numerous job-seekers and fortune-seekers. Many of the fourteenth-century mayors, sheriffs and aldermen came from outside the city, including Henry Darcy and Simond Swanland from Yorkshire, Johan Oxenford from Oxford, Johan Grantham, Simond Corp and William Thorneye from Lincolnshire, William Brixworth from Northamptonshire, Bertelmew Deumars from Essex, and Richer Refham and Roger Forsham from Norfolk.

Wards

Medieval London was – and indeed, the modern City of London still is – divided into twenty-five wards. Each was headed by an alderman, an elected official who in the fourteenth century held the office until he died or was moved to another ward. The wards were, and are, in modern spelling (for the medieval spelling, see Appendix 2): Aldersgate; Aldgate; Bassishaw; Billingsgate; Bishopsgate; Bread Street; Bridge; Broad Street; Candlewick Street; Castle Baynard; Cheap; Coleman Street; Cordwainer Street; Cornhill; Cripplegate; Dowgate; Farringdon (divided into Within and Without); Langbourn; Lime Street; Portsoken; Queenhithe; Tower; Vintry; and Walbrook.

A tax assessment of 1320 showed that Douuegate was the richest ward, with Vinetrie second, while the poorest was Lymstrete, which was also sometimes called Ferthingwarde in the fourteenth century. Only £1 4s in tax was raised in Lymstrete, while Douuegate raised over £106 and Vinetrie £94, and Portsokne, the second poorest, 79s or under £4. By 1368, the richest wards were Cordewanerstrete and Chepe, with Lymstrete still coming last. Money was levied from 'the more wealthy people' in each ward to give to Edward III, Queen Philippa and the magnates overseas with them in November 1339. The sums raised show that Chepe and Cordewanerstrete had the largest number of rich individuals living in them: £36 was levied from each ward. Only £1 was levied from Lymstrete, and the next three poorest were Algate, Portsokne and Bassieshawe, who raised £4 10s each.[1]

The numbers of men chosen from each ward in April 1338 who swore to safeguard the city during Edward III's impending absence overseas give a good indication of the relative size of each ward's population. Six men were chosen in Colemanstrete, Bassieshawe, Alegate and Aldresgate, four in Portsokne, and only three in Lymestrete; these six wards were the smallest. At the other end of the scale, seventeen men were chosen in Douuegate and twenty-one in Chepe, and a total of twenty-six in

Farndone, divided into Within and Without. Of the nine men chosen in Bisshopesgate, one was the Italian Cambin Fulberti and another was Jean of Toulouse, and Johan Horn, one of the eleven Brigge men, was specifically said to be a Fleming. One of the seven Vinetrie men was Ferand of Spain. In 1345, Edward III summoned a contingent of eighty archers from London to fight in his French wars, and the aldermen and commonalty determined each ward's quota. Alegate, Portsokne and Lymstrete only had to provide one archer each, while Cordewanerstrete, Brigge, Tour and Chepe sent six each.[2] Foreigners lived in eight of the twenty-four (later twenty-five) wards in the early 1300s. Vinetrie was the ward with the highest number of immigrants, many of whom were Gascon vintners, while Douegate was home to many Germans and people from the Low Countries, and Cordewanerstrete, Chepe and Langebourne to those from Italy, Spain and Provence.[3]

Wardmotes or wardmoots, assemblies of the 'more trusty and discreet' residents of a ward, were regularly held. Residents were meant to inform the alderman holding the wardmote of possible risks of fire; if any fights or assemblies against the peace were made in the ward and who was responsible; if an outlaw, leper, prostitute, courtesan, 'common scold' or 'common bawd' (i.e. a pimp) resided in the ward; if taverners, brewers or chandlers sold their wares without using 'measures sealed with the seal of the aldermen'; if anyone left their filth outside their own homes or others' homes; if pigs or cows were reared within the ward and annoyed neighbours; if unlawful building work was carried out; if bakers of *tourte* baked white bread or vice versa; if anyone broke curfew; if any city official misbehaved; and if anyone paid labourers more than the set fees. Wardmotes were held either in the alderman's house or in the local parish church.[4]

Farringdon ward was named after Nichol Farndon(e) or Faryngdone, a goldsmith who was its alderman from 1293 to 1334; it was previously called either Flete ward, or Lodgate and Neugate ward. Farringdon was officially divided into two wards, Within and Without, in 1394, making a total of twenty-five London wards, though the divisions already appeared on record at the beginning of the 1300s, and Nichol himself referred to his '*aldermanrie* of Farndon within Lodgate and Neugate and without' in his will of June 1334.[5] Nichol served as mayor of London four times as well as being an alderman for over forty years. In the twenty-first century, Farringdon ward still bears Nichol's name, or rather, his wife Isabel's name: Isabel was the daughter and heir of William Farndone, goldsmith and alderman from 1278 to 1293. Nichol himself was the son of Rauf Fevre, William Farndone's predecessor as alderman of the ward then called Lodgate and Neugate, and took his wife's name. Nichol and Isabel had a daughter, Rohese, who married twice and whose sons Nichol and Thomas also used the name Farndone rather than those of their fathers.[6]

Curfew

A curfew was in place in fourteenth-century London, and it was against the law to be out and about on the streets once the bells of the church of Martin le Grand rang for curfew until the bells rang for Prime the next morning. The exact time of curfew is not clear, but was probably about 5.00 or 6.00pm in winter, and a few hours later in the long light evenings of summer. An entry in the coroners' rolls of 1300 shows that there was a period of a couple of hours between sunset and curfew: the vein in William Hampme's leg burst around Vespers, i.e. sunset, and he died some hours later, at the time of curfew. The seven great gates leading into and out of the city were locked at the 'beginning of curfew being rung', while the wickets, i.e. the much smaller gates located at each side of the great gates for pedestrian use, were locked 'at the last stroke of curfew'.[1] The ringing of the bells lasted for a few minutes, to allow people to hurry home or to hurry into the city if they were on one of the roads leading into it. It was all too easy to find yourself locked out of the city if you arrived late, and in July 1340, Gerard Armourer, Johan Lincoln, a furbour, and Johan Keu, a smith, threatened the bedel of Alegate ward because he refused to open the gate and let them in at midnight.[2]

'Great lords, or other respectable people of note', and their retainers, carrying a light, were allowed to walk the streets after curfew. 'Some man of the city of good repute or his servant' were also exempt from curfew, as long as their journey was 'of reasonable cause, and with light'. Anyone else out and about found by the nightwatchmen was assumed to be up to no good and was called a common nightwalker, and imprisoned in a gaol called the Tun on Cornhull. Being out at night without a light was automatically deemed suspicious behaviour, and, given that assaults and thefts could be carried out with near-impunity in the total darkness of a world more than half a millennium before the invention of electric light, this was hardly an unreasonable assumption. Numerous ordinances were issued throughout the fourteenth century, strictly forbidding 'persons wandering about the city after the hour of curfew'. Johan Sloghtre, a chaplain, was caught and imprisoned in the Tun on Friday, 26 September 1320, and so was Emme Wirdrawere, originally from York, on Sunday, 9 November the same year.[3] The mayor, Henry Darcy, and the aldermen gathered on 14 September 1339 to ascertain which 'boatmen were ferrying disturbers of the peace across the Thames at night'. Thomas Perndon and Richard Boge were found guilty of doing so, despite knowing that their passengers were 'men of evil character' and that they were all breaking curfew. They were imprisoned for a week.[4]

At Christmas 1299, Giles Forner, Hugh Forner and Wauter Fannere strolled about without a light in Walebrok ward after dark, and when members of the Watch challenged them for being out in the streets after curfew, they refused to let themselves be arrested and wounded several nightwatchmen with the 'edged weapons' they were carrying. Subsequently, 'hiding in the shadows', the three men made their way to La Riole in Vinetrye ward. The three men appeared before the mayor's court on 23 January 1300 on charges of breaking curfew and wounding the watchmen. Giles Forner claimed in his own defence that his master, Roger of Derby, had invited his friend William to dine at his home, and ordered Giles to accompany William home after the meal. Giles and his fellow defendants were imprisoned, however.[5]

Nightwalkers could, in the endless dark of long winter nights, attach themselves to a group of nightwatchmen without the watchmen noticing and commit crimes, as Johan Sampson did in January 1304. He thereby managed to enter the house of an unnamed woman, unkindly described as an 'imbecile', between Alegate and the House of the Brothers of the Cross, also known as the Crutched Friars. She raised the hue and cry. Nearby, three servants of Master Johan Sandale happened to be visiting the home of one Roger Frowyk and were carrying a light, and chased after Johan Sampson. He was not, however, easily taken and was desperate to evade capture, and injured all of them. The mayor's court heard that Johan was 'a regular nightwalker who goes out to do harm'.[6]

Despite the often-repeated prohibitions and the threat of imprisonment, it is apparent from numerous sources that the curfew was routinely ignored (which was, of course, the reason for the frequent repetition of the prohibition). After curfew on Thursday, 12 January 1301, for example, a coster came to the top of a street near Graschirche, selling his wares to a number of customers who were all outside when they should have been at home. Gilbert Getyngtone dined at the home of his friend Ivo Percival in Bradestrete ward one Friday evening in September 1323, and walked to his home in Soperslane after curfew. The bedel of Vinetrye ward, Johan Harry, encountered two men walking at La Ryole without a light during the night of Sunday, 28 December 1342, and asked them why they had no light and where they were going. They told him it was none of his business, and a scuffle ensued in which the bedel was wounded in the arm.[7] Taverns were meant to close at curfew, and a typical proclamation was made on 27 August 1342: 'Keepers of taverns, to which evil characters usually resort, shall not keep their doors open after curfew sounds at St Martin le Grand, under pain of imprisonment.' It is apparent, however, that some unlawfully remained open; in 1311, Oliver Multone was said to lure men into taverns after curfew and to cheat them at dice.[8]

Sanitation

There is an idea that if modern people could travel back in time to the fourteenth century, we would need to have our noses cauterised, as otherwise we would be unable to cope with the stench. This may not be far from the truth. Edward II complained on 20 April 1309 that, although London residents were meant to take the ordure from their homes out of the city or to deposit it in the River Thames, they simply threw it outside their house, and the 'streets and lanes are more encumbered than they used to be'. In the future, he said, anyone who threw muck into the street would be liable for a fine of 40*d* for the first offence, and 80*d* for the second. Forty pence represented a few days' income for some Londoners, and for many others, closer to a month's. Partly as a result of the filthy streets, Johan Tygre lost his life during a deadly street brawl in Wodestrete at the beginning of 1322: while being pursued by men armed with swords, cudgels and knives, he 'fell over a heap of dung' and was caught and stabbed to death.[1]

It has to be said that throwing excrement and rubbish into the city's main waterway, the Thames, hardly represented the best solution to the problem of muck-ridden streets. Often, waste was dumped and water collected in the same place: a wharf in Baynardeschastel ward was 'used by people coming and going to the river to draw water or dispose of dung and other things'.[2] In May 1345, an inquisition found that 'the water of Thames in the dock of Douuegate has become so corrupted by dung and other filth' that the carters who carried water from the river at Douuegate throughout the city were no longer able to work. Five carters volunteered to clean the dock and to keep it clean in the future, and for their labour were given permission by the mayor and aldermen to take 1*d* from the crew of every ship and boat landing at Douuegate, and ¼*d* from every cart using the dock.[3]

The Thames was not the only smelly, filthy river, and the ditches around the city were equally unpleasant. In November 1307 Edward II

21

commissioned three men to survey the River Flete, 'its course being so obstructed by filth', and his son Edward III complained about the 'infection of the air, and the abominable stench' caused by the filth from latrines in the ditch around the Flete prison on 29 December 1355.[4] If the smell was bad enough to come to the king's attention in the middle of winter, it must have been far worse in summer. The mayor, Hamo Chigwell, and ten aldermen ordered the cleaning of the city ditches on Tuesday, 6 October 1321, and it took place on five days, from Wednesday, 7 October until Saturday and the following Monday. On each of the five days, men from five of the city wards did the cleaning; on the first day, for example, the cleaners came from Bishoppesgate, Bradestrete, Cornhull, Tour and Billyngesgate wards, and on the second, from Brigge, Langbourne, Candelwikstrete, Walebroke and Alegate.[5]

On Thursday, 19 September 1297, a series of regulations for London was issued. Every resident was ordered to clean the street in front of his or her tenement, and the deadline imposed for doing so was the following Friday at Vespers, i.e. in eight days' time. Pigsties were to be swiftly removed from the streets, and it was forbidden to allow pigs to roam around, on penalty of losing the animals. Boxes or tables placed in the streets for the purpose of selling wares from them were also to be removed.[6] The battle to make London cleaner and less smelly continued throughout the fourteenth century. On Friday, 12 November 1339, at a congregation of the mayor, sheriffs, aldermen and commonalty, the serjeants of each ward were ordered 'to clean the streets and lanes of the city and to remove all dung and rubbish before Monday week'. The aldermen were to 'see that the streets were properly kept and that rubbish and dung were removed, under pain of imprisonment for the serjeants of the wards' in December 1343. In November 1332, Johan Brok was attached (i.e. arrested) after assaulting Richard Tailleboys, bedel of Crepelgate Ward, while the latter was performing his duty of cleaning the streets.[7] One important job was the *rakiere*, who raked out latrines and the streets. Richard Rakiere died a terrible, and ironic, death in August 1326 when the planks of the latrine in his house in Bradestrete ward gave way and plunged him into the ordure below.[8]

Johan Toly, servant of the alderman Henry Gisors, did little to aid the battle to keep the city clean by urinating into the street out of the window of his solar during the night of 15 January 1326. Neither did Thomas Scott, who relieved himself in public somewhere in London in

April 1307. He was assaulted by two men, who told him 'it would be more decent to go to the common privies of the city to relieve himself', and in fact there were at least three public latrines in the city, one on London Bridge, one on Vedastlane, and one at Quenehithe, and surely a few more along the banks of the Thames and the Flete.[9]

Apart from human waste, another major issue was the disposal of the many animal carcasses used for consumption and in processes such as the production of leather, and animal remains and blood were not the only smelly, unhygienic problem: in July 1343, the *dieghere* Simond Warfield was temporarily imprisoned for 'throwing stinking trade-refuse into the street near Fanchirche'.[10] Also in 1343, Mayor Simond Fraunceys, 'for the decency and cleanliness' of the city, leased a piece of land in Secollane to the butchers of the Flehsshameles for 'cleansing the entrails of beasts'.[11] Houndesdych or Hundesdich was a ditch which ran alongside the city wall and outer moat, and was where the corpses of animals, especially dogs, were disposed of. Not everyone, however, bothered to do so. Richard Houndeslowe, a skinner, was summoned to the mayor's court in April 1304 because he buried the carcasses of horses within the walls of the city. He swore on the Gospels that he would never kill, skin or bury animals within the city or city ditches again. The butcher Johan Odierne and his apprentice Robert Odierne were found in February 1338 to have dumped the remains of animal carcasses in the middle of Grascherchestrete, and to have fed their pigs with the carcasses, 'thus defiling the street'. They paid a fine to the sheriffs, Nichol Crane and Wauter Neel.[12] Some people saw an opportunity to make money from animal carcasses: Johan Gylessone from Norfolk admitted to the mayor and sheriffs in May 1348 that he 'found a certain dead sow, thrown out near the ditch without Alegate', flayed it, and sold its meat in various places across London.[13] There was a widespread belief that 'bad air' was hazardous to health, and killing, skinning and burying animals was forbidden within the city walls because it 'corrupted the air' and endangered residents. Johan Maldone died while cleaning a well in Langebourne ward in September 1337, supposedly because he 'was overcome by the foul air and immediately died'.[14]

Pigs found wandering the streets were liable to be killed or at the very least confiscated from their owners, and it is apparent from the regularity of ordinances forbidding people to let their swine roam about that this was an ongoing and common problem. One order to remove 'vagrant pigs' from the streets of London was issued on 9 March 1316, though on the other hand, people were sometimes imprisoned and fined for slaughtering lawfully-kept pigs. William Simond, butcher, had to pay 7s to Idonea Hukestere in 1344 for killing her sow.[15] Joce and Johane Spaldinge complained in September 1322 that their neighbour Rohese Hert, a widow, kept her pig-sty too close to their wall and that the sty was causing the wall to collapse. Luke, parson of the church of Seint Benet Fink, stated in June 1304 that Roger Eucre had torn down the fence around the churchyard with the result that 'pigs and other animals and even men enter it by night and day, and carry off the plants growing there, and commit other enormities in contempt of God'.[16] As well as being unhygienic and eating people's plants, pigs could be dangerous. In May 1322, a 1-month-old baby named Johane, daughter of Bernard of Ireland, was bitten by a sow as she lay in her cradle in her father's shop in Quenehithe. She died a day and a half later.[17]

There is little evidence of how, or how often, people managed to clean themselves, but certainly at least a few people washed in the Thames. This was not without its dangers; firstly, the river had excrement and animal carcasses dumped into it, and secondly, the currents were strong. William Wombe, who worked as a latrine-cleaner, drowned in the Thames near Heywharf around curfew on 2 June 1339, while he was washing himself. The river carried his body as far as the Flete bridge over the Flete river, over a mile away, where it was discovered two days later. The armourer Henry Overestolte drowned a year later on 3 June 1340 while he was washing in the Thames opposite Heywharf, and numerous other people drowned in the river over the years (see 'Rivers' below). In July 1350, Edward III forbade bathing in the river near the Tower and in the ditches around and near the Tower, perhaps a delayed response to the drowning of 16-year-old Johan Redebourne in the Houndesdych, where he was bathing, in June 1337 (bathing in a ditch where animal carcasses were dumped seems an extraordinarily bad idea).[18] The existence of the *Lavenderebrigge*, literally 'Laundress's Bridge' but meaning a jetty or wharf with steps down to the Thames, located in Vinetrie ward very close to where Southwark Bridge now stands, surely reveals that laundresses washed clothes in the Thames there.

Privies

Sessions of the London Assize of Nuisance took place on Fridays every few weeks, with the mayor and some of the aldermen adjudicating, and we are lucky that records of the Assize survive for the entire fourteenth century. Residents could go to a session to complain about their neighbours, and grumbles about privies or latrines were common, particularly because they were often shared.

One issue was privies which stood too close to a common wall, inconveniencing neighbours with the smell or with sewage. At the session held on 10 February 1301, Guillaume Bethune or Betoyne, who came from France and raised a family in London, complained about the cess-pits of the privies belonging to his neighbours on either side, William Gartone and William Sterteford. The cess-pits stood too close to the walls of his house, and the sewage from them went into his cellar. Elias Russel, the mayor, and ten aldermen visited Guillaume's house on 3 March, and ordered his neighbours to move their cess-pits 1½ feet farther away from it. One of the aldermen investigating was Simond of Paris, either Guillaume's fellow Frenchman or at the very least of French origin.[1] The Assize often ordered people to move their cess-pits farther away from their neighbours' homes, or to wall them in stone, or both.

Hugh and Juliane Waltham complained on 14 June 1325 that their neighbour Robert Mustrel, originally from Tonbridge ('Tonebregg') in Kent, had built 'the cess-pit of his privy and a pit called *swelugh* receiving the water from his cistern and from a well not walled in stone' too close to their land. The mayor, Hamo Chigwell, the two city sheriffs, Johan Causton and Benet Fulsham, and nine aldermen went to look, and agreed with the Walthams that Robert's cess-pit and '*swelugh* receiving the water from the well and from a great vessel called a *thityngtunne* are not walled in stone'. He was ordered to remove them to a distance of at least 2½ feet, or at least 3½ feet if he did not wall them in stone. Margerie Rothyng of the parish of Seint Michael Wodestrete was summoned to the mayor's court in March 1305 because she dug a pit in her tenement and 'filled it with filth from the privy', contrary to city regulations.[2]

In December 1330, Johan Melf, a nakerer, and his wife Johane told the Assize that they possessed an 'easement' situated on the land of William Abel, a butcher, in the parish of Seint Nichol Flehsshameles. They had 'access by an enclosed place 7½ feet long and 4 feet wide to a privy', which had a pipe leading to William Abel's cess-pit, and Johan and Johane had 'a door in their solar opening on to the said place'. William had, however, completely removed the privy, pipe and fence and replaced them by 'joists and other constructions', even though Johan and Johane and previous tenants in their house had had the right to use the easement for half a century or more. A jury ordered William to replace the privy and pipe so that Johan and Johane could continue using the facilities, but reprimanded the couple for claiming that the enclosure was 4 feet wide when in fact it was only 3½ feet.[3]

Alis Wade's neighbours in the parish of Seint Michael Quenehithe told the Assize on 9 August 1314 that 'a gutter running under certain of the houses was provided to receive the rainwater and other water draining from the houses, gutters and street, so that the flow might cleanse the privy'. Alis, however, 'has made a wooden pipe connecting the seat of the privy in her solar with the gutter, which is frequently stopped up by the filth therefrom, and the neighbours under whose houses the gutter runs are greatly inconvenienced by the stench'.[4] This particular complaint reveals that not only was Alis ingenious in being able to devise and construct a wooden pipe which carried away her waste, but that she had a privy in her solar, i.e. an upper room of her home. Other entries in the Assize of Nuisance tend to show that privies were built outside, behind people's homes.

A privy in the parish of St Dunstan by the Tower stood in its own room and in 1310 was used by William Busshe, Maud the widow of Johan Heaumer, and William and Richolda Basing.[5] In the early 1330s, William Thorneye, a pepperer who had moved to London from a village in southern Lincolnshire a few years earlier and who later became sheriff and alderman, lived in the parish of Aldermaricherche with Johane Armenters. Johane was the widow of Johan Armenters (d. 1306), a city sheriff in 1299/1300.[6] The nature of William and Johane's relationship is not clear; William might have been Johane's lodger, or perhaps he was her lover. Their neighbours were Thomas Heyron and Andrew and

Johane Aubrey, and the five shared a common privy which was walled, roofed, and partitioned with joists to provide some privacy. The Aubreys complained to the Assize of Nuisance on 25 June 1333 that William Thorneye and Johane Armenters had removed the partitions and roof so that 'the extremities of those sitting upon the [toilet] seats can be seen, a thing which is abominable and altogether intolerable'. The aldermen ordered William and Johane to restore the partitions.[7]

Privacy

The Assize of Nuisance is also fascinating for demonstrating that in the fourteenth century, not usually considered to be an era when privacy was desirable or even possible, Londoners did indeed value their privacy. Even in crowded medieval London, people felt they had a right to it. In September 1301, carpenter William Holebourne and his wife Johane specifically gave their neighbours Johan and Isabel Wyndesore permission to make an opening in their tenement which overlooked William and Johane's tenement, and also gave Johan and Isabel a temporary right of way through their house while the couple repaired, roofed and plastered their own house.[1] Many others, however, felt differently, and complained to the Assize that their home was overlooked by neighbours. Richard Chiggewelle told the Assize on 15 December 1301 that Geffrei Conduit and Imanya Brauncestre on Wodestrete had windows and 'other apertures' in their houses that overlooked his land. Solomon Coteler aka Solomon Laufare, alderman of Bradstrete ward, complained on 7 September 1302 that water from the house of Michael Tholesan in Pultrye flooded his courtyard and submerged Solomon's trees and plants. He added that Michael had torn down a fence, with the result that Michael's tenants could now see into Solomon's courtyard and observe his 'private business'.[2]

A tanner named Johan of London and his wife Johane built three windows 'in the wall of their solar', less than 16 feet above the ground, from which they and their household could see into the chamber and kitchen of their neighbour, clerk Johan Hardyngham. The Assize told them on 1 December 1340 to block up the windows within forty days. On 29 February 1348 (a leap year), Simond Worthstede of the parish of Seint Alban Wodestrete complained that his neighbours Robert Bisshop and Roger Madour had six windows and two apertures in their tenement and could see his 'private business'. Hugh of Huntingdon, resident of Baynardeschastel ward, stated on the same day that the abbess of

28

Burnham owned a tenement next to his, and had four windows less than 16 feet from the ground through which her tenants could see the private business of his own tenants. The abbess was told to block the windows.[3]

Isabel, widow of Johan Luter and resident in Walebrok, kept the Assize busy in July 1341 with complaints about her neighbours. Firstly, the skinner Johan Thorp, whose tenement adjoined her garden, had four windows with broken glass in his tenement, through which he and his servants could see into her garden. Secondly, Johan Thorp had another seven windows in his tenement through which he could see into Isabel's own tenement. Thirdly, Henry Ware had four apertures in his tenement overlooking her own, and the stench from his cess-pit came through them. Fourthly, Johane, daughter of Reymund of Bordeaux and widow of Simond Corp (sheriff of London 1310/11, died 1329), had twelve apertures overlooking Isabel's tenement. Fifthly and lastly, the fishmonger Johan Leche had a 'leaden watchtower' on the wall of his tenement, and he and his household stood there daily watching Isabel and her servants. The Assize found in Isabel's favour in all these matters. By December 1341, Johan Thorp and Johane Corp had not yet complied with the order to block up their windows, and were each fined £2 (480*d*).[4]

There are many dozens of similar examples where Londoners grumbled about their neighbours being able to see into their homes or gardens, and the neighbours were ordered to block up their windows to maintain the right to privacy. Examples of Londoners complaining about neighbours blocking their light or view also exist. In August 1321, Thomas Berkyngge, goldsmith, stated that Henry atte More, another goldsmith, had prohibited him from building a new house on the east side of Henry's own house. Henry explained that the plot where Thomas wished to build his property had a condition attached that no building on it should 'obscure the light from two glazed windows' in Henry's property and should not stand within 10 feet of his home. He produced deeds dating back to 1263/64 in support of his claim. A similar example dates to October 1278, when Reynald Cantebrege (i.e. Cambridge) left various houses in London to his seven sons, 'on condition that one brother does not shut out the window light of another'. Rohese Farndone, daughter of the late alderman and mayor Nichol Farndone, asserted in September 1343 that, as the occupant of 'a tenement abutting on a street or lane', she was, according to city custom, entitled to light, but the building work of her neighbour Hugh Brandon on Goderomlane had obscured it.[5]

Isabel (d. 1349), daughter of Richard Wolmar (d. *c.* 1314), married Hamo Godchep or Goldchep, a mercer and one of the two sheriffs of London in 1315/16. Now Hamo's widow, Isabel went to the Assize of Nuisance on 26 July 1331, and made a complaint against her neighbour Johan Ruddok in the parish of Seint Botolph Billyngesgate. Johan, she said, piled his firewood against the window in the west gable of her house, so high that it covered the window and Isabel's 'light, view, air and clarity' were entirely impeded. She produced a deed dated 1 April 1299, granting her father Richard Wolmar the right to have 'the view, opening, light, air and clarity' from the window.[6] Austin Waleys, who came from Uxbridge, Middlesex and moved into the city, told the Assize in November 1339 that people who had previously lived in his home and in his neighbour William Wetheresfeld's had, back in 1269/70, agreed that they would always leave at least 3 feet between their plots, and 'do nothing to obscure the view and light' of each other's homes. Geffrei and Maud Aleyn of Walebrok complained in July 1341 that they and their predecessors in their tenement had always 'enjoyed the light and view from their windows and open apertures', but that William Stansfield, the local parson, William Hackford and Adam Bury had recently obscured the Aleyns' view with building work. Furthermore, the three men's tenants threw sewage and rubbish into the Aleyns' gutter, and broke their tiles. For their part, the three men accused the Aleyns of deliberately building two of their windows opposite the tenement they owned.[7]

Two Italians, Orlandino Podeo and Tommaso, son of Guidicio, told the Assize on 1 December 1301 that Robert Multone, a tailor, and his wife Anneis, and Wauter Northwyc and his wife Cecile, had built a new house which obstructed the view from their own home 'contrary to the terms' of the purchase of their property. Orlandino's attorney was Laude Ruffini, obviously also Italian.[8] It is interesting to note that the sale specified that the two Italians, like Isabel Godchep née Wolmar and her father, had the right to a view, though unfortunately the Assize did not clarify where in London they owned their house, or what the view was.

Houses

Most medieval London houses and tenements were made of wood and did not survive the Great Fire of 1666, though there is evidence of some stone buildings and walls. A 'stone house' on Medelane next to the Thames, belonging to Johan and Belisant Stratford, is mentioned in August 1306. Idonea of Cambridge owned a tenement in the parish of Seinte Marie Magdalen of Melkstrete, and complained in September 1308 that her tenants' lives were endangered by a ruinous stone wall nearby belonging to Richard Mompesson and Raymond Brouwe. In October 1336, the stone wall on the north side of Henry and Isabel Sutton's house, which faced the street in the parish of Aldermarichirch, was ruinous and about to collapse, 'to the terror of the neighbours and passers-by'. According to a city regulation, stone walls had to be at least 16 feet high, presumably so that they could accommodate a house of two storeys.[1]

A specification for building a house in London, to be made by the carpenter Simond Canterbury for the skinner William Haningtone (who died in or soon before March 1313), still exists.[2] The agreement dates to Saturday, 16 November 1308, and Simond promised to finish the house 'down to the locks' by Easter 1309, i.e. 30 March. In return, William would pay him £9, 5*s* and 4*d*, and would provide the carpenter with furs, presumably because Simond would be working outside all winter. The house would have a hall and a room with a fireplace, with a larder between them; a solar over the room and larder; an *oriole* (bay window) at the end of the hall 'beyond the high bench' (i.e. dais); a covered step from the ground outside into the hall; two cellars beneath the hall; one enclosure for a sewer, with two pipes leading to the sewer; a stable 12 feet wide between the hall and the 'old kitchen', with a solar above and a garret above the solar; a kitchen with a fireplace; and a passageway 8 feet wide between the hall and the 'old chamber'. The references to the old kitchen and old chamber indicate that some buildings already stood on the site. Rauf Beri, a cordwainer, also hired Simond Canterbury in May 1313 to build him a house in Billinggesgate ward, and promised to pay him £36, but unfortunately for Simond, Rauf died before work began and before he received the money.[3]

In the early 1300s, Johan Wallere rented 'a certain small house called *loge*', i.e. lodge, without Alegate near the ditch, 12 feet long and 7 feet wide. He paid only 12*d* a year for this tiny property, though was bound to maintain the road under the gate of Alegate at his own expense. Johan also had a 'turret adjoining Alegate', which Henry Wake rented from him at 10*s* a year. A 'small house outside Alegate' was leased to Phelip and Alis Turnour in 1318, with 10 feet of land, for 4*s* a year. This was, despite the fourfold increase in rent, probably the same house once rented by Johan Wallere, as Phelip and Alis had to 'keep the road under the gate clean, as tenants of the house had been accustomed to in times past'.[4] Another 'certain small house outside Alegate', next to the churchyard of Seint Botulph, was leased to Johan Chaundeler in June 1320. Part of his tenancy agreement stipulated that he had to clean the church gate, and around and underneath it.[5] Wauter Taillour owned a tenement in Alegate in the early 1300s, for which his tenant Richard Bakere, who really was a baker, paid 80*d* annually. Richard also baked a *penitourte*, a loaf of brown bread which cost a penny, for Wauter every week.[6]

Wauter Wynchester, a cordwainer, and his wife Sabine, daughter of Thomas Derby, leased a tenement in Wodestrate to William Partenhale for twelve years in February 1321; he would pay 2 marks (320*d*) annually for the first six years and 2½ marks (400*d*) for the next six.[7] In November 1342, Adam and Alis Westone leased a house on Watlyngstrete in the parish of Aldermaricherche to Alis Spersholte and Roger Wodhulle for twenty-four years. Alis and Roger would pay the Westones 25*s* (300*d*) a year. Johan of Pountoyse (Pontoise, France) rented a house outside Alderichesgate from Reynald Frowyk for a year in September 1300, for which he paid Reynald 40*s* (480*d*). By Easter 1302, however, he had still not vacated the property, and did 100*s* worth of damage to the locks, timber, and various fixtures.[8]

A word that often arises in connection to London houses in the fourteenth century is 'solar', meaning an upper room reached by a narrow staircase or ladder. A case presented to the Assize of Nuisance in 1340 shows that a couple had a solar less than 16 feet above the ground, contrary to city regulations, though the January 1326 death of

Johan Toly, who urinated out of his window and fell, reveals that Johan's solar was 30 feet above the ground.[9] Wauter Heyngham, a tanner, left his son Estephene a 'solar and stable within his great gate, with garden and free entrance and exit through his little gate' in 1289. In October 1307, Maud Barre left a 'house and a stone vault under the solar of Johan Beauflour' near the Tower to Adam Ludekyn, and Henry Chaundeler owned two 'painted solars' at Garlekhuth in 1317.[10] The cutler and alderman Solomon Laufare, aka Solomon Coteler, left his wife Isabel a 'solar extending from the entrance to the Conduit tavern up to the wall of the church of Seint Thomas Acon' in 1312, and in November 1341 the carpenter Simond Canterbury (hired by William Haningtone in 1308/09) left his daughter Alis a *newewodehous*, 'new wood house', with a solar and garret. A solar in Bredstret in the 1320s was called *pavedeloft*, i.e. it had a tiled floor.[11] The narrow steps leading up to solars could be dangerous, and several cases of Londoners falling down them to their deaths are recorded in the coroners' rolls. One victim was Elena Scot of the parish of Seint Benet Wodewharf, who at the end of 1321 fell and broke her neck after slipping on the top step at the entrance to her solar.[12]

In the middle of the night on 16 March 1301, two men known as Credo and Falwey went into a brothel on Fletestrate. They became embroiled in a quarrel with Adam Coteler and chased him to his house with swords drawn. Adam fled to his solar and locked the door, but the furious Credo and Falwey began to break it down. Adam climbed out of his window and managed to escape, whereupon Credo and Falwey beat up his servants instead. In September 1306, Estephene Barber and an unnamed woman went to the Graschirche house of Robert Barber and his wife Maud, and asked (for an unexplained reason) to see their solar and to have a drink there. Maud heard the two making a noise, and when she went to investigate, saw Estephene pulling on his breeches. He hit her over the head with a quart pot and kicked her, and later claimed to the mayor's court that he had only gone to the Barbers' house to drink wine and that Maud and her servant assaulted him first so that he lost an eye. He was, however, imprisoned and had to pay Maud 10 marks (1,600*d*) as compensation.[13]

As well as solars, many London homes had cellars. A Londoner mentioned in a will of 1351 was called Symond atte Holeweceler, 'at the hollow cellar'.[14] A house in Garleckhithe had a *colceler* or 'coal-cellar', Johane Travers owned a big stone hall, a little stone hall, and 'two cellars called *Helle*', and the 1335 will of Juliane Gauger mentions a 'large cellar where she used to reside' in the parish of Seint Michael Paternostercherche which had a hall, larder, parlour, kitchen and *bedchaumbre* above it. Johan Amys from Haveringland in Norfolk, who made his will in Sudbury, Suffolk in April 1340, lived in London for a few years. Among his bequests was a cellar called *yilhuys* ('alehouse') under a brewery also in the parish of Seint Michael Paternostercherche. A will of November 1324 shows that another house in that parish had a bedchamber, a 'little hall', a parlour, two cellars, a chamber with a fireplace, and a privy with 'an alley underneath the cellar leading' to it.[15] In May 1343, William and Juliane Salesbury leased 'a certain cellar under a shop' in Bradestrete to Estephene Hodesdone, a cook, and in March 1349 the goldsmith Johan Walpol left his daughter Margerie a house in Bredstrete ward with a cellar for wood and coal, and a tavern attached.[16] A grim murder took place in Ismongerelane in December 1276: Roger of Westminster cut off the head of his master, the taverner Symond Winchester, as he slept, and hid the body (minus the head, which was never found) in the coal-cellar of Symond's tavern.[17]

William Thorneye, who, with his landlady or lover Johane Armenters, was ordered to restore the partitions of the privy they shared with their neighbours the Aubreys in 1333, launched a counter-accusation against them. He stated that the couple had made a hole in the floor of their house above his and Johane's cellar and were able to spy on his 'secret business', and Andrew and Johane Aubrey were ordered to block up the hole. This shows that London houses tended to be a bit higgledy-piggledy; part of the Aubreys' house lay above William and Johane's cellar, and Johane Armenters complained that the Aubreys had prevented her from building a door in the stone wall of her cellar because they owned the wall from the foundation upwards. Johan Yonge stated in August 1347 that the solar of Henry Yonge and Johan Conyng lay above his cellar in the parish of Marie Abbechirche, and that the pipe of their latrine overflowed into the cellar. William Salesbury tried to prevent William Cornehulle, parson of Seinte Marie Aldermanberi, from building a house next to his in March 1314, because the parson's timbers and brace would be attached to a post in Salesbury's house. The Assize determined that in fact the parson's building work could go ahead, as the brace of a house which had previously stood on the site had been affixed to the post. Cambin Fulberti from Florence (d. 1346) stated in July 1314 that the solar above the entrance to his house on Grascherche was built on the posts and timber of the common wall between his home and the home of his neighbours Geffrei and Cecile Blithe, and that they had prevented him from repairing his solar.[18]

Another common feature of fourteenth-century London houses was gutters. One, in the parish of Marie le Bow, was 3 feet wide and 23 feet long, and another was 7 feet long and 1½ feet wide. Estephene Mazerer of Colmanstrete stated in 1342 that his neighbours Johan and Thomas Gratefige, brothers, needed to construct a gutter 100 feet long to prevent rainwater falling from their tenement onto his.[19] Henry Ku and his neighbour Hawise Rothyng agreed in September 1301 to make a gutter 'running above the kitchen and stable' of Hawise's house and 'along the stone wall between their houses to Wodestrete'. In September 1303, Adam Hallingbury of Wodestrete made a gutter and nailed it to the timber of his house to carry away the water from his house and the house of his neighbours Osbert and Isabel Braye into the street, and seven years later, the Assize of Nuisance told neighbours Simond Corp and Peres Adrian to build a gutter between their homes and to assume joint responsibility for its upkeep. Richer Refham informed the Assize in November 1306 that his neighbours Ranulf and Isabel Balle had contrived to construct a gutter intended to carry off the water from both their houses so that it ran through the middle of Richer's house.[20] In June 1337, Johan, young son of the chaundeler William atte Noke, was playing with a ball upstairs in the home of a neighbour, Johan Wynton, in the parish of Seinte Marie Abbechirche. The ball went out of a window into the gutter, and young Johan climbed out of the window to retrieve it, but lost his balance and fell into the street, and died five days later. The carpenter Robert Berdene fell from his ladder in the same year, while repairing a gutter on the house belonging to Nichol Sandwich in the parish of All Hallows Bredestrete.[21]

At the wealthier end of society, some Londoners' homes were concealed behind gates, such as Margerie Somery's in the parish of Seint Michael Wodestrete in 1314: her house had a 'great hall ... with free entry and exit through the gate with horses and other beasts of burden and carts'. The Heyngham family owned a house – where in London was not specified – with a solar and stable within the 'great gate', plus a garden through a 'little gate'.[22] Other London residents of the wealthier kind, some of whom were knights, owned stables. Sir Francis Vilers of Fletestrete had a stable between his home and the home of Henry Brewere in 1312, and Sir William Langeford had one at his home in Clerkenewelle in the 1340s. Sir James Audley sold houses with stabling for four horses on Cornhull in or before early 1320.[23]

A complaint by the prior of Seint Bertelmew Smethefeld in December 1346 indicates that Johan and Juliane Wroth and Thomas Honilane lived in a tenement next to the property of his church in the parish of All Hallows Honilane, and had ten windows in the tenement through which they and their tenants could see the 'private business' of the prior's tenants. There were also three doors in the tenement through which Johan, Juliane and Thomas and their tenants came and went across the prior's land as they pleased.[24] Johane Luter's complaint of July 1341 against her neighbour, the skinner Johan Thorp, shows that Johan had 'four windows with broken glass' through which he could see into Johane's garden. It is fascinating to note that a skinner had translucent glass windows in his home, albeit broken ones; glass windows were costly and would not become common in England until the seventeenth century, though there is evidence that they were already plentiful in London in the fourteenth. In December 1301, for example, Robert Lasshingdon broke the window of someone's home in Alegate ward, climbed in, and stole some cloth.[25] Austin and Maud Waleys complained in July 1338 that their neighbours Johan Hadham, Johane Algate and Johan Northbrugh all had unglazed windows in their homes, contrary to city custom, and that Hadham, a potter, had four windows in his hall 'only 4½ feet above the ground'.[26]

Some houses and tenements had a lane running between them. In 1339, the timbers of the fishmonger Adam Pykeman's new house in Retheresgatelane extended 14 inches beyond the middle of the lane between his house and the house of his disgruntled neighbour Margarete, widow of Johan Bourne. A few months later, the former mayor Johan Gisors, now about 60 years old, grumbled that his neighbour Henry Vannere, a vintner, had 'built his house extending beyond the middle of the lane' between their houses. Andrew Aubrey, the mayor, and ten aldermen went to look, and listened to the testimony of carpenters and masons who had worked on Henry's house. They found that in fact it was 'an inch or more short' of the middle.[27]

Other houses and tenements were separated by fences or palings which were sometimes made of wattle and daub, stone walls, or earthen walls. In 1325, the wattle and daub paling between the tenements of

Hugh and Juliane Waltham and their neighbour Katerine Rothyng was 40 feet long, and the fence between the Walthams' home and that of their other neighbour, Thomas Marche, was badly damaged. The Assize of Nuisance told the Walthams and Thomas to provide 1½ feet of land each and to share the costs of building a stone wall instead. The earthen wall between the homes of Esmon Grymmesby and Johan Elys in the parish of St Dunstan West was 81 feet long in 1342. Gilbert Marshal complained in September 1302 that his neighbour Gilbert Colchester had refused to mend the fence between their tenements, and the Assize ordered the two men to build a stone wall 16 feet high and 3 feet wide instead (in line with the city regulation that stone walls had to be at least 16 feet, though this seems remarkably high and wide for a partition wall). Hamo Chigwell, mayor of London many times between the late 1310s and late 1320s, lived next to the Thames near Pouleswharf, and in June 1328 stated that the fence between his home and the homes of Joce and Johane Spaldinge and Benet Reyner was 'ruinous and broken down'. Residents often complained that children, dogs, pigs and hens came over ruinous walls or broken fences and trampled their gardens, or that walls were too low and compromised their privacy.[28]

Johan Abel owned a house 28 feet long in Crokedelane in 1331, and the house of his neighbour, the fishmonger Adam Kyngestone (d. 1349), overhung his wall by 14 feet on the east side. In 1348, Richard Rittlyng had a house 36 feet long and 36 feet wide fronting the street in Holbourne. The house was ruinous, and overhung the street; Richard was ordered to demolish it within forty days. Fishmonger Adam Pykeman (d. 1349) built a house in Retheresgatelane in November 1339 that was 25 feet long.[29] A tenement that stood at the junction of Abecherchelane and Candelwikstrete in the 1320s was called *Litelcaponhors*, one in Candelwikstrete was called *Webbeloft*, one in Thamysestret was *Gladewyneshouse*, and others were *Bonsieshous* in Garlekheth, *Horssho* ('horseshoe'), *Irendore* ('iron door'), *Brodedore* ('broad door'), *Crokedehous* ('crooked house'), *Longehous*, *Stonhous* ('stone house'), *Brodegate*, *Horsmelne* ('horse mill'), *Cardinalshat*, *Blakeloft* near Martelane towards the Tower, which belonged to Piers Blakeney, and *Sarasyneshed* or 'Saracen's Head' in Bredstret, which belonged to Michael Tholesan. A building in Estchepe was called *Scholdynghous*, a name which almost certainly means that its inhabitants scalded poultry there.[30]

Hostels

Numerous hostels and taverns catered to the large number of people, both English and from abroad, visiting or temporarily working in London. Hostellers were called *hostelere* in fourteenth-century English or *haubergere* in medieval French, and their establishments were called *hostellrys*, 'hostelries'. Although most *hosteleres* were men, some were women: Beatrice Hynde ran a hostel in Holbourne in the 1330s, and Isabel Toppesham had one near St Paul's brewhouse in Baynardeschastel ward in 1350.[1]

As well as providing a bed for a night or two, at least some London hostels provided long-term accommodation. William Beaubek of Kent stated in April 1345 that he rented a room in Johan Waltham's inn (where in London was unfortunately not clarified) for 1½d a week. He had a key to the room, and believed it to be a secure place in which to keep his deposit box containing 10 marks in cash, gold and silver rings, silver ornaments and dishes, silk purses and girdles, and other valuables. While William was out, however, someone unlocked the door to his room with the garden door key, and stole his box. The innkeeper Johan Waltham blamed his brewer, Roger, as the only other person beside himself who had the key. This interesting case shows that a London inn had its own garden through a door that could be locked, and also that innkeepers were deemed liable for the theft of goods from rooms they let out.[2] To pay 1½d a week for a room in a London inn seems excellent value; in 1324, Edward II gave Beatrice Gos, wife of one of his servants, 12d (1s) to pay for four nights' accommodation in London. Some guests required stabling for their horses, and *hosteleres* were allowed to charge 2d to provide hay for one horse for a day and a night.[3]

A proclamation of August 1343 stated that taverners were to 'warn their guests to leave their arms in their inns before going into the streets', and were 'not to receive strangers for more than a day and a night unless they are willing to vouch for them', so clearly they provided accommodation to people visiting London who might not be aware of the city regulation that no one was allowed to go about the streets armed. In December that year, the two dozen aldermen of London were told to ensure that all innkeepers and hostellers in their wards were 'of good fame', and were reminded that hostellers were under surety not to allow evildoers in their lodgings and were bound to inform officials if any 'suspicious characters' arrived. In April 1338, as part of a series of safety measures to be taken in London while Edward III was absent abroad, 'the better men of every ward' were to examine all hostelries, and innkeepers were told not to 'harbour persons for whom they cannot answer'.[4]

Some London residents made extra money by renting out a room in their home to visitors or newcomers. In 1305, the cordwainer Johan Gaytone, newly arrived in London, hired a room in the home of his fellow cordwainer Roger Lauvare (d. early 1307), 'to sleep in'. The arrangement ended badly, however, when Johan woke up and caught Roger in his room one night attempting to steal his goods (a coat partly furred with lamb's wool, two towels and a rug), and Roger assaulted him, so that he had to flee into the night.[5] And not everyone paid their hostel bills on time. By May 1338, sixteen merchants from Brabant, including Gysemann Cort, Tarus Hale and Frankyn Depe, had fallen behind on the rent they owed to Henry Rombaud for board and lodging, and were summoned to the mayor's court.[6] *Hosteleres* were themselves not always entirely trustworthy; some of them went to Suthewerk to buy horse-bread, i.e. bread of low quality intended for animal consumption (or for very poor people), and sold it to their guests at ½d per loaf, 'whereas four such loaves are really not worth a penny'.[7]

Whenever the king and his massive household of hundreds of people stayed in London, his marshals requisitioned inns and private homes for the royal retinue to stay in, and other officials called herbergers went to the inns and homes and marked the front wall with chalk. In July 1325, one of the two city sheriffs, Johan Causton, got into trouble after his home in Billyngesgate was requisitioned for Edward II's secretary Richard Airmyn and Airmyn's clerks. Causton removed the chalk mark from his wall, and was prosecuted before the steward and chief marshal of Edward's household a few days later. He pleaded not guilty, and was acquitted after citing a 1268 charter of Edward's grandfather Henry III which stated that 'no-one should take a hostel by force in the city'. A month earlier, four of Edward II's hobelars (armed men on horseback) were assaulted and robbed in the Fletestrete home of Robert Gumby, which had been assigned as their lodging by royal marshals.[8]

Edward II and Isabella of France's coronation as king and queen took place at Westminster Abbey on Sunday, 25 February 1308, and Edward's marshals appropriated a number of London inns 'for lodging the great folks' who came to the event, and their retinues. The foreign VIPs included Edward's sister and brother-in-law the duke and duchess of Brabant, his cousin the duke of Brittany, the counts of Luxembourg, Savoy and Foix and the queen's uncles the counts of Valois and Evreux and her brother the count of La Marche, and numerous English earls, bishops and magnates also attended. The 'great folks' and their attendants were allowed to stay in the hostels for free until Thursday four days after the coronation, and if they wished to stay longer were enjoined to recompense the hosteller.[9]

Mansions

On 24 July 1307, there is a reference to a house located in the parish of All Hallows at the Hay called *Coldhakber*. Johan Trumpeshale went before the mayor's court to complain about his trading partner, William Conele, and stated that when he went to *Coldhakber* one afternoon to ask why William had not been present at an audit of their accounts being carried out by Thomas Romeyn and others that morning, William and his servant assaulted him. This is the earliest reference to the famous riverside mansion known as Coldharbour, and a decade later in 1317, *Coldherberghe* was leased by its then owner, Sir Johan Abel, to the draper Henry Stowe for ten years at an annual rent of 33*s* 4*d*.[1]

Coldharbour was situated in Heywharflane and had its own wharf on the Thames, and later belonged to the wealthy merchant Johan Pulteneye, mayor of London in 1330/32, 1333/34, and 1336/37. On 14 February 1347, Pulteneye leased Coldharbour, called *Choldherberwe* in the grant, to Humphrey de Bohun (d. 1361), earl of Hereford and Essex, a grandson of King Edward I. Humphrey would give Johan a rose every Midsummer as nominal rent. Pulteneye's long will of 14 November 1348 mentions Coldharbour, called both *Coldherberuy* and *Choldherberwe* with the usual casual fourteenth-century attitude towards spelling, and he valued it at 1,000 marks or £666.66. Pulteneye's widow Margarete married secondly Sir Nichol Loveyne, and in 1355 they paid 26*s* 8*d* annually to hold *Choldeherberwe*.[2] As well as Coldharbour, Johan owned a property without Bisshopesgate, and another residence in the same parish as Coldharbour, All Hallows at the Hay, was called *Dyneshemanhalle* in 1314.[3]

Two large houses which stood on the south bank of the Thames in Suthewerk opposite the Tower, where City Hall stands today, were La Rosere and La Cage. Edward II leased La Rosere from Dame Anneys de Doneleye (Lady Agnes Dunley) in October 1324 and purchased La Cage next to it from Sir William Latimer in February 1325 at a

41

cost of 20 marks, and spent much money in 1324/26 renovating and improving La Rosere, later called Dunley's Place. The king had a new kitchen installed in the house and had it covered with 800 tiles, and built a covered walkway from the kitchen to the hall which had 200 tiles and its own gutter. La Rosere had a solar above the kitchen, and the king had his own chamber there, presumably also on an upper floor. A plasterer called Watte of Coventry and his assistant Robin worked on the new kitchen and the hall in and after March 1325, and on 9 March 1325 Edward II's chamberlain Hugh Despenser gave a bonus of 20*s* to carpenters working on the house. Edward much improved the *hays*, i.e. hedges or palisades, around La Rosere, and had trees and shrubs planted within its enclosure. Having lavished money and attention on La Rosere, Edward often visited or stayed there, paying boatmen to carry him across the Thames from the Tower. In June 1326, the king had a pentice built between the jetty and the door into the hall of La Rosere which was made of 100 laths (long strips of wood) and fifty nails. Edward II's son and successor Edward III, however, showed little interest in the property, and by 1330 the rent was in arrears and its 'walls against the water of the Thames' were in a perilous state.[4]

Many noble families owned homes or mansions in or just outside London, as did a few of the English bishops. Among numerous other examples, the Audleys, landowners in Staffordshire and Shropshire, owned *Audeleehalle* without Aldresgate; Roger Bigod, earl of Norfolk (d. 1306) owned 'houses and a little garden' at Brokenewerf (close to the modern Millennium Bridge); the Hastings family, earls of Pembroke for much of the fourteenth century, owned *Pembrokesyn*, 'Pembroke's Inn', in the parish of Seint Martin Lodgate; and Giles, Lord Badlesmere (1314–38) owned a tenement with seventeen shops and an adjacent garden within Alegate, and a tenement and enclosed garden in Lymstret. A will of 1349 mentioned the 'palace ... towards the east end' of the highway of Lothebury.[5] The massive Palace of Westminster, birthplace of Edward I in 1239 and his brother Edmund in 1245, burned down in 1834 and was rebuilt as the Houses of Parliament.

The greatest London residence of the fourteenth century was the Savoy, then spelt *Sauveye* or *Saveye* and located on the Straunde between the city and Westminster, which had gardens running down to the Thames and became an enormous, opulent palace. Edward I granted the site to his brother Edmund, earl of Lancaster and Leicester, in the early 1290s, and it had once belonged to their great-uncle the count of Savoy, hence the name. In March 1327, the Savoy was called 'a plot of land on the bank of the Thames … which is worth nothing except in the fruit of a certain tree'. This was a pear-tree; Edmund of Lancaster's son Henry (d. 1345) kept treasure buried beneath it, but one night in or before July 1335, thieves dug it up and stole it.[6] Henry's son Henry, first duke of Lancaster (d. 1361), inherited the Savoy in 1345, and spent tens of thousands of pounds – tens or even hundreds of millions in modern terms – building it into a great palace. It passed into the possession of Duke Henry's son-in-law John of Gaunt, son of Edward III, and was destroyed during the Great Uprising of 1381.

Gardens

Part of the area north-west of the city, north of Holebournestrete, was given over to gardens, vineyards, pastures and arable land, to the point where medieval London presented a greener aspect than one might imagine.[1] Although this area stood outside the city walls, it is apparent from the Assize of Nuisance, wills and other sources that numerous inhabitants within the walls also owned gardens, not only magnates and bishops but ordinary people. In the early 1300s, Richard Meldebourne paid 12*d* a year for a garden 'near London Wall, near Aldresgate towards Crepelgate', and in 1317 Elyas Toundor requested in his will that his garden in the parish of Seint Olouf (Olaf or Olave) be sold to pay off his debts. Johan Lawe left three houses and gardens in the parish of Seint Giles Crepelgate to his wife Lucy in April 1301, and six years later the goldsmith Richard Stanes left shops in Everardeswellestrate with adjoining fountain and garden in the same parish to his wife Emme.[2]

Roger atte Watre and his wife Cecile, daughter and heir of Richard Weston, owned a garden called 'Hermitage' on the south side of Alegate, and leased it to a blader named Peres Staundone in July 1325 at an annual rent of 10*s*. In 1320 a 'certain small garden' adjoined Ledenhalle, opposite the choir of the church of Seint Peres Cornhull. This garden belonged to Sir Johan Neville in 1343, and was called, not very creatively, *Ledenhall gardyn*.[3] The 'king's garden' in the *Roumelond* near the Tower is referenced in 1330, a garden in the ward of Bradestret was called *Lovelane*, and another in Aldergatestrete, which belonged to Reymund of Bordeaux, was called *Jewesgardin* or *Juesgardyn*, i.e. 'Jew's Garden'. The cordwainer William Dode inherited a garden from his sister Maud Hannam, and in early 1342 leased it to Thomas and Maud West; it stood in the parish of St Michael in Bassieshawe ward, 'near the tenement of Johan Huntecook, and extending up to the garden of the Guildhall'.[4]

Cristine Tylly and Henry Denecombe told the Assize of Nuisance on 5 November 1322 that although an open drain was meant to carry away rainwater from their adjoining houses, their neighbour Nichol Perndon had blocked the drain, so that when it rained, their garden and the plants were flooded. Cristine and Henry were not a couple and lived in different houses, but obviously shared a common garden. Johan Gisors (*c*. 1279–1351), mayor of London 1311/13 and 1314/15, lived in the parish of Seinte Marie atte Naxe, close to where the building nicknamed the Gherkin now stands. He went to the Assize on 24 May 1325 and stated that the earthen wall between his land and the land of the prior of Holy Trinity was so decayed and broken that it no longer served as a viable boundary, and that the prior's tenants often entered his garden and damaged it.[5]

Hugh and Juliane Waltham of Cornhulle, who complained about their neighbour Robert Mustrel's privy in 1325, went to the Assize again on 8 June 1330. Another neighbour, Thomas Marche, had prevented them building an earthen wall between their garden and his. The mayor, Simond Swanland, one of the sheriffs, Richard Lacer, and six aldermen told them that Thomas must provide 4½ feet of land and that the Walthams must pay for the wall, which ran from the corner of their house next to a well on the south, as far as the garden of the prioress and convent of St Helen's, and was about 118 feet long. The same session of the Assize heard that Richard atte Pole was building a new house also on Cornhulle, and that a stone wall ran from the churchyard of St Michael on the north to the corner of Richard's new parlour on the south, and was adjacent to the garden belonging to Richard Leukenore on the east. The wall was about 132 feet long.[6]

In October 1302, Brother Henry Sutton, described as the 'guardian of the Friars Minor', i.e. the Franciscan order, made a complaint against the dean and chapter of the church of Martin le Grand, and specifically against Master Robert Staundone and William Hottokeshathere (this extraordinary-looking name means Uttoxeter, Staffordshire). He claimed that they had refused to mend the fence between their garden and the Franciscans', and that the Franciscans' garden was now 'ruinous and broken down so that the fruit and plants are carried off and trampled down and other evils and enormities are inflicted upon them'. The garden of the priory church of St Bertelmew in Aldresgate ward was used for criminal purposes in March 1325. Johan Fuatard and his mistress Isabel climbed over an earthen wall into the garden in the middle of the night, intending to burgle the home of the carpenter Richard Rothyng, which stood next to it.[7]

A 'certain tenement in the parish of All Hallows near London Wall' belonged to the cordwainer Robert Stratford and his wife Dionise in 1348, and although they leased the tenement out for 20*s* a year, Robert and Dionise 'reserve to themselves the right to half the fruit growing on the fruit-trees on the premises'.[8] The alderman Solomon Coteler or Laufare (d. 1312) had a herb-garden in the courtyard of his home in the parish of Seinte Mildred, close to the River Walebrok, and in 1314 the prior of Holy Trinity stated that people and animals went into his garden in the parish of St Botolph without Alegate over a broken wall, and stole the fruit growing there.[9]

Professional gardeners existed in fourteenth-century London. The gardener of the Tower doubled up as the gardener of the Palace of Westminster (see 'Tower' below), and the large gardens of the nobility and episcopate next to their London mansions would have required much work. The 'gardeners of the earls, barons, bishops, and of the citizens of the city' petitioned Mayor Johan Hamond in August 1345. They wished to continue selling the garden produce of their employers in the same place where they had sold it of old, in front of the Church of St Austin, at the side of the gate in St Paul's churchyard. Hamond and the aldermen, however, decided that this fruit and vegetable market was a 'nuisance to the priests who are singing Matins and Mass' in St Austin's and to clerks and laymen passing by 'in prayers and orisons'. Local residents had also complained about the 'scurrility, clamour and nuisance' of the gardeners' market, and they were therefore ordered to move to the space between the south gate of St Austin's churchyard and the garden wall of the Blackfriars' convent.[10]

Hospitals

A fourteenth-century 'hospital' had nothing to do with a modern hospital. In 1318, the staff of the hospital of Seinte Marie without Bisshopesgate in London were named as the 'prior, canons, brethren and sisters', which makes it apparent that it was a religious house.[1] Hospitals did their best to look after the poor and sick who came in, but had little if any medical training and little if any equipment and medicine. Edward I's nephew Henry, earl of Lancaster and Leicester, owner of the Savoy, founded a hospital in Leicester in 1330 said to be for 'poor persons and pilgrims' and staffed by four or five chaplains.[2] This makes clear that fourteenth-century hospitals provided beds for the poor and infirm and for travellers, and that the guests' religious needs were catered for, but little else.

It is apparent from the extant London coroners' rolls how rarely a person who suffered an accident or was attacked was taken to a hospital. In December 1325, when Rauf of Nottingham was badly wounded in the head after being assaulted outside a tavern at the north end of London Bridge, he was carried into the home of the vintner James Beauflour, because it was nearby. James and his wife Emme did not summon a physician; they summoned a priest, who gave Rauf the last rites. After the saddler Johan atte Vyse was horribly beaten and stabbed by half a dozen goldsmiths in Chepe in November 1325, his friends could think of nothing better to do than to carry him, 'groaning', into his own home in nearby Goderomlane, where he died. When Wauter and Cristine Arderne found Wauter Benigtone lying unconscious outside a brewhouse in Brigge ward one night in March 1325, having been hit on the head with a cudgel, they carried him to a fountain in Crokedelane, then in the morning took him into a nearby house belonging to Geffrei Warde, where Wauter died. Johane Cotekyn fell downstairs and 'fatally crushed her body' in Brigge ward one evening in August 1324. Her neighbours carried her to her father Johan's house in the same ward, and she died there two and a half days later.

The pregnant Lucy Barstaple was beaten up by a woman with the odd name of Anneis Houdydoudy near the Tower of London on 30 June 1326. Lucy's friends found her and carried her into the hospital of Seinte Katerine, but only because the hospital was close by. When Thomas Northampton was wounded by robbers opposite the hospital of Seint James the Apostle in February 1339, he did not even go to the hospital, but walked the 3 miles to the home of a friend or relative in Langebourne ward and died there a few days later. After Thomas Hodesdone (Hoddesdon, Hertfordshire) suffered a severe head injury and his friends took him into London for treatment in April 1325, he died in a house rented by Estephene Hodesdone in Walebrok ward.[3] His friends' instinct was to take him to the home of a city resident whom they knew from their native village rather than to a hospital.

Other than Lucy Barstaple, the only example in the coroners' rolls of an injured person being taken to hospital is that of Phelip Asshendone. At Vespers on Monday, 7 December 1321, William atte Rowe relieved himself into a public urinal at the top of Vedastlane, and some of the urine went onto the shoe of a man standing nearby. When the man complained, William punched him with his fist, and Phelip Asshendone, also nearby, remonstrated with him. William hit Phelip on the forehead with a stick and inflicted a deep wound. Onlookers, the saddler Johan Waledene and Thomas Welde, who worked for Richard Hakeneye, one of the sheriffs of London, carried Phelip to the hospital of Seinte Marie without Bisshopesgate, and he died there on 2 January 1322.[4]

The pepperer William Grantham left generous bequests in his will of December 1350 to the poor residents of several London hospitals: the hospitals (plural) of Seinte Marie without Bisshopesgate, Seint Bertelmew Smethefeld, Seint Thomas of Suthewerk, Seint Giles near Holbourne, Seint James near Westminster, Seinte Marie within Crepulgate, and Seinte Katerine near the Tower.[5] Seinte Katerine was probably the city hospital mentioned most often in fourteenth-century records, and was founded in 1148 by Matilda of Boulogne, wife of King Stephen (r. 1135– 54). It fronted onto the Thames, east of the Tower of London and outside the city walls. When Edward I wished to enlarge the Tower in the late thirteenth century and to build a ditch and wall around it, he had to take some of the hospital's land to do so, and promised them an annual payment of 5 marks.[6]

Elyas atte Park, from Bedfordshire, worked as a mason in the Tower of London, and in November 1324 quarrelled with his brother Johan within the Tower grounds. Elyas drove Johan 'up to the Tower wall by the Thames' with the intention of killing him, but Johan managed to draw his own knife and stabbed Elyas in the heart. He then climbed over a building where munitions were kept, dropped into the Tower ditch, and sought refuge in the church of Seinte Katerine hospital, where he confessed to his deed after his and Elyas's other brother, Roger atte Park, found Elyas's body and raised the hue and cry.[7] As well as a church, the hospital had houses and stables within its complex, which in the 1320s belonged to Sir Johan Cromwell, former constable of the Tower, and his wife, Idonea Leybourne née Vipont. The couple kept their horses, war-horses and falcons there.[8] Juliane Prykafeld, a *lavendere*, died in the Seinte Katerine complex around midnight on 17 September 1337. She lived in one of the houses within the hospital, and a skinner named Thomas Longe from Sandwich in Kent broke into her home with the connivance of 'a certain Anne, a courtesan' who also lived there. Thomas stole a strong-box containing money and jewels from Juliane, and killed her by stabbing her in the chest and throat.[9]

One London hospital was called 'the new hospital of Seinte Marie without Bisshopesgate' in the thirteenth and fourteenth centuries, though it had been founded in 1197.[10] There were also houses and a church inside the complex, and it had a total frontage of about 544 feet.[11] Another hospital was Seint James the Apostle, which probably stood on the site where St James's Palace was built centuries later and which treated women with leprosy, and yet another was Seint Bertelmew or St Bartholomew in Smethefeld, founded in 1123 and still extant (and often called Barts). In the 1320s, its master was Brother William Rous.[12] The hospital of 'St Thomas Acons' is mentioned in 1315, and in 1320 appears as the 'hospital of St Thomas the Martyr of Accon'. In the fourteenth century, it was believed to have been founded by King Richard Lionheart (r. 1189– 99). In fact, it was founded in the 1220s as the 'Hospital of St Thomas the Martyr of Acre', and was the headquarters of the Knights of St Thomas, named after their patron saint Thomas Becket, archbishop of Canterbury (d. 1170), a native Londoner. In 1327, 100 years after its foundation, its master was Nichol Clifton.[13] In the early 1320s, Edward II ordered the mayor and sheriffs of London to arrest 'persons pretending to be proctors' of the hospital of 'St Thomas the Martyr of Dacorum' from collecting alms.[14] William Rothyng, a merchant, left money in his will of 1349 for 'a lamp to burn by night among the weak and sickly' in the hospital of St Thomas.[15]

William Elsyng or Elsinge, a London mercer who died in the plague year of 1349, founded a hospital on 19 July 1330, and called it 'the New Hospital within Crupulgate' or 'the hospital of Seinte Marie within Crepilgate'. Others often called it Elsyngspital or Elsinggespitele. In his will, William specified that the hospital was for the 'poor, blind and indigent of both sexes, under the direction of a prior and convent', and in 1340 stated that 'a master and four secular priests' should work there.[16] As early as 3 November 1330 within months of its foundation, Thomas Leyre left £5 to the hospital.[17] Finally, a hospital for lepers called *Loke* or *Lok* ('Lock') is mentioned in wills of 1356 and 1361 and was located in Suthewerk, and another will of 1349 left money to 'poor lazars [lepers] without Suthwerkbarre and at Hakeneye'.[18] Later writers stated that the *Loke* was founded in 1321 by Edward II, which is possible, though records are missing. In March 1346, Edward's son Edward III banished persons 'smitten with the blemish of leprosy' from London, claiming that they actively endeavoured to contaminate others 'by the contagion of their polluted breath ... [and] by carnal intercourse with women in stews and other secret places ... to the great injury of the people dwelling in the city'. The unfortunate victims of the disease were given fifteen days to leave London.[19]

Roads

In his will of March 1348, the mercer Thomas Burton left tenements in Gropecountelane in the wards of Seint Pancras and Seinte Marie Colcherche to his colleague and nephew-in-law Johan Howle.[1] 'Grope' means the same as in modern English, and the Middle English word *counte* is now a four-letter word ending in 'nt'. Another fourteenth-century London street with a hair-raising name was Shitteborwelane, with numerous variant spellings, now called Sherborne Lane. Peres Brauhinge left houses in Schitebuelane to his daughter Johane in June 1300, though specified that she could only receive the rents from tenants once she had married, and in 1304 Robert Wodere owned shops and Alis Lauvare owned a tenement in Shiteburuelane. The tapicer William Palmere left a corner tenement in Schittebournelane to his daughter Cristine in 1348, with building material and £10 for finishing the work.[2]

Edward II granted a vacant plot of land to his clerk Master William Maldone in June 1312, which lay west of a house that belonged to the king's cousin Johan of Brittany, earl of Richmond, east of houses that had once belonged to Henry Waleys, a former mayor, and between 'our highway which extends from Ivylane to Eldedeneslane' and the north wall of the bishop of London's palace. In the absence of useful later inventions like house numbers and grid references, this was a typically long-winded way of describing a section of Paternosterstrete just north of St Paul's between Chepe and Lodgate. The mayor, Johan Gisors, and the aldermen pointed out that if Maldone built a house on this land, it would be a 'nuisance and annoyance' to everyone, and to the king and queen in particular. It would narrow the king's passage through Chepe to Westminster too much, and the queen's carriage would not be able to pass another carriage or to turn easily. Furthermore, the new building would hinder carts carrying items to and from the wharf of Baynardeschastel.[3]

Just how narrow London streets and lanes could be is revealed by a case at the Assize of Nuisance in August 1306. The commonalty complained that the prior of Seint Bertelmew had narrowed Medelane (presumably by building on it) by 1½ feet, and that the lane should be 5½ feet wide but now only measured 4 feet. The residents of Fisshyngwharflane in the parish of Seinte Marie Somersete stated in February 1346 that William Trig blocked the lane with wooden stalls, wood and 'other things' and that they no longer had access to the Thames. William countered that the lane had always been too narrow to be used by carts because they could not turn in it. One lane leading from Thamestrete to the river was 5.8 feet wide, and another, Desebournelane, was 215 feet long and 7 feet wide at the Thamestrete end, but only 45 inches wide by the river.[4] In 1312, it was ordained that all the lanes leading to the Thames should be 'well and stoutly chained'.[5]

A channel, gutter or open drain, *canellum* in Latin, was sometimes made in the middle of streets and lanes to carry away wastewater and rainwater either to the Thames, Flete or Walebrok rivers or to a marshy area north of the city walls called the *More* or 'moor' (the sogginess of the *More* is revealed by the fact that in June 1301, a group of men required a boat in order to make an inspection of it). Thomas Leggy, the mayor, gave the fishmonger Johan Gildesburgh permission in September 1348 to make a gutter along Desebournelane down to the Thames, to 'draw off the water from the highways in the neighbourhood'. The royal highway outside Bisshopesgate had a ditch, *fossatum*, running down the middle which carried away rainwater from the fields behind the hospital of Seinte Marie to the More, and another such channel took water to the Houndesdych through an aperture in the city wall. Other people made use of sinks or soakaways in their gardens.[6]

Tolls were sometimes exacted from highway users, especially carters, to pay for repairs to the roads. In March 1344, for example, one penny was levied on all carts passing between Hollebournebrigge and the bishop of Ely's house, and in July 1345 on all carts passing through Bishoppesgate. Persons leading a horse carrying merchandise paid ¼d.[7] In 1282, for a few months, a toll was imposed on everyone using London Bridge to pay for repairs to the bridge: ¼d for pedestrians, 1d for riders, and ½d for every horse-load.[8] In an attempt to protect the roads, it was forbidden to bring carts with iron or partly iron wheels into London.[9] In 1304, Richard Wollechirchehawe gave £19 'for the repair of the pavement within Bishoppesgate', and an inquisition of 1307 found that although the guardians of the Flete prison were liable to repair the woodwork of the Fletebrigge, the sheriffs of London were bound to pave the bridge.[10] A salter, Gilbert Palmere, left money in his will of 1349 for 'the repair of highways within a circuit of 20 miles of the city of London'.[11]

Broken pavements were a hazard in the narrow city streets, and residents were responsible for repairing and maintaining the pavement outside their homes. Johan Waldene was told to lower the pavement outside his house in April 1309, as 'private persons and strangers walking and riding there' were inconvenienced. The abbot of Reading, the prior of the new hospital of Seinte Marie without Bisshopesgate, and William Causton, all of the parish of Seint Benet atte Wodewharf, had neglected to repair the 'broken and worn-down' pavements outside their tenements by December 1341, which endangered pedestrians and riders.[12] Another hazard lay above one's head: pentices, i.e. the extended eaves of a house or solars jutting out over the street. A city regulation stated that a person on horseback must be able to ride easily beneath pentices, and they were not allowed to extend more than 2½ feet beyond a house, though this rule was flexible in wider streets. Complaints that pentices built across narrow streets which impeded those riding through the streets on 'great horses' occurred fairly often, and it was declared that pentices and solars must be at least 9 feet above the ground.[13] As noted in 'Sanitation', Londoners often unlawfully threw their waste and excrement outside their homes, so in addition to the hazards of broken pavements, narrow streets, overhanging pentices, churned-up mud and horse manure, walking the streets of fourteenth-century London is unlikely to have been a pleasant or fragrant experience.

Trading

The Middle English words *chep(e)* and *cheping(e)*, meaning a market, were often used in fourteenth-century London. The street-name Chep(e), now Cheapside, has nothing to do with the modern adjective 'cheap' but reveals that the street was the main trading area of medieval London, and the names of towns like Chipping Sodbury and Chipping Norton come from the same root. Another word was *evecheping*, 'trading at night', which was forbidden. A writ of Edward II in July 1323 states that about forty phelipers sold old clothes, shoes and other goods on Cornhull at night, though such sales were lawful only between sunrise and sunset. In future, the king decreed, these goods must not be sold after Vespers rang at the hospital of St Thomas the Martyr of Acre. The phelipers included Roger Penyfader of Houndesdiche, Wauter Radioun of Clerkenewelle, William Beverle of Suthwerkbarre, and three married couples.[1] Edward II had also proclaimed in June 1310 that no one was allowed to hold a market in Chepe after the hour of None, or anywhere else in the city except Cornhull. This was probably a reference to a fair called *Neue Feyre* ('new fair') which was held on Soperelane in the afternoons, and which the king's father Edward I had banned in June 1297 – evidently to little effect – because it had become a magnet for cutpurses and murderers.[2]

Henry Waleys, mayor of London several times in the late thirteenth century, owned a house called the Stokkes, i.e. Stocks, adjoining the churchyard wall of Wollecherche. In the tenth year of Edward I's reign (November 1281 to November 1282), Henry assigned this house as the place where meat and fish could be sold in the middle of the city, and it was an excellent location, in the large open space at the junctions of Pultrye, Walebrokestrete, Bradestrete, Cornhulle and Langbournestrete. The only other places where selling meat and fish was allowed were Bruggestrete in Estchepe, Eldefisshestrete, and 'the Weststrete of the butchers in the parish of Seint Nichol'. The money paid by traders to rent market-stalls in the Stokkes went towards maintaining London

Bridge, and those whose payment fell into arrears were banished from the market until they had paid in full. In April 1323, the guardians of the Bridge, Johan Sterre and Roger atte Vine, complained that some fishmongers, including Anneis Greilond and Benet Shorne, set up their stalls elsewhere. The fishmongers were ordered to desist.

At a congregation of the mayor (Johan Hamond), the sheriffs, the aldermen and the commonalty held at the Guildhall in July 1345, it was stated that 'the king's highway between the place called the Stokkes and the conduit … was so occupied on flesh-days by butchers and poulterers with their wares for sale, and on fish-days by fishmongers' that the road was partially blocked. The traders were all reminded of the rule that meat and fish could only be sold at the Stokkes and not on the roads near it, and that if they broke this rule again their wares would be confiscated. Four butchers had their meat seized shortly afterwards 'because they obstructed the street of the Pultrye with their benches, placed there for selling their meat'.[3] This ordinance makes clear that meat and fish were sold on different days ('fish-days' and 'flesh-days'), and also that meat stalls were inside the Stokkes while fish stalls were located 'beneath the pentices' adjoining the Stokkes enclosure (i.e. under a sloping roof or a covered walkway).

A set of regulations for London cornmongers was issued in 1315 or 1316, and shows that corn could be sold at four places in the city: Billyngesgate, Grascherche, Quenehithe, and in front of the house of the Greyfriars (Franciscans) at Newegate. Nineteen men were elected in April 1322 to guard Quenehithe and Billyngesgate in order to prevent corn from being taken out of the city or removed unsold from the market. 'Strangers', i.e. non-Londoners, could bring corn by the river to Quenehithe and were allowed to sell it there once the bells of St Paul's rang for Prime, under the careful supervision of four city cornmongers. In 1298, it was ordained that corn which was to be ground should be delivered by weight to millers, who were to return the same weight in flour, and in 1300 that 'by ancient custom in London', bakers and brewers had to pay for transporting the corn purchased at Quenehithe to their homes. From Quenehithe 'through all streets and alleys to Westchep, Horshobrigg and Wolsiesgate in the Ropery' cost ¾d; 'beyond to Fletebrigge, Neugate, Crepelgate, to the opposite side of Berchenereslane on Cornhull, Estchep and Billingesgate' cost 1d; and 'as far as the Barres of the suburbs' cost 1¼d.[4]

Traders and shops clustered together, and the names of streets which still exist in modern London show what was sold there in the fourteenth century: Melkstrete, Bredstrete, Honilane, Pultrye, and so on. The fishmongers worked on Briggestrete and the goldsmiths on Chepe, the 'goldsmithery'. Shops opened Mondays to Fridays, and on Saturday mornings and early afternoons. The articles of the cutlers stated in 1344 that cutlers should not work on a Saturday after None, and should not keep their shops open on Sundays. If a 'strange person' passing through London urgently needed a knife or blade, however, it was permitted to sell him or her one from a private house, without opening the shop.[5]

Richer Refham (d. 1328) was a wealthy mercer, alderman and knight, and mayor of London in 1310/11. He complained in March 1314 that although he had recently bought a shop on the corner of Sopereslane next to Chepe, Johan Botoner had 'a very small shop in the corner of the same, under the first storey', which was about to fall down. The Assize agreed that the shop was ruinous and dangerous and ordered Johan to demolish and rebuild it, and to provide a new post at the corner of Chepe and Sopereslane the same thickness as the old one (12 inches), together with the joists, planks, plates and 'everything else necessary', except the wall his shop shared with Richer's. The dimensions of Johan Botoner's tiny shop – where he presumably, given his name, either made and sold buttons or worked in the cloth trade – are provided: 5.8 feet long, 5.4 feet wide, 8 feet high on the Sopereslane side and 8.75 feet high on the Chepe side. Johan was allowed to fix the iron hooks for the shutters over his windows to the timber of Richer's adjoining shop.[6] Thirty years later, Richer's grandson Johan Refham leased the shop Richer had bought in 1314 to Johan Dunle, a pepperer, for 20s a year.[7] In July 1318, Johan Wentgrave, the mayor, Johan Priour, one of the sheriffs, eight aldermen, and a master mason and a master carpenter went to measure a shop in Bredstrete which was disputed among a number of co-heirs. The shop was used by a *fourbour*, William Neve, and measured 27.4 feet by 29.3 feet. It had a solar to which a pentice was fixed to shelter the shop windows and steps from rain. Johane Tayllour, a *selkwyf*, leased a shop in Sopereslane from Master Johan Botoner, a rector, in the late 1340s, and before 1349 the *thredwomman* Isabel Wybourne left shops in Bredstrete to her kinswoman Margerie Wybourne.[8]

A word that often appears in medieval London records is *seld(e)*, meaning a warehouse or storage space with lockable cupboards. In July 1310, a 'painted seld [*peinteselde*] in Westchep' is referenced in the will of Estephene Coventre, and it belonged to his mother Rohese, whose own will of early 1318 calls it her *brodeselde*, 'broad seld'. There are other references to 'the great seld of Rohese Coventre in the mercery of London': Johan Sturmy leased a 'piece of ground in the great seld of Rohese Coventre' to the mercer Hamo Godchep in 1317 for eight years at 20*s* annually, and a will of 1354 still called the seld Rohese's, thirty-six years after her death, and makes clear that it had a gate.[9] Johan Blount, mayor 1301/08, left a seld called *Andovreselde* in Walebrok ward to his son Edward in his will of early 1313, and had inherited it from his father, also Edward (d. 1278). The 1327 will of the mercer Robert Worstede mentions his 'aumbry [cupboard] and chest with two covers' in a seld belonging to Alis Arraz, which was called *Brantefeldesselde,* and Robert Meldeburn left a chest in St Martin's seld near Soperlane to his son Richard. Bertelmew Arnald, a tanner, left his sister Rohese 'a seld with chamber within, situated at the west end of his tenement in Lymbrennereslane, for life; the same to be kept in repair against wind and rain' in 1348.[10]

Food

In an age when few people enjoyed an abundance of food and deaths from starvation were not uncommon, people who sold food to the public and broke the rules and regulations were punished harshly and subjected to public ridicule. Mayor Richer Refham and several aldermen examined the bread of baker William Somerset in August 1311, and discovered that it was 'putrid and altogether rotten', to the point where those who ate it 'would be poisoned and choked'. Richer therefore sent one of the city sheriffs to arrest William.[1] Most probably, he was either locked into the pillory or dragged on a hurdle (see 'Punishment' below), as happened to baker Richard Davy in October 1299 for selling inadequate bread. Richard Lughteburghe and Aleyn Lyndeseye were dragged on the hurdle in May 1316 for selling *pain demaign* 'made of bad dough within and good dough without' and halfpenny *wastel* loaves that were too light. Some millers got into trouble in 1324 for mixing chalk, white sand and bran into their flour, and in 1335 a group of bakers were accused of 'carrying on their business secretly, hiding themselves like foxes'. Such behaviour was automatically deemed suspicious and probably criminal.[2]

In January 1310, nine *baksteres* of Stratford-le-Bow were accused of selling halfpenny loaves at a lesser weight than they should be; the women included Godiyeva Foting and Johane Cauntebrigge. Later in 1310, two other *baksteres* were named as Richolda and Mabel Stratford, and the area of Stratford was the breadmaking centre of the city.[3] Bakers either had to make *tourte* or white bread such as *wastel* and *pain demaign*, but not both, a regulation dating to 1281, and the cheapest *tourte* loaves cost ¼*d*. Bakers were not allowed to sell their wares in their homes or 'in front of their ovens', but only 'from boxes and baskets in the market', for which they paid a toll of ½*d* per basket.[4]

The penalty for those who sold rotten meat was to have the meat burnt beneath you while you were locked in the pillory. This unenviable fate befell William Sperlyng of Westhamme in November 1319 when he attempted to sell two beef carcasses in the Stokkes. The 'wardens for overseeing the meat' sold there, Adam St Albans, William Ramme, Nichol Dereman and Gilbert Dullyngham, noticed that William's beef was 'putrid and poisonous', and that the cows had died of disease. William claimed to a jury that the meat was 'good and clean', but to no avail.[5] Esmon Ware and Reynald Bridel also suffered this fate in April 1350 after selling 'putrid meat' in the Flehshammeles.[6] Something of the fury contemporaries felt at wasting their hard-earned money on bad meat is apparent from the accusation hurled at the cook Henry Walmesford in 1355, that he had sold veal that was 'stinking and abominable to the human race'. In 1351, Henry Pecche bought two capons baked into a pasty at the Stokkes for himself and two friends, and described the meat as 'putrid and stinking, and an abomination'. Henry Passelewe, the cook, was condemned to the pillory.[7] Butchers were not allowed to cut meat for sale after the bells of St Paul's rang for None, and any meat they had already cut had to be sold by Vespers. The pork and beef of three butchers, Johan Perer, Johan Esmar and Reynald atte Watre, was confiscated in November 1320 as they were alleged to have tried to sell it by candlelight.[8] The assumption was that anyone trying to sell meat in inadequate light was trying to pass off bad meat as good.

The dean and chapter of St Paul's grew crops in the fields of Stebenhuth, and the fields were guarded at night; in August 1325, seven servants performed this task.[9] Desperate, hungry times created desperate, hungry people, and this was just a few years after the Great Famine of 1315/17, when it barely stopped raining in northern Europe for many months and crops were ruined in the waterlogged fields, and the harvests failed catastrophically. Up to 10 per cent of the population starved to death or died of disease and malnutrition in those dreadful years, and despite Edward II's efforts to fix the prices of basic foodstuffs so that people could afford to eat, costs went up and up. The plight of Londoners, who had less opportunity than rural dwellers to grow their own food, was particularly dire, and chroniclers say that two small onions cost 1*d* in Chepe.[10] For most Londoners, this sum represented a few hours' wages; imagine having to work for half a day or more just to be able to afford two small onions. Edward II's regulations of early 1316 reveal the costs of food: two dozen eggs cost 1*d*; a 'fat chicken' 1½*d*; three pigeons 1*d*; a 'fat capon' 2½*d*; a 'fat shorn sheep' 14*d*; and a 'live fat cow' 12*s* (144*d*).[11] Alis Goldenlane, a beggar on Pultrye, was one of those who starved to death in London during the Great Famine: in 1315, she collapsed and died under the wall of St Mary's chapel 'of bodily weakness and lack of food'.[12]

Traders were forbidden to buy victuals before Prime was rung at St Paul's, though, as often happened, buyers for the king and for 'great lords of the realm' were exempt. Johan Broun, poulterer, was imprisoned on 19 November 1341 for purchasing twenty-four partridges and thirty-four larks at Ledenhalle before sunrise. 'Forestalling', when a trader bought up the entire available supply of a food product at a higher than usual price before markets opened, and thus deprived other traders, was forbidden, and in 1309 Edward II appointed four men to 'punish cases of forestalling'. In March 1350, the poulterer William Tythynglomb was found guilty of a second offence of forestalling, and was sentenced to the pillory. Five years earlier, a brewer named Johan Erdele was convicted of meeting merchant Peres Kyngeston outside the market of Grascherche and buying up all his malt, though as it was Johan's first offence his only punishment was to forfeit the malt. Two women and four men were accused of forestalling the corn market in February 1338, though only one man was found guilty, and six men were acquitted in December 1337 of 'entering boats and buying oysters before the recognised hours of sale'. Supposedly they had kept the oysters until they were 'stinking and putrid', then mixed them with fresh ones.[13]

Both men and women earned a living by fishing in the Thames west of London. Edward II's accounts of the 1320s record Alis atte Churche and Isabel Fissher near the royal manor-house of Sheen (later Richmond Palace), 'the fisherwomen of Lambehuth', and seven fisherwomen near Kennington. In October 1324, Edward II, staying at the Tower of London, bought fish and seafood plus butter and onions from local fishermen, including Robyn Sharp and Cock Swete. His oysters cost 5*d*, sixty unsmoked herrings cost 5½*d*, three large eels and seventy-three lampreys cost 5*s* and 11*d*, four large stockfish cost 10*d*, and twenty roach and 100 smelt cost just a few *d*. The king dined on eels at his house of La Rosere in Suthwerk opposite the Tower in late June 1326, and personally went out to the postern gate of the Tower in September 1326 and bought two large salmon for 3*s* from the fisherman Richard Marbon.[14] A city regulation stated that lampreys had to be offered for sale immediately on arrival in the city, under the wall of the church of Seinte Margarete in Briggestrete. Hugh 'Huchon' Madefrey or Matfray, a fishmonger from a family of fishmongers, got into trouble in 1311 after storing pots of lampreys from Nantes in Brittany in his house for several days.[15]

As noted in 'Gardens', a few Londoners grew their own fruit, vegetables and herbs, and some people worked as *fruteres*, *frutesteres* and *costers*. Pearmains and costards are two of the varieties of apple we know were consumed in England in the fourteenth century, and costards are believed to have been cooking apples rather than dessert apples. Pears, quinces, plums and cherries were also popular. A pear-tree grew in the garden of a house in the parish of St Michael Paternostercherche and was valued at 5*s*, and another pear-tree stood in the garden of the Savoy in the 1320s and 1330s.[16] Vegetables often eaten included onions, garlic, beans and leeks, and fruits and vegetables were grown in sizable quantities in the London gardens of the well-to-do.[17]

The reference to Henry Pecche buying a pasty with two capons baked inside shows that hot, takeaway food could be purchased at the Stokkes market. A coster sold his apples in the streets in January 1301, presumably from a cart or from a tray on a strap around his neck, and in the summer of 1326, Roger Styward sold eels from a bucket in Cordewanerstrete.[18] As well as fixed market stalls and shops, therefore, food-sellers sometimes walked the streets to find potential customers.

Drink

In a census of 14 February 1309, according to the annalist of St Paul's, there were 354 taverns in London and 1,334 brewers and brewsters. Assuming a city population of 80,000, this equates to one tavern for every 225 people.[1] A popular tavern stood at the head of London Bridge and belonged to Thomas Drinkewatere, and therefore was called *Drinkewaterestaverne*. In 1319, the vintner James Beauflour leased it from Thomas. A clerk, Rauf of Nottingham, was attacked with a *shovele* (shovel) outside the tavern in December 1325, and died of his injuries a few days later.[2] The Frenchman and London alderman Guillaume Betoyne owned a tavern in Westchepe which bore the name *Ubi le Bere tombeth*, meaning 'Where the bear tumbles' in a mixture of English (*bere tombeth*), Latin (*ubi*) and French (*le*). Almost certainly, the name means that the tavern featured a dancing bear. Guillaume left the Tumbling Bear to his son Richard in 1305, and Richard, mayor of London in 1326/27, left it to his daughter Johane in 1340.

Johan Oxenford ran a tavern in Lymstrete ward in the early 1320s which had a solar, and Godwin Hodere (d. 1313) owned a tavern on Cornhulle which had 'a hall built over it and chambers'. The skinner Thomas Leggy, mayor of London in 1347/48, owned a tavern in Westchepe called *Taverne atte Groot*, which looks more like Dutch than Middle English. In 1350 Roger Brewere had a tavern called *Atte Mayden en la Hope* ('At the Maiden in the Hoop'), and others were named *Hors atte Hope, Helm on the Hoope, Hert on the Hop, Scotothehop, Cok in the Houpe, Aungell on the Hoop, Belle on the Hop, Pecok on the Houp* and *Bere on the Hoop*.[3] Tavern signs, called 'ale-stakes', were often carved with the subject of the sign and hung within a hoop, hence the many 'hoop' names. It was ordained that no London tavern should have a stake which extended more than 7 feet into the street, with a penalty of 40*d* imposed for longer ones.[4]

There was a city regulation, repeatedly proclaimed, that tavern customers had the right to see their ale or wine properly drawn in the rightful measure from a cask. Taverners Roger Torold and Nichol Blake were fined 80*d* each in 1350 for refusing to allow a customer, Johan Cortoys, to see his wine drawn.[5] It was forbidden to hang a cloth or curtain in front of the door leading to the cellar where wines were stored, and one customer from each party of friends was permitted to descend and inspect the casks and drinking vessels. Taverners were also strictly enjoined not to mix bad wine with good or old wine with new, as some of them did so 'to the corruption of the bodily health of the purchasers'. Edward III fumed in November 1327 that London taverners mixed 'weak and bad' wine with other wine and sold it at the price of 'pure wine'.[6] Edward II ordered the mayor and sheriffs in December 1310 to visit all the taverns in London – 354 of them – and test their wines. Any found to be bad were to be destroyed. A few weeks later, the king issued a series of regulations for the sale of wine in London, which specified that dregs should be poured into 'wines of lower price', that each tun of wine should be marked with its value on the front so that customers could easily see it, and that wine merchants and wholesale dealers (*grossours*) were not allowed to keep taverns.[7]

In November 1306, Henry Scheleford and his friends visited a London tavern run by Robert and Ellen Wych. Henry drank a gallon and a quart of wine and ate a halfpenny loaf – revealing that taverns offered basic food as well as drink – and offered to pay 3¾*d* for the wine rather than the 4*d* per gallon which the taverners charged. They demanded the full price, and when Henry refused to pay, Robert and Ellen claimed to the mayor's court that he assaulted them. Henry, for his part, stated that they imprisoned him in the tavern until the middle of the night.[8]

Thirty-six years later, 4*d* was still the maximum price permitted for a gallon of Gascon wine, and Johan Beauflour, vintner and son of James (d. 1328) of the *Drinkewaterestaverne*, got into trouble for selling it at 6*d* a gallon. He was released on mainprise (meaning that three other city vintners stood as guarantors for his good behaviour), but immediately committed the same offence, and therefore was imprisoned on 4 March 1342. Johan Pynsone sold wine at 5*d* a gallon in Holebourne in June 1345, but was released on mainprise. An ordinance was made on 2 July 1331, and repeated on 17 December 1339, that *Renys wyn* or Rhenish wine could not be sold for more than 8*d* a gallon. As well as red and white wine, sweet wines were sold: Crek or Cret (from Crete), Vernage or Vernache (from Tuscany), Ryvere, Malveysin or Mauveysyn, and

Romeneye. Taverners who sold sweet wine were not allowed to sell red or white wine as well, and it was forbidden to keep Gascon wine and Rhenish wine in the same cellar.[9]

In July 1331, the mayor, Johan Pulteneye, four aldermen and the commonalty revealed the names of twenty-nine taverners who had closed the doors of their taverns and refused to agree to sell Gascon wine at only 4*d* a gallon. Two were women, Alis atte Laneende ('at lane end') and Anneis Ballard, and the rest were men.[10] Another female taverner was Katerine Oveseye, who leased a brewhouse with garden from the vintner Simond Leuesham and his wife Alis in Bassyeshawe ward in the 1320s and early 1330s. Hugh Strubby, a spurrier, left his wife Sarra his tavern in Fletestrete with eight shops around it in his will of November 1316, and in 1341 the carpenter Simond Canterbury left his tavern to his wife Isabel for life, when it would pass to their daughter Alis.[11] Brewing ale was a job often done by women in the thirteenth and fourteenth centuries, and they were called *brewstere* or *brewyfe* ('brew-wife'). Female tavern-keepers were called *tap(pe)steres*.[12]

In May 1320, the mayor, Hamo Chigwell, forbade the sale of ale on London Bridge, and the five men who did so, Robert Amyas, Roger Ceynturer, Henry Flete, Thomas Hide and Anselm Latoner, thereafter had to ply their trade elsewhere. Edward II had it proclaimed in London on 20 September 1316 that ale must not cost more than 1*d* per gallon, and it was sold by the gallon (3.8 litres), *pote(l)l* (half a gallon, 2 quarts, or 1.9 litres), or quart. Turners were the people responsible for making liquid measures, and six turners promised in December 1310 only to make gallons, potells and quarts and no false measures called *chopynes* and *gylles*.[13] When workmen were hired for temporary labour, they were usually given an allowance on top of their daily wage to buy ale and food: a generous 4*d* or 5*d* a day. This money was called *nonschenche* or 'noon's quench'.[14] In July 1326 during a brutally hot summer, Edward II gave twenty-seven ditchers cleaning the ditches around a cottage he owned near Westminster Abbey 20*s* to buy themselves ale.[15] This would have bought each man almost 9 gallons each.

At the junction of Chepe and Pultrye stood the great conduit, an impressive piece of thirteenth-century engineering which brought fresh water to the city centre from the Tibourne river several miles away. In July 1345, Edward III stated that the conduit's purpose was for 'rich and middling persons' to have fresh water to prepare food and for the poor to have something to drink.[16] This presumably means that poor residents could not afford ale and had to make do with water. Guardians of the conduit were appointed regularly and given the keys; in 1325, for example, they were William Latonere, Johan Albon and Richard Gaunter, though only two months later Albon and Gaunter were replaced by Geffrei Gedelestone, a cutler, Henry Ware, and Benet of the Guildhall. The oath taken by the guardians is recorded in November 1310: 'he will well and trustily, with the greatest diligence, cause the conduit in Chepe to be kept, so that neither brewers nor fishmongers shall waste the water thereof; nor shall he sell the water thereof to anyone'.

The water from the conduit was free to most residents, though brewers, cooks and fishmongers had to pay, as they used larger quantities than anyone else. Roger of Paris, Ranulf Balle and William Hardi were appointed in 1312 to collect the fees which these groups of people paid to use the conduit, and the money was used to repair and maintain it.[17] The accounts of the wardens Richard Gaunt and Thomas Peautrer show that they received £6 18*d* from brewers for filling tankards and vessels called *tynes* (large tubs) in 1333, and £6, 6*s* 6*d* the following year. From the money they received, the two wardens paid £4 22*d* for 'making a clay wall around the head of the conduit at Tyburne'.[18]

A complaint was made in November 1337 that people who kept brewhouses in the streets near the conduit used *tynes* to take water without permission and without paying, to make malt and to brew ale. The keepers of the conduit, Johan atte Barnet and William Peautrer, were told to confiscate *tynes* in future, as their use hindered other residents from drawing water. Fishmongers were also reminded on this occasion that they were forbidden to use the conduit's water to wash fish unless they paid for it.[19] The wardens of the conduit, Robert Fundour and William St Albans, presented an account in November 1350. One payment of 32*s* 2*d* was made to 'investigate the conduit for poison', an intriguing entry not explained, and another of 33*s* 6*d* to repair the 'fountain-head', which was washed eight times a year. Over 6s was spent repairing the *spurgail*, a Middle English word apparently meaning an overflow tank, at the Fletebrigge.[20] In addition to the great conduit, a fountain in Crokedelane is mentioned in 1325. Margerie Somery had her own well outside her home in Wodestrete in 1314, and so did Hugh and Juliane Waltham in Cornhulle in 1325 and Simond Wenlok in Pultrye in 1346. There were also public wells which local residents could use, and one, in the parish of St Dunstan by the Tower, was called *Draghewell* or 'drawing-well'.[21]

Drunkenness

In a case heard before the mayor's court in March 1306, the mayor, Johan Blount, heard that Thomas Blendesowe 'goes to the tavern at night, gets drunk and is quarrelsome, and is a nuisance to the neighbours'. He was, therefore, expelled from his ward.[1] Which ward was not specified, though it is interesting to see that a person could be expelled from their home and area of the city if s/he routinely became drunk and disturbed the peace.

Luke Havering was a very busy man at the start of the 1300s: as well as practising his profession as a corder, he was chamberlain (chief financial officer) of London and one of the two city sheriffs between September 1300 and September 1301, and also held the office of king's butler. Luke lived and worked in Roperestrete, and invited his friend Henry Curteis to his home on Friday, 28 October 1300. Henry became exceedingly drunk as the evening progressed, and while attempting to descend a flight of steps from Luke's hall, missed his footing, fell, and hit the right side of his head very hard. He died around midnight. Another unfortunate incident befell Richard Brewere, who earned a living brewing ale in Brigge Ward, a few weeks later on Wednesday, 14 December 1300. Drunk, presumably on ale he had brewed himself, as Richard carried a bag of malt up the steps of a house belonging to William Cross he stumbled from a step and fell, 'rupturing his bowels and diaphragm'. He died the following Friday.[2]

Staircases could be lethal to those who had imbibed too freely: William Hamond was drunk one evening in September 1339 in the home he rented from the draper Geffrei Weston in Bredstrete ward, fell down the stairs, and broke his neck. William Bonefaunt, a skinner, rented a house from William Bokkyng in Candelwykstrete. Around the time of curfew on Sunday, 31 August 1337, Bonefaunt was drunk, and stood naked at the top of the steps in his home to relieve himself, presumably into a urinal or other receptacle, though this is not stated. He lost his balance and fell down the stairs, and died. Dancing while inebriated could also be dangerous. One evening in August 1339, the goldsmith Johan Markeby was 'drunk and leaping about' in his home in

Mogwellestrete with his daughter Alis and his servant Robert, when he managed to stab himself in the thigh with his own knife.[3]

Alis and Johan Quernbetere lived in Crepulgate ward. Alis was very drunk after Vespers on Wednesday, 30 August 1301, when she came into Wodestrete at the corner of Selverstrete and saw workmen, hired by one Thomas Sely, preparing the ground for the walls of a new house Thomas was having built. Being inebriated, Alis thought it was a good idea to provoke the men, and shouted that they were *tredekeiles*. One of them took her by the hand and told her that she should join them in treading the earth, then deliberately bumped her to the ground. Alis went home and complained to Elena Scot, who owned the house where Alis and her husband lived. Elena duly went to shout at the workmen and called them ribalds, and the matter blew up when a man named Johan Melkesham passed by and reprimanded Elena for scolding the men, whereupon she called him a thief and he called her a whore. She stomped home, told two of her other tenants and her chaplain, Wauter Elmeleye, to avenge her, and they went looking for Melkesham in the house of Anneis of Nottingham, a taverner. In the ensuing fight, Melkesham stabbed Elmeleye in the shoulder, and he died. Alis and Elena were arrested; Johan Melkesham fled, but subsequently joined the king's army in Scotland, and Edward I pardoned him for Wauter Elmeleye's death on 23 February 1302 as a result of his 'good service'.[4]

The ship *Seinte Marie Cogge* was moored at St Laurence wharf near the Tower in late 1336, and one of the crew was Elyas Ide. On 21 November, Elyas came back to the wharf very drunk, and decided it would be a good idea to climb up the mast of the ship. Probably inevitably, he fell, and drowned in the Thames. One of the investigating jurors was the local shipwright Martyn Palmere of Petiwales, and one neighbour questioned was Richard Councedieu, also a sailor, who came from Sandwich in Kent and lived in London for decades. Laurence Brauhyng, captain of the *Seinte Marie*, was also questioned. Two more sailors, William Hampton and Pieter Skomakere from Flanders, drowned in the Thames on 5 and 12 December 1339. Both men were supposedly very drunk, both decided to stroll alone on a wharf – William on St Botolph's wharf in the port of Billingesgate and Pieter on the one belonging to William Box in Tower ward – after curfew on a Sunday evening in winter, when it would have been completely dark, and both lost their balance and fell in the river. The similarities of these two deaths, exactly a week apart, seem odd and somewhat suspicious.[5]

Misadventure

When a Londoner died unexpectedly, his or her death was investigated by a number of jurors, a minimum of a dozen and sometimes as many as thirty (and always male), from the dead person's ward and several of the adjoining wards. If the person died in an accident, a fine called *deodand* had to be paid to the king to the value of the inanimate object which caused the accident, but only if the object was or could be in motion, or could cause a person to be in motion. *Deodand* was not payable if a person died in bed, but was if s/he fell down steps or from a ladder or a horse. Johan atte Wode from Suffolk was killed around Vespers on 11 November 1300, outside Adam Drayton's house in Chepe between Honilane and Melkstrete, by a piece of falling timber. The timber had been affixed to Adam's solar 'for the purpose of drying saddles', and inflicted a wound 4 inches long and 2 inches deep on Johan's head. Jurors from four wards asked a large number of passers-by whether anyone had moved or touched the beam, and discovered that although William Branthingge had been inside Adam Drayton's house, shearing cloths, he 'did not move his hand', i.e. did not touch the timber. The jurors decided, however, that as the beam had killed Johan by falling, *deodand* of a penny was payable.[1]

When Henry Curteis died in his friend Luke Havering's home on 28 October 1300 when he fell down some steps, the jurors solemnly noted that 'the right side of the head appeared broken', and stated that Luke's steps were worth 12*d* as *deodand*. The jurors who investigated the death of Richard Brewere in December 1300 valued the steps of William Cross's house, where Richard fell while drunk, at 2*s* to be paid as *deodand*, and when 80-year-old Alis Pursere fell down the stairs and died in her home in the parish of Seinte Marie Colcherche on the last day of 1325, the stairs were valued at 4*d*. After Isabel Pampesworth hanged herself during a *frensy* in November 1321, the cord and beam were worth a farthing (¼*d*) as *deodand*. The carpenter Hugh St Albans fell from a ladder and 'fatally broke his head' in April 1324, while working on the gate of a house in Baynardeschastel ward that belonged to Sir Roger Waltham. His colleague Richard Rothyng carried Hugh almost a mile to his (Richard's) house in Aldresgate ward, but he died five days later, and his ladder was valued at 4*d*. Henry Callere, who 'fell down and died' in his home in Crepelgate ward in 1340, was walking upstairs when he passed away, and his stairs were valued at 18*d*, a surprisingly large sum.[2]

After sunset on Thursday, 4 May 1301, 3-year-old Pernel was playing in the street near her parents' home in Crepulgate ward when Hugh Picard, servant of the clerk Master William of London, lost control of his white horse as he rode. The horse's front right foot caught Pernel on the head, and she died the following day; the horse was valued at 1 mark (160*d*). Thomas atte Chirche, a squire who worked in the household of the half-Italian earl of Arundel, Edmund Fitzalan (1285– 1326), rode along Tamestrete towards the Tower in the evening of 19 October 1321, in the company of a 'certain unknown man'. The two men rode too fast and carelessly, and as they passed the house of Olive Sorweles, a widow, Thomas atte Chirche's horse almost knocked an unnamed woman carrying her infant to the ground. Local resident Johan Harwe shouted to Thomas that he should ride more carefully, whereupon Thomas leapt from his horse, drew his sword, and plunged it 5 inches deep into Johan's right side. Johan died the following morning, and the jurors who investigated the matter ordered the arrest of Thomas atte Chirche and his companion, who had fled in the direction of the Tower. The value of Thomas's horse should have been payable as *deodand*, but as Thomas fled while riding it, the jurors had no means of valuing it.[3]

Elena Gubbe drowned in the Thames on 22 October 1324 while filling two pitchers at the Lavenderebrigge, and the step of the wharf from which she slipped into the river was valued at 4*d*.[4] The unfortunate Johan Bone died in the parish of Seint Andrew Estchepe in Billingsgate on 28 August 1340. Johan had dropped a bucket into a well, and as he attempted to retrieve it with a pole, fell in. Sensibly, the dozen jurors who investigated his death asked the sheriff Roger Forsham for permission to stop up the well, which he granted, and they valued the pole at 1*d* as *deodand*. A similar case had occurred at the end of September 1324, when Richard Herkyn of Tower ward let himself down a well in a bucket to retrieve a board, but fell and drowned. In this instance, the coupere William Stiward found Richard's body and raised the hue and cry, and jurors valued the hemp cord and bucket at 12*d*. The well was also blocked up.[5]

Murder

The murder rate in fourteenth-century England rose inexorably as the century passed and reached levels rarely seen in the modern world except in warzones, and between 1300 and 1350 a depressingly large number of Londoners stabbed or bludgeoned each other to death, often during a quarrel or while drunk. Research suggests that the murder rate in medieval London was fifteen to twenty times higher than one would expect in a modern town of similar size.[1] An eyre (a circuit court held by itinerant judges) held in London in 1321 heard details of 699 killings, of which the judges held twenty-five to have either taken place outside the city and therefore to be outside their jurisdiction, or to have been committed in self-defence.[2]

In an attempt to avert violence and murder, only city officials, sergeants-at-arms of the king and queen, and great lords and servants 'carrying their lords' swords in their presence' were allowed to carry arms on the city streets.[3] It is apparent from the number of murders and assaults, however, that numerous people did carry knives, swords, cudgels and other weapons, including: *Irysshknyf* (Irish knife), *bidaw(e)* (long, broad knife), *thwitel* or *twytel* (large knife), *misericorde* (long, narrow knife), *bal(gh)staf* (cudgel), *anelaz* (dagger), *panade* (poniard, a small dagger), *fauchon* (falchion, a one-handed, single-edged sword), *pol(l)ax* (poleaxe), *sparth* (axe) and *gisarme* (halberd).[4] Even some children carried weapons. The brewer William Kempstone was working in a brewhouse owned by Wauter Seynmore in Farndone Without ward on 23 August 1339, and saw a young boy steal a hood from a female customer. He gave chase and caught up with the boy on Secollane, but the boy stabbed him in the belly with a knife. William managed to stagger back to the brewhouse, and died the following day. It was the custom for men to wear cloaks with hoods, and during an attempted abduction of a young woman named Emme Pourte from her home in Brigge ward in March 1325, eighteen men put stones in their hoods as well as the swords and knives they carried.[5]

70

After curfew on Thursday, 12 January 1301, a coster, name not recorded, came to a street near Graschirche in Kandelwykstrete ward, crying out 'Costard apples for sale'. Two local residents called James Kyng, known as Copin, and William Osbern bought some apples from him but also tried to steal five, and their neighbour, Thomas Brewere, heard the coster's protestations and remonstrated with the thieves. The men got into an argument which turned violent, and Brewere hit Copin on the left side of his head with a staff. Copin died two weeks later. Although witnesses stated that Thomas Brewere had acted in self-defence and that Copin Kyng had tried to steal the coster's apples, Thomas was imprisoned in Neugate. On 10 February 1303, Edward I pardoned 'Thomas May, brewer', for Copin's death as he had killed him in self-defence.[6]

Joce Spaldinge, who lived near Pouleswharf and appeared before the Assize of Nuisance to complain about a neighbour's pigsty in 1322, killed a draper named Thomas Kyrkeby in April 1325 after the two men quarrelled in the church of All Hallows on the Cellar. Thomas chased Joce out of the church to the stone wall of the house belonging to Ydonia Leyre, punched him in the face, and drew his knife. Joce drew his own *anelaz* to defend himself, and in the ensuing struggle stabbed Thomas in the chest and killed him. Joce was imprisoned in Neugate but not executed, and eight months later Edward II pardoned him on the grounds that he acted in self-defence. He was still alive in June 1328.[7] Johan Pope stabbed Robert Curteis to death in Distaflane in May 1322 after Robert assaulted Johan's wife Amice outside their shop. Johan was imprisoned in Neugate, and Edward II ordered him to be bailed six months later as he killed Robert 'without malice aforethought'.[8] Roger Styward was killed in Cordewanerstrete in August 1326 as he sold eels from a bucket, and deliberately dropped eel-skins on the ground outside the shops of Simond Peckham and Johan Keslyngbury. Johan's apprentice Richard Keslyngbury and Simond followed Roger up the street, hit him round the head and kicked him, and killed him, apparently inadvertently. They were both imprisoned in Neugate. Simond was pardoned and released a few weeks later, and lived until 1339, having fathered a son named Johan in 1338. Richard Keslyngbury was perhaps the man of this name who was mayor of London in 1350/51.[9]

Johan Lyncoln, son of a London cordwainer also named Johan Lyncoln, travelled towards Rochester ('Roucestre') in Kent early one Friday morning in May 1322, and started talking to an unnamed man journeying in the same direction. As the two men were crossing Blackheath ('Blakehethe'), the traveller pulled Johan's own *thwitel* from its sheath, stabbed him in the stomach, tied him up, and made off with all Johan's goods. The unfortunate man lay there for twenty-four hours until a passing carter found him, untied him and 'for charity's sake' took him on his cart to Grenewych. Here a group of boatmen 'for the love of God' took Johan up the river to St Botolph's wharf, where friends carried him into the home of one Anneis St Neot, another friend or relative of Johan or perhaps his lover, on Cornhull in the middle of the city. Unhappily, Johan died of his injury on Monday evening a few days after the incident, and his attacker was never identified or caught.[10] This case reveals that although some people were willing to commit murder for the sake of stealing a few possessions, others gladly helped a stranger in dire need. It is a sad irony that Johan Lyncoln had probably considered it safer to find a travelling companion than to journey alone on the dangerous roads and paths of fourteenth-century England.

In late July 1322, Johan Pentyn, a *neylere*, decided to hang himself in the home he rented from Mabel Gisors, sister of the former mayor Johan Gisors, in Aldresgate. His wife Clemencia raised the hue and cry, and Johan Chiggewell, *copresmyth*, was one of the neighbours who rushed into their home to help. He paid for this diligence with his life: Johan Pentyn hit him over the head with an iron staff, and he died a few days later. Pentyn was forcibly prevented both from killing himself and from escaping, and was imprisoned in Newegate but bailed in April 1323.[11] The jurors who came to investigate Johan Chiggewell's death specified that the iron staff wielded by Johan Pentyn caused a wound 3 inches long and 5 inches deep in the victim's head, though jurors who investigated murders on behalf of the coroner could be squeamish when it came to head wounds. When Roger of York, a cordwainer, assaulted the bedel of Bredstrete ward, Richard Leving, in 1302, he 'maliciously threw down the said Richard so that he fell against the pavement and broke his head'.[12] 'Broke his head' or 'fatally broke his head' is a common expression in the coroners' rolls and court rolls. Lucy Faukes of Alegate ward made the fatal error of believing that Richard and Cristine Sherman were good friends of hers, and went to spend the night of Sunday, 20 September 1322 with them in their shop, as she had often done before. The cold-blooded couple, however, decided to murder her

72

and steal the good-quality clothes she wore. Richard took a *balstaf* and struck Lucy on the top of her head, and, said the jurors, 'mortally broke and crushed the whole of her head'.[13]

Some of the chief justices of the realm held an eyre at the Tower of London in 1321, including Hervey Stanton (d. 1327), Geffrei Scrope (d. 1340, ancestor of the Lords Scrope of Masham), William Denum, and Johan Herle, and it was the first eyre held in London since 1276. The extant roll of pleas reveals some of the appalling cases the judges heard: two men who had taken a prostitute to a latrine argued over who should go first, and one man struck the other dead; a man's head was discovered in another latrine, but no one knew what had happened; and a chaplain killed a young man who was bestowing his sexual favours on him by sodomising him with a stick. The shocking case of a Gascon merchant, Menald Porte, gives us another horrifying and disturbing glimpse into the London underworld. He induced a brothel-keeper named Anneis Rousse to procure a child for his pleasure, and abused the girl so abominably that he broke her back and she died two weeks later.[14]

Theft

In a society where most people had few possessions, theft was judged harshly, and if a person stole items with a greater value than 12½*d*, s/ he was executed. Alisandre Nedelere stole a tunic belonging to Johane Lavendere in August 1328, though as it was only worth 10*d*, he was imprisoned in Neugate for forty days rather than being hanged at the Elmes.[1] On 6 March 1327, Edward III granted the mayor of London the rights of *infangenthef* and *outfangenthef*. These are Old English words meaning 'thief seized within' and 'thief seized without', i.e. the right to judge and hang thieves captured in London who had committed their crime there, or who were captured elsewhere. A few weeks later, the first judgements on thieves were recorded, often using the words 'with the *mainour*', i.e. the thieves were caught red-handed with the stolen items (from the French *main*, 'hand').

Johan Reynham stole a surcoat and hood from Roger Child on Ismongereslane on 1 November 1326, but as the clothes were only worth 10*d*, he was sentenced to be flogged then set free. Robert Milleward stole clothes and pieces of cloth worth 40*s* from William Prentiz in Quenehithe ward on 1 May 1326, and was hanged; William Owyas, caught in possession of a mazer worth 10*s* which he stole from Gilbert Mordon, one of the sheriffs in 1325/26, was also hanged. Three other men were hanged in 1327 after being convicted of stealing a gown of bluet cloth and 18*s* 6*d* in cash from Johan Emelyn in *Drinkewaterestaverne*. Wauter Barry was hanged at the Elmes in August 1339 after being caught with an overtunic of *appelblome* (apple blossom) and a tunic of blanket cloth which he had stolen from a tailor named Roger Barkworth. Execution followed just two days after the theft. Johan Duk was hanged in June 1346 after he broke into the house of a skinner named Roger Shrouesbury (Shrewsbury, Shropshire) in Wolcherchehawe, and stole 'four white furs of lamb' and a furred *courtepy* (short jacket) of gold.[2]

Johan Brewere drowned in the Thames in November 1338 while being pursued by two merchants of Florence, whose names are recorded as Johan Bercard and Alisandre Gydetty, from whom he had stolen money and goods on the road between Romford and Brentwood ('Brendewode') in Essex. The merchants searched the streets of London for Johan and his four criminal associates between sunrise and Terce on 17 November 1338. Johan saw them coming for him in the parish of Seint Nichol Flehshammeles, and ran half a mile to Pouleswharf. As the Thames was low, he hid in the water, intending to make his way along the wharves to the Flete river and to escape at the Fletebrigge; but the tide rose, and he drowned. The huge sum of 160 florins (640*s* or 7,680*d*) which Johan had stolen from the Italians was found on his body and returned to them.[3] Another Johan, Johan Barkere, moved to London from Elsham in Yorkshire. In the summer of 1337, he stole a blanket, four sheets and a coverlet from Aleyn Osgodby, who, judging by his name, was Johan's fellow Yorkshireman, and was probably Johan's landlord. Johan confessed to the theft, but escaped before he faced justice; perhaps he returned north.[4] A cutpurse named Johan Mulleward came to a sticky end in February 1336: he attempted to rob Thomas of Bristol in St Paul's churchyard, but found himself on the wrong end of Thomas's *trenchour*, yet another type of knife. Thomas was said to have lost his right eye, though whether this happened in the struggle with the cutpurse or in a previous incident was not explained.[5]

Thomas Beneyt turned up at the house of the mayor, Andrew Aubrey, on Wednesday, 9 May 1341. He claimed to be a member of the household of William Montacute, earl of Salisbury (d. 1344), and bore a letter in which Salisbury supposedly asked the mayor to lend him £40, giving the money to Beneyt to bring to him. Aubrey became suspicious when he noticed that the seal attached to the letter was clumsily placed, and it occurred to him that he had never seen Thomas Beneyt before. Realising that his subterfuge had been discovered, Beneyt crept away while the mayor was at Mass, but Aubrey ordered his doorkeeper to go and find him, and the man found Beneyt near St Paul's, wearing a different set of clothes. Beneyt was imprisoned inside Aubrey's house and admitted the forgery, and was handed over to the earl of Salisbury himself to deal with.[6] This case shows that even in London, people's faces were recognised; Mayor Aubrey knew the members of the earl's retinue by sight, and realised that Thomas Beneyt was not among them. Another example is the case of the squire Thomas atte Chirche, detailed above, who in 1321 nearly knocked down a woman and her infant by riding too fast. Atte Chirche worked in the earl of Arundel's household, and was recognised by witnesses who were able to tell the investigators his name and position, though his companion was not.

Assault

On 28 October 1300, two Frenchmen named Pierre of Artois and Reymund Bernard entered the home of William Tailor and his wife Cristine Morel in the parish of Aldermarichirche (which they rented from Thomas Romeyn, alderman and later mayor), and accused William of stealing a coat which belonged to Reymund and of subsequently selling it. During the ensuing quarrel, Reymund kicked Cristine Morel just under the navel and knocked her to the ground. She died early on Sunday morning, 30 October, and the jurors who investigated her death noticed that her 'belly appeared blue and inflamed' below the navel. Immediately on hearing of Cristine's death, Reymund's mistress Magote advised him to flee, but his associate Pierre of Artois was caught and taken to the sheriff Luke Havering's house.[1]

One night at the end of March 1301, Johan Sherman and Augustine Curzon were out and about after curfew, unlawfully, and broke into the Smethefeld home which Adam and Alis Cobel rented from the prior of St Bertelmew. They launched a brutal attack on Adam after he discovered them ransacking his home, and when Alis tried to protect her husband, they assaulted her too. Alis was pregnant, and gave birth to a premature child soon after the attack. She never recovered from her injuries, and died two months later on 31 May. Another pregnant woman attacked was Lucy, wife of Richard Barstaple, beaten and kicked to the ground by Anneis Houdydoudy near the Tower in late June 1326. Lucy gave birth prematurely three weeks later and herself died a month after the attack. And Emme Whitewell, a 'poor woman', was assaulted in her home by William Ammory on Ash Wednesday in 1355, 'so violently and in so horrible a manner that she gave birth to a dead child and kept to her bed for seven weeks'. Sadly for Emme, a jury found Ammory not guilty.[2]

Filippo Gerardini worked in London for the Spini, a trading company of Florence. One Saturday evening in July 1301, Filippo and his companions were sitting at supper in their lodging when they began to 'magnify and praise' King Philip IV of France (r. 1285– 1314) and to 'vituperate and despise' King Edward I of England. One of their English servants, Johan Lung, overheard and made his outrage known, so Filippo hit him. Johan fled from the lodging, whereupon Filippo and his companions pursued him down the street towards the church of Seint Esmon with swords drawn. People came out of their homes and asked the Italians why they 'made so great an uproar, terrifying the neighbourhood', and Filippo cursed them and yelled that they were *Englishoundes*, 'English dogs', revealing that he had learnt some of the local language during his stay in London. The situation grew serious when Filippo and the others retreated to their home and threw stones out of the windows at their neighbours, and they were joined by a number of other Italians including Cose and Pouch Lombard, Bonaventure, Bynde, Simonet, and Rogaz (last names not given). In the end, the mayor, Elias Russel, had to come and deal with the matter in person, and shortly afterwards held an inquest at which it was stated that the Spini, the Frescobaldi, the Pulci and other Italian trading societies 'raised uproars in the city of London by day and night'. Furthermore, they dragged any woman or girl passing into their lodgings to violate them, 'to the damage and scandal of many women, and in contempt of the English'.[3]

The extant sheriffs' court roll of 1320 reveals a large number of assaults in London that year, several of which were carried out by women. Anneis atte Marche assaulted Roger and Margerie Rede on 15 May, Dulcia Paramour assaulted Alis Reyle 'with force and arms' in Phelipeslane on 26 August, and Isabel Seint Cler wounded the clerk Alisandre Lincoln in the left eye with a stick on 1 September. Richard Cordewaner and his wife Dionise assaulted Maude Berkyng on 28 July: they beat her up, shoved her to the ground, and stole two veils she was wearing. Johane of Cateloigne, i.e. Catalonia, Spain, was accused of wounding William of Newcastle in the left ear with a knife on 8 June.[4] Twenty years earlier, Eve Callestere was imprisoned after being convicted of assaulting Johan Fuatard and biting his finger when he went into her house to confiscate 'false grain measures'.[5]

In early 1306, William Hoggenortone 'threw down' Johan Lincoln, 'so that he fell in the mud and turned over three times before he could rise'. William also grabbed Johan's sword and would have struck him with it, except that neighbours pulled him away. A year later, Richard Costentyn and Peres Berneval 'abused each other at the door' of the

Guildhall, and Richard tried to punch Peres but was dragged off by onlookers so that he 'only touched him with his fingers'. The mayor, sheriffs and aldermen took a dim view of brawling in the Guildhall, so imposed a fine of half a mark (80*d*) on Richard and imprisoned him.[6] Thomas Lauda of Wales, a tailor, and Richard of Kent, a cobbler, appeared before the mayor and sheriffs in July 1341, accused of throwing stones at Peres, bedel of Bassishaw ward, while he was on his watch. The unfortunate Richard Tailboys or Tailleboys, bedel of Crepelgate Ward, was assaulted in November 1332, and again in December 1342. On the latter occasion, Thomas Goldsmyth of Faversham in Kent, out and about after curfew, met Tailboys and other nightwatchmen on his way home to Melkstrete, called the men 'ribalds', and broke Tailboys' left arm with a staff. Street brawls were not uncommon, and one took place in Chepe in August 1345; Johan Comberworth was committed to Newgate for drawing his knife during the brawl. Johan Berkyng, a latoner, was charged with affray in August 1339 after punching Henry Asshindon, a tiler, under the jaw because Henry 'used abusive words to him'.[7]

One argument in 1342 had far-reaching consequences. When Gilbert Stayndrop, a goldsmith, was walking along Fridaystrete on 1 September, a passing horse struck him lightly with its hoof. Gilbert reacted by calling the horse's rider a 'ribald' and struck him with his fist, and then with a knife. The rider retaliated by wounding Gilbert quite seriously with his sword. Gilbert soon found himself in big trouble, because the unnamed rider was a servant of Henry, earl of Derby (b. *c.* 1310/12), who was the king's cousin, heir to his extremely wealthy father the earl of Lancaster and Leicester (*c.* 1280– 1345), the future first duke of Lancaster, and the builder of the great Savoy Palace. An inquest held two days later stated, predictably, that the affair was entirely Gilbert's fault; Gilbert demanded another inquest; and the second came to the same conclusion as the first. Even so, the earl of Derby threw a massive sulk, and stated that he, his knights and squires and his entire retinue of soldiers would not cross the Thames to participate in the king's wars. He added that he 'would visit his enmity upon all citizens of London wherever he found them'.

Faced with such obvious blackmail and with being held responsible for the absence of the earl's massive contingent from Edward III's wars in France, Mayor Simond Fraunceys, the aldermen, and an 'immense commonalty' realised that their only choice lay between offering Derby a gift and incurring his lasting displeasure. Several aldermen and commoners went to placate him and gave him 1,000 casks of wine, and begged him not to hold the city responsible because of Gilbert Stayndrop's assault on his servant. The earl, highly delighted with the free wine, accepted, and invited them to dine with him. Having evidently had quite enough of over-sensitive noblemen, however, they politely declined. As for Gilbert, he survived his sword wounds and his experience with the wrathful earl, served as sheriff in 1351/52, and died in 1355.[8]

Disturbance

Fourteenth-century London could be a raucous, dangerous place. Edward II ordered the mayor and sheriffs to 'make diligent search for the armed vagrants who disturb the peace of the city by day and night' in January 1310, and a few months later, complained to Mayor Richer Refham about the 'many robberies, murders, and diverse other trespasses' in London. City chroniclers spoke of the *riffleres* and *roreres* terrorising the streets.[1] At Christmas 1298, Roger Rous of Alegate ward was said to make 'a great roistering with minstrels, tabor-players [drummers] and trumpeters, to the grave damage and tumult of the whole neighbourhood', and at the same session of the mayor's court, it was found that Peres Portehors 'is a receiver by night of unknown depraved men and prostitutes'. Another session of the mayor's court was held on 23 June 1300, and Rauf, a chaplain who lived in Porthesocne ward, 'was a receiver of thieves and prostitutes'; Wauter Coupper was a nightwalker who 'made disturbances' in various inns after curfew; and 'a certain chaplain', unnamed, in Belleryteryslane did the same thing 'to the terror of the neighbourhood'.[2]

Manet or Manett (his name appears in the Latin form, *Manettus*), son of a barber, appeared before the mayor's court in June 1302. The jurors heard how three nights earlier, in the middle of the night, Manet had 'filled an empty cask with stones ... and set it rolling through Graschirchestrate to London Bridge, to the great terror of the neighbours'.[3] Almost certainly, Manet was Italian, as every other instance of the name 'Manettus' or 'Maynettus' in the thirteenth and fourteenth centuries referred to an Italian. Twenty years later, fourteen men's disturbance of the peace had tragic consequences. William Grimsby owned a shop on Bradestrete, and during the night of 31 January 1322 was prevented from sleeping by the men's 'singing and shouting, as they often did at night' outside his shop. Furious at their refusal to let him and his neighbours sleep in peace, and goaded beyond endurance by their taunting him to come out of his shop if he dared, William ran outside with a *balstaf* (cudgel) and bludgeoned Reynald Frestone to death.[4] In April 1338, a proclamation was made against 'any person making cry or noise near the windows or doors of houses and shops'.[5]

Oliver Multone was indicted before the mayor, Richer Refham, in March 1311 for enticing men into taverns after curfew and cheating at dice in the wards of Chepe and Crepulgate, and for being a bruiser, nightwalker and *rorere*. He was imprisoned, though the length of the sentence was not stated, and his friend Simond Braban was found guilty of the same offences. At the same process, Johan Rokeslee was imprisoned after the jury found him guilty of being a nightwalker, beating men, causing much mischief in the city, and 'unlawfully frequenting taverns with harlots' in Crepulgate ward. Peres Taverner was found guilty of breaking curfew 'with sword and buckler and other arms' in Douegate ward, Johan Blome was found to be a common *wagabund*, and Thomas, son of Sarah Bredmongestere, to be a nightwalker and disturber of the peace. Vagrancy was forbidden in London: Edward II ordered the mayor and sheriffs in 1310 to search for vagrants (all of them, not only the ones disturbing the peace, as above) and to subject them to 'due punishment'.[6]

Richard Heryng was accused in 1311 of being a nightwalker and bruiser, even though he was a chaplain, and much evidence indicates that London chaplains often, despite being ecclesiastics, behaved astonishingly badly. Some years earlier, in 1305, Heryng had wounded Robert Bissheye in the left arm and head with a sword, after Bissheye attempted to stop him and eleven associates assaulting the rector of Holy Trinity the Less. Bissheye 'was confined to his bed for half of a quarter of a year' after the chaplain's attack. Another chaplain, Pynchard Wynchecoumbe (i.e. Winchcombe, Gloucestershire), who served in the church of St Dunstan by the Tower, lay in wait for William Noreys one night in January 1340 after they had a quarrel, and stabbed him to death.[7]

In July 1339, twenty-five residents of Farndone ward presented 'a number of disorderly persons and nightwalkers' to their alderman, Richard Lacer. Some of these 'disorderly persons' were arrested and imprisoned in Neugate, though were subsequently released on bail. At the same meeting, Lacer and twelve jurors indicted Thomas, son of Simond Nichol, for beating his father, and for being the leader of a gang of disorderly persons who terrorised the neighbourhood of Smethefeld; Thomas Hundesmor 'for being an armed bully and a harbourer of women

City of London Ward Map (1870)

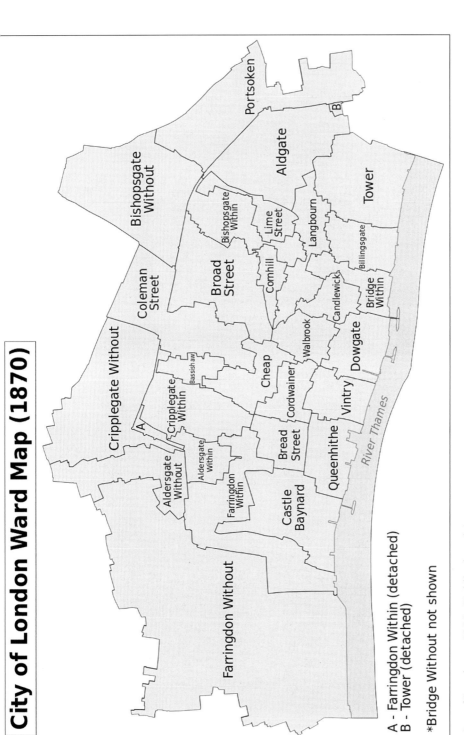

A - Farringdon Within (detached)
B - Tower (detached)

*Bridge Without not shown

Map of London c. 1300. (Public domain)

Portsoken

Bishopsgate Without

Aldgate

Bishopsgate Within

Lime Street

Langbourn

Tower

Coleman Street

Broad Street

Cornhill

Billingsgate

Cripplegate Without

Bassishaw

Candlewick

Bridge Within

Cripplegate Within

Cheap

Walbrook

Dowgate

A

Aldersgate Within

Cordwainer

Vintry

Aldersgate Without

Farringdon Within

Bread Street

Queenhithe

Farringdon Without

Castle Baynard

River Thames

B

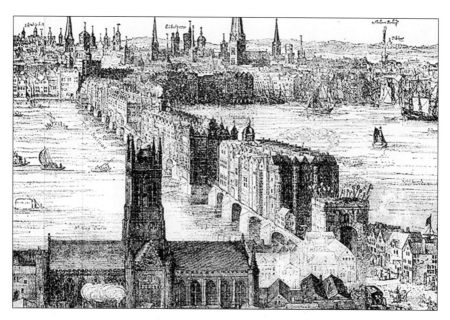

London Bridge in 1616. (Public domain)

London Bridge today. (Author's Collection)

Panorama of London in 1616. (Public domain)

City Hall, which stands on the site of fourteenth-century houses called La Rosere and La Cage. (Jorge Armando Garcia Galvez on Flickr)

Above and overleaf: Tower of London. (Author's Collection)

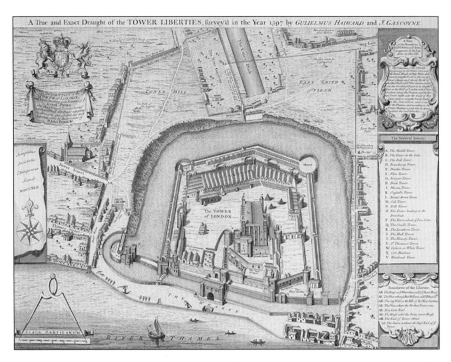

Plan of the Tower in the 1590s, with Tower Street and Thames Street leading to the city on the left. (Public domain)

St Paul's Cathedral, built in the early 1700s on the site of the medieval building that was destroyed in 1666. (Author's Collection)

Old St Paul's; a 1913 reproduction of a sixteenth-century image. (Public domain)

Modern Cheapside, the main trading centre of fourteenth-century London. (Author's Collection)

Cheapside, 1837. (Public domain)

River Thames from London Bridge. (Author's Collection)

Westminster Abbey. (Author's Collection)

Palace of Westminster, now the Houses of Parliament. (Author's Collection)

Houndsditch, the modern street that in the fourteenth century was a ditch where dead animals were disposed of. (Andrew Milligan on Flickr)

A section of the original Roman and medieval city wall near Tower Hill underground station. (John Winfield on Wikimedia Commons)

The Gherkin, real name 30 St Mary Axe, which stands close to where Johan Gisors (c. 1279-1351), three-times mayor of London, lived in the 1320s. (Andy Wright on Flickr)

Newgate Prison in the early 1800s. (Public domain)

The Pool of London in the 1930s. (Public domain)

of ill fame'; and several others, both men and women, 'for keeping disorderly houses, receiving armed nightwalkers and committing assaults, in consequence of which the neighbours did not dare to come out of doors at night'. Hundesmor and his wife Isabel were called 'a source of danger to the neighbourhood' where they lived, and to have 'associates [who] were dangerous persons'.

In 1340, Andrew Brewere 'sleeps by day and wanders about at night', and William Taillour of Sholane 'lies hid at night, springing out on honest men passing by'. Andrew and Beatrice Wrenne were 'common evildoers and disturbers of the peace' who had assaulted three men, and Hugh Staunton was also a common evildoer and 'frequents the house of Alis Stanewell'. Wauter Walteshef, Gracian Palmere and Johan Walssh were well-dressed and lavish with their money, though no one knew how they made a living, and would sooner associate with people of bad character than with those of good report.[8] Suspicion fell on those who wore fine clothes yet had no obvious means of supporting themselves, and in 1311 Johan Rokeslee, Thomas Bery and Nichol Brigge were among them. Johan, nightwalker and frequenter of taverns, had 'no business whereby to maintain himself nor private means' and neither he nor the other two received income from rents, yet they were 'well-clothed'.[9]

Punishment

Anyone who saw that a crime had been committed or was being committed had to make a noise to alert anyone in the vicinity, so that the criminal could be pursued, captured and handed over to the sheriffs or their deputies. This was called the hue and cry, and it was 'raised by horn and voice'. There were fines for failing to do so and failing to respond to it.[1] As there was no such thing as death row in fourteenth-century England, execution often followed remarkably swiftly after conviction; William Sawiere was hanged six days after he killed Cristine Menstre in 1300, and Wauter Barry was hanged two days after stealing a tunic in 1339.

Sir William Wallace, the Scottish patriot made famous in the film *Braveheart*, was hanged, drawn and quartered at the Elmes in Smethefeld on 23 August 1305. He was tried in Westminster Hall and dragged from Westminster to the Tower on the same day, and then through the city to the Elmes. The day after, the paternostrer Roger Southcote went to 'look at the head of William le Waleys' in 'the road on the north of St Michael atte Corne', i.e. Neugatestrete (where Southcote was arrested for 'making a disturbance'). Wallace's head was spiked on the southern gatehouse of London Bridge, though the fact that Roger Southcote went to look at it on Neugatestrete the day after Wallace's execution implies that his head and perhaps the four quarters of his body were first taken through London for residents to gawp at.[2]

The English nobleman Sir Henry Tyes (b. 1285), wearing a gown quartered with green and purple, was hanged in London on or just after 3 April 1322.[3] Henry and around twenty other noblemen and knights who had taken part in a rebellion against Edward II's powerful chamberlain and favourite Hugh Despenser (b. *c.* 1288/89), and whom the king called 'Contrariants', were executed in March/April 1322, though only Tyes was hanged in London. Hugh Despenser himself, lord of Glamorgan, fell from power in 1326 and was hanged, drawn and quartered in Hereford on 24 November that year, and on 4 or 6 December, his head was carried down Chepe to the sound of trumpets and spiked on London Bridge. It remained there for four years.[4] Despenser's downfall was brought about by Roger Mortimer (b. *c.* 1287), a nobleman who escaped from the Tower of London in 1323, and Mortimer's hanging at the Elmes on 29 November 1330 brought this cycle of executions to an end.

At the end of August 1340, a congregation took place in the Guildhall, attended by the mayor, Andrew Aubrey, the sheriffs, William Thorneye and Roger Forsham, the two dozen aldermen, and the commonalty. Edward III was absent from his kingdom for much of 1338 to 1340, and emergency measures were in place to safeguard the city (see 'Defence'). Earlier that month, a massive argument had taken place between groups of fishmongers and skinners, and the fishmonger Rauf Turk was stabbed to death by several skinners including one called Lyttle Jakke. The quarrel blew up into something deeply serious when a violent fight between the two misteries took place in Briggestrete and resulted in the fishmonger Thomas Haunsard threatening Mayor Aubrey with a drawn sword. Johan Brewere hit the mayor's sergeant Simond Berkyng on the head and felled him to the ground, and 'his life is despaired of'. Thomas Haunsard and Johan Brewere were brought into the assembly and admitted their guilt. No fewer than 528 members of the commonalty stated on 30 August 1340 that the two men should be beheaded by the Stonecrouche in Chepe, and the sheriffs Thorneye and Forsham carried out the sentence immediately. Edward III indemnified everyone involved in the executions in June 1341, stating that he had 'charged them to keep the peace in his absence and to inflict swift punishment on any who broke the same'.[5]

The chief London prison in the fourteenth century, and long before and after – it was opened in the twelfth century and not closed until 1902 – was Neugate or Newegate, a notorious hellhole where 'gaol fever', i.e. typhus, ran rampant. Gaolers had no obligation to feed the incarcerated, so if prisoners had no friends or family to bring them food, or money to pay the guards for it, they starved to death. Three men died of starvation in Neugate in 1322 alone, all of whom had been convicted of theft: William Brich, Thomas atte Grene and Adam May.[6] The Neugate warders were not always above suspicion themselves. Edward II removed Esmon Lorimer, 'keeper of Neugate', from his position in 1319, after Esmon broke into the park of Estephene Gravesend, bishop of London, at Haryngeye.[7] In addition to breaking and entering, jailers could also be corrupt. James Galduches, a former prisoner in Neugate, complained in September 1314 that Richard Honewyk, keeper of the gaol, handed him over to his sergeant Johan Parker, and 'although the complainant ... ought not to have been placed in the depths of the gaol as a felon or thief, [Parker] did so immure him so that he might extort money from him, and detained him there, placed with notorious felons and thieves and horribly laden with iron fetters'.[8] Edward III stated in March 1333 that Hugh Croydon and other Neugate guards 'have been guilty of oppressions and extortions' by putting men incarcerated for minor offences in the same cell as 'notorious felons', by committing torture, and by taking bribes and ransoms from prisoners.[9]

For all its notoriety, however, Neugate was not always secure. In March 1315, the prison had 'certain chambers which are in a ruinous state to the ... danger of the escape of prisoners'.[10] Estephene Dunheved was imprisoned there in July 1327 but escaped shortly before 7 June 1329, and was still at large at the end of March 1330.[11] Nichol atte Mulle or Westmille, the gatekeeper of Neugate, was stabbed to death by four escaped prisoners in the high street of Farndone Within in June 1325. Supposedly two women, Alis, the wife of Roger Barber of Croydon, and Alis Ellefeld, sister of the dean of St Martin le Grand, connived at Nichol's death and supplied his killers with knives, though their motive for doing so was not explained.[12] In January 1325, Edward II pardoned Reynald Conduit and William Prodhomme, the city sheriffs of 1320/21, for the escape of Robert Bakere and Estephene Thresk from Neugate, and two years later Edward III pardoned the former sheriffs Benet Fulsham and Johan Causton for a mass escape in September 1325 (the city sheriffs were officially in charge of Neugate). Around midnight on Saturday, 7 September, ten men escaped through a hole in Neugate's western wall. Five were soon recaptured by warders, aided by local residents, and the other five fled into sanctuary and subsequently abjured the realm (see 'Abjurers').[13]

As well as Neugate, there was the Tun on Cornhulle, where nightwalkers were imprisoned; it stood near a bakehouse, and was built by the mayor Henry Waleys in 1282/83.[14] An early reference to the Marshalsea prison appears on 23 June 1308, when Robert, son of Margerie Hedonne, escaped after two fellow prisoners let him down from a window using a towel. Robert's brother Richard had visited the prison three days earlier and planned the escape. Although the Marshalsea later stood on High Street in Suthewerk, and became infamous as a debtors' prison, the prison window through which Robert escaped was on Lymstrate.[15] There was another prison in Suthewerk in the early 1300s: Edward II's over-mighty chamberlain Hugh Despenser (executed 1326) imprisoned Sir Johan Inge, formerly a loyal adherent of Despenser and sheriff of Glamorgan, there in *c.* 1323. Despenser also imprisoned the members of Inge's council in Suthewerk at the same time, and one of them, Thomas Langdon, died in prison.[16]

A *stokfisshmongere* who made his will in 1349 left money to 'prisoners in Neugate, Templebarre, and the Flete'.[17] The Flete prison stood next to the Flete river outside the city walls, and had a ditch around it; Edward III complained about the stench in 1355, and an inquisition held soon afterwards stated that the ditch was meant to be 10 feet wide and 'have sufficient water to float a vessel freighted with a tun of wine'. The prison was rebuilt around 1337: in August that year, the king ordered Esmon Cheyne, 'keeper' of the prison, to allow Richard Potenhale to carry away the 'stones of the walls of the ancient Flete prison', and the stones were valued at 10 marks.[18] The Sench or Shenche family, who owned a house and garden on Fletestrete, had the hereditary custody of the Flete prison, for which they received *6d* a day from the sheriffs of London, and every prisoner was also bound to pay them *2s 4d* a year. Johane Sench was the daughter and heir of Estephene Levelonde, and inherited the custody of the prison from him. She died in September 1332 and her son Johan Sench, born *c.* 1306/08, was her heir, but Johane's second husband Esmon Cheyne outlived her, and had the right, by a custom called the 'courtesy of England', to act as the prison's custodian and to receive the payments until he died in February 1339. Johan Sench then took over. He died on 7 October 1349 in his early forties, leaving his 1-year-old daughter Margarete, named after his wife, as his heir.[19]

Crimes that were not serious enough to merit the death penalty or imprisonment were punished by the pillory, a wooden post with a frame into which the victim's head and hands were locked (the stocks, also sometimes used as punishment, secured the feet, but not the head). One London pillory stood on Cornhulle near a bakehouse and the Tun prison, and another stood at or near the junction of Chepe and Wodestrete. The standard sentence was between one and three hours.[20] In 1310, William Croton of Suffolk was condemned to the pillory for 'pretending to be a serjeant of the sheriffs of London' and demanding a bribe from the *baksteres* Richolda and Mabel, pushing their carts of bread into the city. People who sold bad meat or bread were often locked into the pillory (see 'Food'), and one was William Clerk of Higham Ferrers, Northamptonshire, in 1320. William tried to sell 'putrid and poisonous' meat from an animal that had died of disease, and was put on the pillory with the meat burning beneath him. Johan Sharryngworth, called a *faytour*, was put on the pillory in July 1355 'for being an able-bodied vagabond, who would not work and pretended to be an invalid'. In the same year, Johan Godard was locked in the pillory for three hours 'as a warning to other evildoers' after pretending to be a member of the household of Edward III's eldest son the prince of Wales and obtaining ale without payment.[21]

Later in the century, from *c.* 1364 onwards, a special London pillory for women called the *thewe* is mentioned several times. Alis Salesbury, a beggar, was locked into it for one hour after kidnapping Margarete, young daughter of Johan Oxwyke, in the Roperie in 1373; she intended to force the child to beg with her in order to increase her takings. Alis Shether of Tower ward suffered the same penalty in 1375 after she was found to be a common scold who sowed envy and discord and who used malicious and abusive words.[22] Another punishment sometimes used in lieu of the pillory was to be dragged on a hurdle, i.e. tied to some kind of wooden contraption and pulled around the streets by a horse. There is evidence that a minstrel playing a drum or trumpet accompanied the victim, and that the punishment ended at the person's home.[23] This seems designed to draw more attention to the person and to make their ordeal even more humiliating, and to ensure that their neighbours saw them. Given how filthy the streets were (see 'Sanitation' above), we can assume that the unfortunate victim was dragged through heaps of muck and excrement. In 1316, this punishment was meted out to half a dozen bakers for selling loaves of bread that were too light, including Gilbert Pany. As this was Gilbert's third offence and third time on the hurdle, he had to 'forswear the trade of a baker in the city forever'.[24]

Abjurers

Those who knew they were likely to be sentenced to death often took another way out before their trial. Criminals had the right to seek sanctuary within a church or other religious house, and within forty days of their crime, while still in sanctuary, could announce to the sheriffs or the coroner their wish to abjure the realm; that is, to exile themselves from England permanently.

Abjurers had to leave sanctuary bare-headed and barefoot (even in winter), carrying a cross, and dressed only in a shirt and hose for men or a shift for women. They made their way to a port assigned to them by officials, via the route prescribed and in a specified number of days. Once there, they had to 'cross the sea at the first tide', or rather, board the first ship whose crew agreed to transport them. All their belongings, and property if they owned any, were forfeit. On arrival overseas, perhaps in France or Spain or the Low Countries, the abjurers had to make a new life for themselves, without money and even, supposedly, without shoes or warm clothes. Only the king had the right to pardon abjurers, and if they were seen in England after they should have departed, they were declared 'wolf's head', i.e. outlaws. Edward III pardoned William Wit in August 1337 for stealing a horse in Suthewerk and for abjuring the realm, but other examples are few and far between.[1]

Juliane Aunsel and her accomplice Johan Multone admitted to the killing of her lover Esmon Brekles (see 'Adultery' below) to the sheriffs on 11 June 1324, four days after the murder, in the church of St Helen Bisshopesgate. They both chose to abjure the realm, and were both assigned Dover as the point of departure. Johan was given four days to reach the port, travelling via Dartford ('Derteford'), Newington ('Neuentone'), and Canterbury; Juliane was given five days, and was ordered to stay one night in Dartford, Rochester, Sittingbourne, and Canterbury on the way. Johan departed two days later on 13 June and Juliane on 16 July, the month's delay presumably being intended to prevent the couple meeting up again in Dover or on the way there. Johan Burgeys of Barnwell, Cambridgeshire kept the sheriffs busy on 11 June 1324 by admitting to them, in the church of St Sepulchre without Neugate, that he had killed Robert Seleby in Myton, Yorkshire on 10 September 1320. He agreed to abjure the realm and was given three days to reach Dover, spending the first night in Rochester and the second in Canterbury.[2]

Johan Whetley from Chester killed Johan Belringere on Thursday, 23 May 1324 as they sat drinking and playing dice together in Roger Haverynge's house in Douegate ward. Whetley fled to the nearby church of All Hallows at the Hay, and admitted his crime to the sheriffs shortly afterwards. Unusually, he was allowed to choose his port of departure, and selected Bristol. The sheriffs, Adam Salisbury and Johan Oxenford (who became mayor in 1341), gave him five days to get there, and told him where to spend each night: High Wycombe, Buckinghamshire; Oxford; Highworth, Wiltshire; and Malmesbury, Wiltshire. William Tollere of Lincolnshire and his friend Roger Leche of Shropshire admitted in London on 27 June 1325 that they had murdered William of York around Christmas 1322. Tollere was assigned Dover as his port of departure, and Leche was assigned Harwich and given three days to reach the port from London. Johan Bedewynde and Wauter Gomme sought sanctuary after breaking out of Neugate prison on 7 September 1325, and asked to abjure the realm. The sheriff, Johan Causton, assigned them both Southampton and gave them four days for the journey, spending one night in Cobham, Surrey; Farnham, Surrey; and either Alresford, Hampshire in Bedewynde's case, or Winchester, Hampshire in Gomme's. Bedewynde and Gomme's fellow Neugate escapees, Adam Nouneman and William Soutere, were both assigned Dover. Wauter Gomme had returned to England by early 1340 and must have been pardoned by Edward III.[3]

The experiences of abjurers show that officials in London in the fourteenth century had an excellent idea of routes to other parts of the country, which towns abjurers would pass through, and how long their journeys should take. Each stage of the route Adam Salisbury and Johan Oxenford gave Johan Whetley from London to Bristol in 1324 covered between 20 and 30 miles a day; the longest day was the first, from London to High Wycombe, and Whetley would have to walk about 25 miles on three of the five days. In 1324, Juliane Aunsel was given five days to walk the 70 miles to Dover, Johan Multone four, and Johan Burgeys only three. The following year, Adam Nouneman was given four days to reach Dover and William Soutere three; apparently Burgeys and Soutere were younger and fitter than the others. Johan Bedewynde's journey to Southampton in 1325 required him to walk almost exactly 20 miles each day, and the sheriff Johan Causton could hardly have planned the route better if he had had access to Google Maps.

Defence

London was a walled city for many centuries from Roman times onwards, and in the fourteenth century there were seven massive wooden gates into the city plus a small postern gate by the Tower. From west to east, the gates were Ludegate, Newegate (which housed the famous prison of the same name), Aldresgate, Crepelgate, Bisshopesgate and Alegate, and the seventh stood at the south end of London Bridge. The medieval gates were pulled down in the 1760s, and the remnants of the great city walls were gradually demolished in the eighteenth and nineteenth centuries, though some parts were incorporated into other structures and some fragments are still visible. The most impressive section stands just outside Tower Hill underground station, and is 35 feet high. By 1300, London had spread well beyond its walls, and more gates, called 'bars' to differentiate them from the seven great gates, were erected along the main roads leading into the city to mark its boundaries. Originally they were little more than chains stretching across the road, and were later built as elaborate gateways.

With massive stone walls and seven heavy gates that could be locked and barred, it was easy to keep people, or an army, outside the city, though conversely, this meant that it was also easy to become trapped inside London. This happened to the unpopular Edward II in 1321 when a group of baronial rebels placed their armies around the walls to stop him leaving the city, and five years later he was forced to leave London to prevent it happening again. In the twenty-first century, when London has a population 100 times greater than its fourteenth-century population, and sprawls for mile after endless mile and it is hard to tell where it stops and the rest of the country starts, it takes some imagination to visualise the city as it was 700 years ago: a fortified castle writ large.

Once the bells rang for curfew in the evening and the city gates were locked, the nightwatchmen took up their positions above the gates and on the walls, and if they saw anyone or anything which signified danger, they would sound their horns. Thomas Romeyn, the mayor, decreed in early 1310 that the aldermen could levy a penny or half a penny on each household in their wards to pay for 'strong and well-armed men' to guard the city gates at night. On 14 August 1311, Richer Refham, then the mayor, met the aldermen in the Guildhall to lay down some rules for the safe-keeping of the city. Two or three men were entrusted with the keys of each gate; at Lodegate it was Roger Bristowe and Richard Dokesworth, and at Alegate, Esmon Taylor and Phelip May. Two small houses were built at each gate for the keepers, and wickets, narrow gates for pedestrians, stood on both sides of the much wider and higher gates intended for use by those on horseback and those driving carts pulled by horses. As well as locks, each gate had a heavy iron chain across it, and a portcullis. Twenty men-at-arms from three or four wards were appointed to guard each gate at night. Crepelgate, for example, was guarded by men of Crepelgate, Chepe and Basseshawe wards, and Neugate by men of Neugate, Baynardeschastel, Quenehithe and Cornhulle. Twelve men kept watch at the postern gate near the Tower, and thirty-eight men guarded the banks of the Thames: six from Douegate, twelve from Vinetrie, twelve from Quenehithe and eight from Baynardeschastel. A minimum of 200 watchmen guarded the streets during the night, while four 'good and strong' boats with armed men patrolled the river at night, two on each side of London Bridge.

Emergency measures were put in place in early September 1312 after a bad quarrel between Edward II and the earls of Lancaster, Warwick, Hereford and Arundel which brought the kingdom close to civil war, and the earls brought their armies within 25 miles of London. All the aldermen were enjoined to remain in the city and to ensure that each gate had at least twelve and preferably sixteen strong, armed men guarding it in the daytime. A watchman was to stand on each gate and alert the guards as soon as he saw anyone approaching. The portcullis would be raised to allow 'peaceful folks' on foot or on palfreys, i.e. riding horses, to pass; any men riding 'great horses', meaning those trained for war, would not be allowed through unless they had permission from the king.[1]

Edward III claimed the throne of France in 1337, and spent most of the period between July 1338 and November 1340 outside his kingdom, seeking allies against the French. On 20 April 1338, the king ordered the mayor, Henry Darcy, and the aldermen to produce a plan to defend London while he was overseas. Darcy, the aldermen and an 'immense commonalty' subsequently met at the Guildhall to discuss the measures they would take. Simond Turgys, with six men by day and twelve by night, was appointed to guard the postern gate next to the Tower with one springald (a large catapult-like engine that threw heavy missiles). The aldermen and men of various wards would guard sections of the Thames, 'from the Lion Turret to the Stonewharf by the Woolwharf', from the Stonewharf to London Bridge, the Bridge itself, and Ebbegate to Baynardeschastel. Four springalds were erected in the Lion Turret to Stonewharf section. Those present at the assembly agreed that piles should be driven into the Thames so that only one ship at a time could pass, and two aldermen and two commoners were appointed to supervise this work.[2]

There was a genuine fear in 1338/39 that Philip VI of France, whose throne Edward III had claimed, might invade England. The 'common serjeant' of London, William Ilford, travelled to the abbots of Lesnes and St Augustine in Kent in July 1338 with a request from the mayor and commonalty to light *bekenes* (beacons) on Sheterselde and other places, 'so that notice might be given to the inhabitants of Kent, Surrey and London of the approach of the enemy'. The following March, further arrangements were put in place to guard the Thames in London at night 'for fear of foreign invasion', and four aldermen were assigned to watch over the river with the 'good men' of their wards. It was believed that 'the king's foreign enemies were about to attack the city with a great number of galleys and other ships of war'.[3] The unfortunate Luke Carpenter, who really was a carpenter and was called an 'old man', ascended a ladder 'to repair a new building for the city's defence near the Tower' around Vespers on Thursday, 5 November 1338, and fell. His colleagues carried him to the house of the Crutched Friars not far away, but he died the same night.[4]

Fire

In an era when most houses were made of timber, fire was an ever-present danger, and the coroners' rolls and other sources indicate that falling asleep with a candle still alight was hugely risky and caused many serious fires. In greater residences, the kitchen stood separately from the rest of the house to lessen the risk of fire spreading, though this was hardly possible for the large majority of London residents, and most people could not afford to build houses made of stone. After the Frenchman Jean de Chartres de Montlhéry was murdered by his accomplices, William and Johane Wodeford, during their break-in at Pandulf of Lucca's house in October 1323, they tried to burn his body in the fire in Pandulf's kitchen. Phelip Bret bequeathed a solar with a fireplace to his stepdaughter Isabel in 1316, so evidently the kitchens and the higher storeys of some London houses had fireplaces.[1]

Residents of each ward were to tell their alderman when he held the regular wardmote if they knew of any defective oven, furnace or fireplace that was likely to cause a fire, and a city regulation stated that only wood and charcoal could be used as fuel for fires. Residents were also to tell the wardmote if they knew of any houses roofed with reeds or straw rather than tiles, lead, or stone. In January 1302, Thomas Bat bound himself to keep the city of London indemnified 'from peril of fire and other losses which might arise from his houses covered with thatch'. He agreed that he would have the houses' roofs tiled instead by Pentecost, i.e. mid-June.[2] Each of the two dozen London wards was meant to keep something called a *wardehoke*, 'ward hook', an implement used to pull down burning thatch from a roof during a fire. In 1314, the residents of Bradestrete ward stated that an elm, growing by London Wall near Bisshopesgate, was very old and dry and liable to fall onto the nearby shop of Roger Poyntel. They asked if they might cut it down, sell it and use the proceeds to buy rope for a *wardehoke*, as Bradestrete was missing one.[3]

The regulations for the spurriers of London in August 1345 stated that the men 'blow up their fires so vigorously, that their forges begin all at once to blaze', which endangered both the spurriers themselves and their neighbours, who lived in dread of the sparks that 'issue forth in all directions' from the chimneys in the spurriers' forges. The men were therefore ordered not to work at night, at least.[4] Robert Barber complained to the Assize of Nuisance in March 1305 that his neighbour in the parish of All Hallows Grascherch, William Mareschal, kept his fireplace too close to their shared wall, thus risking fire in Robert's home.[5] At the beginning of October 1302, William Basinge's house in Manionelane was badly damaged by fire, for which William blamed the carelessness of his neighbour, Maud Lou.[6] Mayor Johan Gisors and the aldermen who refused permission for the royal clerk William Maldone to build a house in June 1312 because it would narrow the king's highway too much, stated further that if a fire broke out in Maldone's house, the church of St Paul's might be put at risk because it stood nearby, and 'might, in case of such fire, be all the sooner destroyed and burnt, which God forbid'.[7] Their fear that St Paul's might be destroyed by fire came true 354 years later, though they could hardly have guessed the appalling extent of the Great Fire.

Robert Kent, a cordwainer, lived in a 'high solar' in Chepe ward with his wife Maud and their sons William and Johan. During the night of 28 April 1322, a lighted candle which Maud had attached to the wall fell onto her and Robert's bed and caused a fire which destroyed their home. Robert and his son William were caught in the flames and died, though Maud herself and Johan managed to escape the conflagration. The investigating jurors who examined Robert and William's bodies noted that their heads, legs, arms and torsos were 'burnt and almost utterly destroyed'.[8]

Alis and Johan Ryvet ran a shop in Aldresgate ward, and lived above it. During the night of 8 September 1326, a fire broke out in the shop, and as they ran outside, Johan shouted that his wife was to blame by leaving a candle alight, and pushed her back inside. Alis died of her burns the following day, though lived long enough to receive the last rites, and Johan fled. The sheriffs, Gilbert Mordon and Johan Coton, ordered him to be arrested ('attached') wherever found.[9] Maud Cambestere and her daughter Margerie, who tragically was only a month old, also perished in a fire in Maud's shop in Walebrok ward on 4 April 1337. Again, Maud had left a lighted candle on the wall, and during the night it fell onto some straw. A group of jurors investigated Maud and Margerie's bodies and stated they had suffocated, i.e. died of smoke inhalation, before their neighbours could do anything.[10]

Children

We catch a glimpse of the sad and hard life endured by a number of fourteenth-century London children in a tragic entry in the coroners' rolls. Johan Stolere, just 7 years old, a pauper and a beggar, sat on Chepe around sunrise on 24 May 1339, relieving himself. A cart carrying a large container of water and pulled by two horses, driven by 12-year-old Rauf Mymmes, came past, and a wheel crushed little Johan. He died immediately, and the horrified Rauf fled, leaving the cart and horses behind. The idea of a 7-year-old forced to fend for himself on the dangerous city streets, and crushed to death, is a difficult one to bear. This heartrending case also reveals that a 12-year-old was already working at sunrise in a job that he was evidently, judging by his inability to gauge a safe distance between his cartwheels and a small child or to control the horses, too young to perform.[1]

Some people, however, did their best to look out for children's welfare. On Saturday, 23 January 1305, 'a certain boy carrying water in a tankard' stood opposite the shop of the cofferer Adam Boctone near the conduit on Chepe, and an unnamed cook and a clerk called William Radendene decided to torment him. Various bystanders began to worry that the boy might be killed, and Adam St Albans intervened and moved the boy out of their way. The clerk bit Adam and the cook punched him, but he gave as good as he got, and when it came before the mayor's court, sympathetic witnesses pointed out that if the two men 'received any harm, they had no cause of complaint'.[2]

One-day-old Dionise, daughter of Johan Snowe, died in her parents' home in Crepulgate ward at sunrise on 15 June 1339, a 7-day-old infant named Johane died in her father Johan Parlepott's home on Cornhulle on 17 May 1340, and Johan, the 9-day-old son of the cardemakere Johan Russel, died on 19 July 1340 in his parents' home in the parish of Seinte Werburga.[3] Given that the infant mortality rate was extraordinarily high, there must have been some reason why the sad deaths of these three

97

infants were deemed suspicious enough for the coroner to investigate, and provides evidence that some people concerned themselves with children's welfare. The jurors reported, however, that all the deaths were natural. Another case involving the death of a child was investigated in 1324, after 5-year-old Johan Burgh went into the house of his neighbours Richard and Emme Latthere in Farndon Without ward around Vespers on 30 April. The little boy playfully picked up a parcel of Emme's wool and placed it under his cap, whereupon an annoyed Emme smacked him under the left ear. Johan's mother Isabel heard him weeping and raised the hue and cry, and carried her son into the home of another neighbour, Wauter Hengham, but it was too late and Johan died around curfew that evening. Emme fled, but later gave herself up and was imprisoned in Neugate.[4]

Eight-year-old Richard, son of Johan Mason, drowned in the Thames on Friday, 21 July 1301. While crossing London Bridge on his way to school, Richard climbed over the side of the bridge and held himself up by the arms from a beam, but was unable to cling on, and dropped into the river. The water around the bridge was always turbulent, and the boy drowned in the presence of a large number of shocked onlookers before anyone could help him. The current carried his body to the strand of Quenehithe, where it was later retrieved.[5] Evidently at least some London children did attend school at the beginning of the fourteenth century. There is no more evidence, however, of the school that Richard attended, or where it was located. Nichol Picot, an alderman, stated in his will of *c*. October 1312 that his sons Nichol and Johan were 'to study and attend school' and to learn how to write, and the *stokfisshmongere* Richard Gubbe left £10 to his nephew and godson Richard Gubbe the younger in April 1335 'for his maintenance at school'.[6] When a clerk was taught how to write in 1326, a feather, to make a quill pen, and an inkhorn for storing his ink were purchased for him at a cost of 6*d*.[7]

The skinner William Hanington(e), who hired Simond Canterbury to build him a house in 1308/09 and died in 1313, left two sons named Johan and Richard and a daughter named Rohese. Laurence Hanington, probably William's brother, became Johan's guardian, but seven months after William's death, a complaint was made to the mayor and aldermen that Johan 'had not been decently maintained'. The mayor ordered Laurence 'to provide him yearly whilst at school with a furred gown, a coat of Alemayne with tunic to match, four pairs of linen cloths, sufficient shoes and a decent bed', and 10*d* a week for expenses. The reference to the bed implies that Johan Hanington slept at the school, and the matching tunic and German coat (whatever a German coat was) might imply a kind of school uniform. Johan Hanington declared himself of full age on 1 April 1316, though the mayor and aldermen decided that he was too young to take care of his own affairs and asked his stepfather Hervey Beri to guide him and look after the £8 Johan inherited from his late father.[8] 'Of full age' normally meant 21 for a male, though from the context it appears that Johan was younger than this.

Although 7-year-old Johan Stolere was forced to fend for himself in the late 1330s, there were procedures in place for orphaned children, and the unfortunate boy may simply have fallen through the cracks. The story of the 'vagrant orphan' Wauter, son of the late Richard Cook, had a happier ending than little Johan's when Andrew Horn (d. 1328), fishmonger and city chamberlain, became his guardian in 1320. Andrew had also been appointed guardian of the 1-year-old orphan William Fullere in August 1315.[9] Wills and city letter-books indicate that numerous other orphans were placed with guardians until they came of age. Sometimes men specified that after their deaths, their wives should have custody of their children, which in the fourteenth century was not a given. If the mother was dead, other relatives were made guardians of their orphaned grandchildren or nieces and nephews wherever possible, in accordance with a city custom that the nearest family members 'to whom the property of the said children would not descend at their death' should be appointed to look after them.

The will of cordwainer Henry Coventre of the parish of Marie Somersete was proved in October 1313, and in it he mentioned his children Johan, William and Johane, and the child with whom his wife Isabel was pregnant. By December 1315 Isabel had married her second husband Johan Wight, and they were granted custody of her and Henry's children, 7-year-old Johane, 6-year-old William, and 2-year-old Johan, Henry's posthumous son. The older Johan had died in the meantime.[10] In the absence of relatives, the dead person's executors or friends were often appointed as guardians. Johan Greyland stated in 1344 that his wife Johane should have custody of their daughters Anneis, Avice, Maud and Johane, and that if she died before they came of age, his former apprentice William Chaumberlayn should become the girls' guardian. Beatrice Hynde of Holbourne specified in 1337 that her mother Alis

Hynde should have custody of her son William Coblyngton after her death as long as Alis lived, 'to be succeeded by Robert Mareschal, goldsmith' (d. 1354).[11]

Johan Storteford or Stertford of the parish of St Dunstan by the Tower died in late 1298, leaving his young children Adam, Gilbert, Cecile and Margerie; he also had two older daughters, Amice and Juliane, from his first marriage. Johan's widow Laura was dead by April 1301 when the mayor and aldermen appointed Johan Botoner as the guardian of 3-year-old Adam and 9-year-old Cecile, and Johan Lucas as the guardian of 12-year-old Gilbert and 4-year-old Margerie.[12] These two men were probably relatives of the children, perhaps their uncles, or husbands of their older half-sisters. Isabel, widow of the goldsmith Nichol Brun of Fletestrate, died in or before March 1310, and custody of her son Giles was given to her brother Thomas Flete, a chapeler. Giles was not mentioned in his father Nichol's will, proved in November 1305, so was probably born posthumously. Rauf Beri, a cordwainer who owned tenements in Tamestrete and Ropereslane, died in October 1313, and his widow Amice married Richard Pikeman before November 1316. Richard claimed to be the rightful guardian of his stepchildren, Rauf and Amice's children Johan, Esmon, Lettice and Rohese, but their uncle Thomas Cumbe demanded custody of them, and it was granted.[13]

In some cases, children were given guardians who would teach them a trade when they were old enough. Hamo Paumer died in or before April 1306, and his mother Edith died around the same time; his wife had already passed away. The mayor and aldermen assigned custody of Hamo's four sons, 12-year-old Nichol, 11-year-old Edward, 10-year-old William and 8-year-old Thomas, to four different men: a mercer (William Causton, d. 1354), a chapeler (Geffrei Langeleye), a corder (Johan of Paris) and a fishmonger (William Edmund, d. 1332). In Nichol Paumer's case, William Causton promised to 'instruct his ward in his own trade for eight years'. Nichol duly completed his apprenticeship as a mercer in July 1314 when he was 20, by which time his brother Edward was already dead.[14]

William Twomer, a tanner of Morestrete outside Crepelgate, made his will in May 1337 and died in or before October that year. His widow Idonea died in January 1340, and guardians were found for William and Idonea's 9-year-old son William, 8-year-old daughter Anneis, and their daughter Johane, age not given. Another daughter, Alis, was mentioned in William's will, but must have died in the meantime. Anneis Twomer married Henry Myre, a saddler, in April 1349 when she was 17 or 18. Hugh Mockyng, warden of the fishmongers, and his wife Maud were both ailing by September 1339, when their daughter Alis was 13 (though Hugh did not die until the following July). Alis Mockyng was given into the care of her maternal grandmother Alis the elder and her second husband Nichol Bokehurst or Brokhurst. The elder Alis's first husband William Braye, young Alis's grandfather, died in 1328 or 1329, and left his infant granddaughter an annual rent of 80*d* on a tenement in the parish of St Olave; she also inherited a house in Crokedelane from her father. Alis's brother Richard Mockyng, apparently already of age in 1339/40 as no guardian was assigned, died in the plague year of 1349.[15]

Margerie of Bredstrete died in 1316, and was the widow of Johan Longe, with whom she had no children, and Wauter of Bredstrete, a cordwainer who died in 1307. Margerie looked after her namesake granddaughter, her and Wauter's late son Falk's daughter, and her grandsons William and Herman, her late son William's sons (Falk and Herman's names imply some German ancestry in the family). Johan Alegate, a potter who died in late 1324 or early 1325, was the guardian of his granddaughters Marie and Johane, his late son's Esmon's daughters. In his will, Johan appointed his servants Bertelmew and Katerine Thephord to take care of the girls after his death. Isabel, widow of the cheesemonger Johan Writele (d. 1306), made her will in 1332. She was the guardian of her late son Wauter's four children, and appointed her other son William to look after them when she passed away. Isabel also left bequests to her daughters Alis and Emme, and Emme's three sons William, Thomas and Johan Rokele.[16]

Concern was shown for illegitimate children as well (and see 'Adultery' below). The will of Henry Burel, mercer, was proved on 29 April 1325, and he mentioned his daughter Anneis and his son Johan; whether they were legitimate or not is unclear. Henry's lover Margarete Swafham was pregnant when he made his will. On 22 May 1325, Henry's son Johan was said to be a year old, and Margarete had given birth to another son called Johan, now 8 weeks. The mayor, Hamo Chigwell, assigned custody of the two babies to Johan Dallinge, Henry's executor, though sadly one of them died in November 1331. The fate of Henry's daughter Anneis and his lover Margarete Swafham is uncertain.[17]

The *wollemongere* Richard Hakeneye, alderman of Billingesgate ward and sheriff 1321/22, died in or shortly before May 1343. His widow

Alis made her will on 15 April 1349, which mentions her and Richard's children Aleyn, Richard, Neel, Johane, Lecia, Cristine, Pernel and Isabel. In February 1350, custody of Isabel, the youngest Hakeneye child, was committed to Isabel's brother Richard the younger. Alis Hakeneye was pregnant with Isabel when her husband the alderman made his will on 20 February 1342 the year before he died, and Isabel married William Olneye (d. 1375), a fishmonger, around 16 August 1362 when she was 20; their son Johan Olneye died in 1410 when his wife Johane was pregnant. The grant of Isabel's wardship to her brother specified that Richard Hakeneye the younger was not allowed to arrange her marriage without the mayor's permission, so the 1362 match with William Olneye must have been approved. Richard died *c.* April/May 1363, married but without children, and left his Olneye brother-in-law 'the tenement wherein he dwells'.[18]

The unlicensed marriages of children did sometimes take place, however: Henry Suttone was imprisoned in August 1342 after 'carrying off' 7-year-old Alis, daughter of the late Johan atte Marche, and marrying her to Thomas Staunesby. William Huberd, a minter who lived without Aldresgate, died in March or April 1328, and custody of his 10-year-old son Robert was given to Johan Spray, who also lived without Aldresgate, that August. On 20 November 1331, Robert Huberd, now 13, was abducted from his guardian's home by William Rameseye, his wife Cristine, his father William the elder and a few others including the chaplain of Wolcherche, and was forcibly married to William and Cristine's daughter Anneis. The Rameseyes appeared before the court of the mayor, Johan Pulteneye, a few days later, and 'inasmuch as the marriage could not be annulled', Robert Huberd was given the choice of remaining with his in-laws or returning to his guardian. He chose the Rameseyes.[19]

In April 1315, concerned adults removed 8-year-old Anneis Laurence from the custody of her mother Maud Laurence and stepfather Simond Burgh, on the grounds that Maud and Simond 'were contriving to marry' Anneis to her stepbrother Thomas, Simond's son, a boy 'not yet 11 years old' (one might note here that they knew Thomas Burgh's exact age, over 500 years before the invention of birth certificates). The banns of marriage had been published, and wedding clothes and a feast prepared, when the unnamed but worried friends of the girl discovered the plot, as they called it, and took Anneis to the mayor and aldermen at the

Guildhall. The mayor, Estephene Abingdon, brought the matter to the personal attention of Edward II, who decided there was insufficient reason to remove Anneis from her home and ordered her to be restored to her mother and stepfather. Showing once again that some people truly did take children's welfare to heart, the mayor and aldermen bravely announced their dissatisfaction with the king's pronouncement and stated that Simond and Maud should not have custody of her daughter.[20] Wauter Mordon, fishmonger, called himself the 'next friend of the children of Paulin Turk', a fishmonger who died in 1325. Wauter raised the alarm in 1331 when he discovered that the Turk children's guardian and stepfather Johan Comptone had 'wasted their property and left the city'. Comptone was finally captured in early 1335, and imprisoned in Neugate.[21]

Women

There is no doubt that English law of the fourteenth century favoured men. Inheritance law regarding lands which were held directly from the king followed the system of primogeniture: the eldest son inherited everything while younger sons, and daughters wherever they came in the birth order, received nothing. On the other hand, numerous occasions arose when there was no male heir, and women inherited instead. In this instance, they received equal portions of an inheritance, and being the eldest daughter conferred no advantage. Thomas and Juliana Romeyn had four daughters, of whom two were nuns, and the other two, Rohese Burford and Margerie Weston, inherited equal parts of their parents' properties in London, Middlesex and Surrey on Juliana's death in 1326. A widow was entitled to hold a third of her late husband's (or husbands') estate until she died, regardless of whether she married again or whether the couple had children. A man who married an heiress was entitled, by a custom called 'the courtesy of England', to hold all his late wife's estate for his life if she died first, but only if the couple had at least one child together who lived long enough to draw breath; if not, the woman's entire estate passed to her rightful heirs on her death.

Only the most important people in the country were tenants-in-chief, i.e. they held their lands directly from the king, and were therefore subject to strict inheritance laws and primogeniture. Others were free to dispose of their houses, lands and goods however they wished. It is revealing to note the numerous male Londoners who willed property and goods to their wives, daughters, sisters and nieces, and did not favour their sons over their daughters. To give just a handful of examples from hundreds, in 1307 Laurence Lillebourne ordered his tenement outside Aldresgate to be sold and the proceeds to be divided equally among his children Johan, Peres and Isabel. In 1316/17, Johan Dittone left jewels, linen cloth, beds and chattels to his daughter Isabel, unspecified other 'chattels' to his daughter Johane, and sums of money to his sons

Thomas and Richard and the unborn child his wife Isabel was carrying. At the same time, the vintner Estephene Feryng left his tenement in Billingesgate to his children Robert, Henry and Isabel in equal parts. Johan of Paris left his tenements without Neugate, without Lodgate and near the Flete bridge to his sons Johan, Roger and Estephene and his daughters Maud, Dionise and Anneis in his will dated 20 July 1321, and a few days later, Roger of Paris, a mercer, requested that after his death, his corner shop in St Pancras should be sold. The proceeds were to be distributed not only among his own two sons and two daughters, Simond, Johan, Maud and Johane, but to his stepdaughter Alis, his wife Margarete's daughter from a previous marriage. In April 1349, the pepperer Simond Brunnesford left his son William £5, but gave £20 to each of his four daughters.

Roger Waltham, a corder, divided his goods, houses and wharf in All Hallows at the Hay equally among his children Alis I, Cecile, Sibil, Isabel, Katerine, Alis II, Johan and Thomas in July 1342, and the master shipwright Martyn Palmere left three unfinished boats to his son Johan and his daughters Cecile and Johane in September 1344. Adam Kyngestone, fishmonger of Crokedelane, made his will on 10 February 1348 and died in or before January 1349; he left all his goods to his daughters Cecile Paterlyng and Juliane Swift and their children. Another fishmonger, Simond Turnham, left his goods, properties and money in March 1346 to his daughter Alianore and Alianore's daughter Johane, and his son Hugh, Hugh's wife Alianore, and their children Johan and Isabel. In his long 1349 will, the alderman and former sheriff William Thorneye left a parcel of land called *Personbroderove* in Leverington near Wisbech, Cambridgeshire to five women: Alis Saleman, Johane Rolle and Maud Bageys, daughters of his late sister Lettice Bageneye, and Alis and Johane's daughters, both named Margerie, William's great-nieces.[1]

Taking several years entirely at random, twenty-five people made their wills in London in the twenty-ninth year of Edward I's reign, which ran from November 1300 to November 1301, of whom five were women. In Edward II's first regnal year, July 1307 to July 1308, fifty people made their wills, and ten were women; in his sixteenth year, July 1322 to July 1323, four of the thirty-one were women. In the eighth year of Edward III's reign, January 1334 to January 1335, four of the twenty-four will-makers were women.[2] This indicates that roughly 15 to 20 per cent of London will-makers in the first half of the fourteenth century were women. Generally speaking, a married woman was not permitted to make a will, and the female will-makers were, therefore, all widows.[3]

Alis Frowyk lived at Ebbegate, a watergate on the Thames, and had separated from her husband Thomas. As a woman living alone, Alis was vulnerable, especially as she was well-off (Thomas Frowyk came from a family of wealthy goldsmiths and pepperers). Shortly before 15 December 1305, a thief named Roger Rokesle and no fewer than eighteen of his associates broke into Alis's home, assaulted her and threw her out into the street, and stole her gold and silver jewels which she had stored in cupboards and coffers to a value of £40.[4] This distressing situation does at least reveal that some women lived alone in London in the early 1300s, and that some marriages broke down and the couples thereafter lived separately. Johane Cotekyn, who fell down the stairs of her rented home in 1324, apparently lived alone, as her friends carried her to her father's house after her accident, and she was not married. The 1343 will of Thomas Baudry, however, left his house to his wife Elena and his brother Johan jointly 'if they shall live together' with Thomas and Elena's two underage children after his death, so he believed there was a possibility that his widow would not wish to live alone.[5]

Some professions were only open to men, or at least women were discouraged from entering them, but widows could and often did lead the trade practised by their late husbands, and some trades were often practised by women: there were many *brewsteres*, *baksteres*, *bredmongesteres*, *frutesteres* and *cambesteres*. The cloth trades also attracted women, and many worked as *websteres* and *spinsteres*, though it is almost impossible to find examples of female carpenters, masons, pepperers and so on. A city letter-book of 1309 to 1314 records a number of women instructing apprentices, including Anneis Evre, wife of the cornmonger Johan Coventre, instructing Johan Staundone; Anneis, widow of the bureller Johan Wynchester, instructing Johan Snel; Alis, widow of the currier Johan Byford or Bifold, instructing Henry Feltham; Alis, widow of the butcher Johan Osebern; and Katerine, working with her husband Henry the Surgeon, as noted in 'Health' above. Two female fishmongers, Isabel Ware and Johane Chigwell, are also mentioned, and were both widows.[6]

Maud Myms or Mymmes of Pultrye left 'the third best part of copies and instruments appertaining to the making of pictures, and one of her best chests for keeping them in' to her apprentice William in 1349. Maud was married to the *ymaginour* Johan Myms, and the couple, who died just a few days or weeks apart in 1349 (almost certainly victims of the plague), also owned and ran a brewery in Conynghoplane.[7] Maud Fattyng is listed as a butcher instructing two apprentices between 1303 and 1312, and was probably the widow of a butcher, though is never specifically identified as such.[8] Some men stated in their wills that their apprentices should continue working for their wives after their deaths. Fishmonger Johan Croydon left 'the remaining term of Wauter his apprentice' to his wife Rohese in 1334, and weaver Johan Alisaunder and skinner Johan Trappe did the same, both in 1344.[9]

All London officials, from the mayor, sheriffs and aldermen down to bedels, were men; all jurors who investigated sudden deaths were men; all jurors who sat on inquisitions, commissions and proofs of age were men; all the guardians of the great gates, London Bridge, the conduit and so on, were men. The same applied to officials everywhere else in England, and the fourteenth century was certainly not an age when women played a full and equal role in public life or when they were anywhere close to legal equality with men. They could and sometimes did, however, own lands and become wealthy, and at the London level, some women were influential and well-off, such as Juliana Romeyn née Hauteyn and her eldest daughter Rohese Burford née Romeyn. Rohese had her own business exporting wool as well as running her late husband Johan Burford's spice business, and was a talented seamstress: Edward II bought a cope which she had embroidered as a gift for the new pope, John XXII, in 1316, and paid Rohese 100 marks for it. Rohese was wealthy enough to lend a man 1,000 marks (£666.66) in 1325.[10] In the 1320s, Eleyne Glaswreghte ran her own successful glass-making business in London, Margerie Faderwyf and Sabyne Warin stitched sail-cloths, Maud Ropere made rope, and Johane of Rochester and Eleyne del Hethe weaved hemp baskets. Johane and Eleyne's work was skilful enough for Edward II to employ them in the Tower of London.[11]

Families

Families could often be quite large; Mayor Johan Gisors, for example, had four younger brothers and four sisters. Roger Mertone, who owned a tenement near Tamestrete and died in May 1317, had one son, Johan, and five daughters, Margarete, Helen, Maud, Alis and Rohese, while the corder Roger Waltham (d. 1342) had six daughters and two sons. The November 1334 will of Hugh Waltham, who held the office of 'common clerk of London', named his sons, Estephene, Hamo and Wauter, and his daughters, Cristine, Cecile, Johane, Margerie and Anneis, a nun. William Hedrisham, one of the many victims of the Black Death in 1349, stated in his will that he had seven brothers and two sisters, though did not name them, and the alderman Richard Hakeneye and his wife Alis had three sons and five daughters. Roger Ely (d. 1349), fishmonger and sheriff 1322/23, had four sons and four daughters, Johan Coroner of Quenehithe (d. 1349) had five sons from his first marriage to Diamanda and another three from his second to Rohese, and Johan Westwyk of Bradstret (d. 1349) had seven sons.[1]

The child mortality rate was, however, horrific. To give just a handful of examples, the will of the *wodemongere* Benet Alfox was proved on 29 July 1314, and he bequeathed tenements to his children Thomas, Johan and Juliane. The rightful inheritance of Thomas, aged 8, and Juliane, aged 3, was confirmed on 30 August 1314, but Johan Alfox was already dead.[2] Thomas Berkyng or Berkinge, one of the wardens of the goldsmiths, made his will, which mentioned his children Roger, Idonea and Alis, on 9 August 1329, and died shortly before 27 January 1332. Roger Berkinge was still alive on 14 November 1332, aged 12, but dead by 3 September 1333.[3] Robert Cook's will was proved on 15 October 1313, and in it he mentioned his children Johane, Anneis and Johan. Johan Cook was dead by 16 January 1314.[4]

Phelip Lucas, a *stokfisshmongere* of Crokedelane, made his will on 3 January 1331, and died before 11 March 1332. He and his wife Anneis, whose maiden name was also Lucas – or more probably, Phelip took his wife's name – had a son they called Adam after Anneis's brother, and daughters Johane, Cecile, Juliane, Alis and Isabel. All the children were underage in 1331, and Phelip specified that Anneis should have custody of them after his death. By the time Anneis Lucas died in early February 1349, her daughters Cecile and Juliane were married with children, and her brother Adam Lucas, sheriff of London 1340/41, had fathered four daughters before he died in 1347. Anneis left money and tenements to her two daughters and their children, and to her four nieces, but her other three daughters and her son are not mentioned, and presumably all died between 1332 and 1348. Cecile Lucas married William Wetheresfeld of Brigge ward, also a *stokfisshmongere*, and, like her mother, died in February 1349; perhaps both women were victims of plague. Adam Lucas himself directed in his will of October 1347 that his tenements in London should be sold and that his wife Maud should use the proceeds 'for advancement in marriage of their daughters', whose names were Alis, Idonea, Cecile and Marion.[5]

Many Londoners did not have children, or at least had no surviving children, and in such cases tended to leave property, possessions and money to siblings, stepchildren, nieces and nephews, and for 'pious uses'. Johan Wade died *c*. November 1307, and left tenements and a brewhouse in Garlekheth and Quenehithe to his brother Adam, sister Avice, and niece Maud, daughter of his late sister Cecile. Richard Gubbe, a well-off *stokfisshmongere*, made his will on 10 April 1335 and died before 8 May. He left £10 to his nephew and godson Richard Gubbe for his education; £10 each to two unnamed nieces, his brother Roger's daughters; a tenement to his niece Juliane and her husband Johan Syward, his former apprentice; and more tenements to his nephews Andrew and Johan, his late sister Isabel's sons. His shops were to be sold and the proceeds given to his brothers Roger and Henry, and the 'residue to pious and charitable causes'.[6]

It is a common modern myth that in the Middle Ages, everyone married in childhood or at the start of their teens. While this was indeed frequently the case for those of royal or noble rank, the same did not apply to people further down the social scale. Evidence indicates that the common people of England in the fourteenth century, with few exceptions, tended to marry in their twenties or thirties, or late teens at the earliest. Mayor Thomas Romeyn and Juliana Hauteyn's eldest daughter Rohese, born *c*. 1286, married Johan Burford sometime before

December 1312, and gave birth to her son Sir James Burford in *c.* 1320 when she was about 34, though her daughter Johane was older. As noted above, Anneis Twomer married Henry Myre in 1349 when she was 17 or 18, and Isabel Hakeneye married William Olneye in 1362 when she was 20. Johan Sherewynd of St Pancras was 27 when he 'promised to marry' Alis Cotesmor in February 1329, and in the same month, Robert Tylere also of St Pancras was 29 when his wife Johane gave birth to their son William. Johan Pulteneye, mayor, was at least 45 when his son and heir William was born in late 1340 or early 1341, and William Thorneye, alderman and sheriff, was at least 40 when his son Johan was born in 1347. Andrew Aubrey, mayor, was at least 30 when he married the widowed Johane Evenefeld sometime after 1328.[7]

Another modern misconception is that everyone in the fourteenth century died young, and although the huge number of deaths in childhood pulled down the average age and it was common to die of diseases or infections which are now easily treatable, many people lived a long life. Johan Gisors, three-times mayor, lived into his early seventies; William Curteys of Brixworth, sheriff 1336/37, lived to about 70; Thomas Maryns, apothecary and chamberlain of London, was about 60 when he died in 1349, perhaps of plague; the carpenter Simond Canterbury had already qualified as a master carpenter by 1308/09 and must have been in his twenties or older then, and lived until 1341; the French girdler Robert Amyas was at least a teenager and perhaps in his twenties when he had a violent row with Robert Brewere in 1301, and lived until 1342; and the mercer William Causton was old enough to take on an apprentice and to act as an executor in 1306, and lived until 1354. Alis Warle, wife of Phelip Taverner of Grascherche then of Johan Ingelard, gave birth to one of her five children in 1317, so is unlikely to have been born much after 1300 and was perhaps born well before that, and died in 1361.[8]

Second marriages were extraordinarily common, for both men and women. Rohese Burford's sister Margerie, born *c.* 1290, married Robert Upton before December 1312, and with him had a daughter whom she named Juliana after her mother. Before June 1326, Margerie married her second husband William Weston, with whom she had a son, Richard Weston.[9] The July 1311 will of Anneis Hengham of the parish of St Sepulchre without Newgate mentions her two late husbands, Robert Hengham and Roger Lauvar(e). Presumably, as Anneis named Robert first in her will, he was her first husband, and she kept his name throughout her second marriage to Roger Lauvare, a cordwainer who died in February 1307 (and who tried to rob his lodger Johan Gaytone in 1305; see 'Hostels'). Anneis had a daughter, Cecile, who in 1311 was married to Wauter Chipstede and had a son named Johan Carlisle; it would seem that Cecile married twice as well.[10] The will of Henry Merlawe, a cutler, was proved in October 1313, and his widow Anneis married William Dorkyngge before October 1318. Anneis and William were the guardians of her and Henry's children Wauter (b. *c.* 1301), William, and Alis, who was Henry's posthumous daughter.[11]

Robert Convers, a goldsmith who owned tenements in the parish of St Vedast and in Fletestrete, died shortly before 27 July 1310, leaving his children Nichol, Henry and Katerine, aged 7, 3 and 1 respectively. His widow Rohese married David Cottesbroke very soon afterwards, before 29 August 1310, and thirdly Nichol Stratstede before June 1321.[12] Katerine, widow of Nichol Crane, alderman of Aldresgate ward, also remarried quickly after her husband's death. Nichol made his will on 15 April 1342 and it was proved on 27 May; Katerine was married to Nichol Poure of Bletchingdon, Oxfordshire by 17 August 1342.[13]

The master shipbuilder Aleyn Palmere of Petiwales near the Tower made his will on 23 February 1335 and died before 1 May. He bequeathed the tenement and wharf he inherited from his father William to his son Phelip from his first marriage to Cecile. King Edward II, who knew the Palmere family well, paid all the expenses of Cecile's funeral in November 1324, and had given her money for medicines.[14] By the time of his death, Aleyn had married a second wife, Emme. Aleyn and Cecile's son Phelip Palmere also became a shipwright, and made his will on 11 July 1339, leaving the tenement and wharf which had belonged to his father and grandfather to his wife Anneis for her life. It would then pass to his children, who were still underage. Aleyn's younger brother Martyn Palmere made his will on 29 September 1344, and died before 15 November. He left unfinished boats on his wharf to his youngest son Johan and his daughters Johane and Cecile, whom he and his wife (name unknown) had named after his late sister-in-law, Aleyn's first wife. Johan Palmere married Amy, and they both died during the plague year of 1349; they named their son after Johan's uncle, Aleyn. All the Palmeres were buried in their local church, All Hallows Berkyngcherche, now called All Hallows-by-the-Tower.[15]

Second marriages meant that a lot of Londoners had stepchildren, and were often close to them. Phelip Bret, who made his will in July 1316, left tenements and shops in Fynamoureslane to his own children Laurence and Cristine, and Cristine's husband, Nichol FitzRobert. He also left 'a solar with a fireplace' to Isabel, daughter of his late wife Maud from her previous marriage. William Russel made his will about three months later, and left houses in the parish of Seint Giles without Crepelgate to his wife Johane and her son William, his stepson. The will of Henry Chaundeler of Garlekhuth was proved in February 1317, and he left his stepson Moris, his wife Isabel's son, his shop and 100s worth of candles. Richard Kyng, a butcher, left money to his own daughters Emme and Isabel and to his stepdaughter Millecent, his deceased first wife Johane's daughter, in 1347. Roger Forsham, mercer and sheriff 1339/40, who had no children of his own, left bequests in May 1348 to his wife Alis's daughters Maud and Cristine, his sister Lucy's daughters Anneis and Cecile, and his sister Margarete's daughter Anneis. Johan Hamond, mayor 1343/45, made his will in September 1346 and died in early 1349. He also had no children, and left properties, money and possessions to his three stepchildren, Thomas, Johan and Alis, the children of his wife Anneis and her first husband Adam Salisbury, and Alis's four children.[16]

Some men willed shops or homes to their wives on condition that the women remained unmarried and 'chaste'. If they did remarry or even became intimate with another man, they would lose possession of the property. In August 1328, William Braye left his house in the parish of Seinte Margarete Matyns to his wife Alis 'so long as she remains in pure widowhood'. Alis, however, decided to marry Nichol Brokhurst, and in February 1345 was evicted by Juliane Braye, her late husband's niece, with the aid of Juliane's stepfather Andrew Turk.[17] Andrew Staunford left houses in Walebrok ward to his wife Emme and their son Johan in October 1319, but if Emme married again or 'knew any man carnally', Johan would become the houses' sole owner. William Hundesdich, who had a son Thomas and daughters Maud and Cristine, died in May 1307. William left his wife Elisia or Elena a tenement without Bisshopesgate 'so long as she remains continent and without a husband'; otherwise it would pass to their son. In fact, Elisia married her second husband William Poumfreyt (i.e. Pontefract, Yorkshire), a skinner, in or before early 1310, but her son Thomas and daughter Maud had died by then. Elisia and her second husband were appointed guardians of her only surviving child Cristine, born *c.* 1303, in July 1310, and kept the tenement.[18]

Names

The first half of the fourteenth century was an important era in the development of fixed surnames in England. Surnames evolved as a way of differentiating the many people with the same given name, and as there was a paucity of first names in medieval England, numerous diminutives and pet forms evolved as well (see Appendix 1 for a list). A huge percentage of all the English people alive between 1300 and 1350 were called Johan, Thomas, William or Robert, or Anneis, Johane, Isabel or Margarete. Most fourteenth-century Londoners also bore the same few first names repeated over and over, though there were a few unusual names: Alemanna Triple, Bonajoia Beleverge, Basa and Aureus Wodere, Clarekin Fylin, Basilia Monoye, Castanea Dernigton, Mauth Wyke, Gencelina Wollemongere, Guiot Cutepointer, the siblings Erneburga, Salerna and Wolvin Cote, Pentecost Oistremongere, Pentecost Russel and his mother Alveva, Anabilia Grapefige, Argentilla Blound, Loth Sampford, Tydeman Cowfot, Wymarkia Tuler, Diamanda Coroner, Fresaunce Picard, Scolastica Hurer, Boydin Fader, Reiner Piggesflesshe, Massilia Tiffeld, Hercellin Schipwreyte, and Albrica Dokesworth.[1] People were often named after a grandparent, such as Alis Mockyng (born *c.* 1326), daughter of Hugh Mockyng and Maud Braye and granddaughter of Alis Braye, or after a godparent. The *stokfisshmongere* and sheriff Wauter Mordon's second son was called Thomas after his godfather Thomas Chetyndon, and Wauter Mordon was himself the godfather of Wauter Pole, son of Mordon's apprentice Adam Pole.[2]

Mayhew Chaundeler made candles for a living, and was known as Maykin, the typical fourteenth-century diminutive of his name. In December 1300, he tried to get out of a charge before the mayor's court on the grounds that a previous judgement against him had been made under his real name, and that now the pet form was being used.[3] As well as the numerous diminutives of given names, some nicknames appear on record. Thomas Hertford, resident in the parish of Seint James

Garlekhuthe in 1301, was known as *Naverathom* or 'never-at-home', and Robert Tillere, a nightwatchman in Clerkenewelle also in 1301, was called *Renaboute* or 'runabout'.[4] Richard Gravele, who finished his apprenticeship as a fuster in 1311, was called *Bokskyn*, 'buckskin', and Wauter Hore, another London apprentice in 1312, was known, for some mysterious reason, as *Starling*. In 1301, Roger Rede of Alegate referred to his brother Henry as *Rofot*, 'roe-foot', i.e. one who was as swift-footed as a roe deer. William Keu, one of the men who attacked and killed Johan Felton in Bredestrete ward in February 1326, was called *Maucovenaunt* or 'evil covenant', and a messenger of the archbishop of Canterbury who brought letters to Edward II in London in July 1325 was called *Copernowe*.[5] Calling slightly-built men 'little', spelt *litel*, *littele* or *lyttle* in fourteenth-century English, was extremely common. A man summoned to the mayor and aldermen in 1301 was Littele Hobbe ('Rob'), a 'certain Robert' who lived near Grascherche in 1324 was nicknamed Litelrobyn, and Johan of Cornwall was called Lyttle Jakke in 1340.[6] Tall men and women were often called *longe* and well-built men *grete*, i.e. 'great' or 'big', and a man found guilty of affray in Quenehithe ward in June 1344 was Longe Watte.[7]

One of Edward II's servants was Esmon Fissher or Fysshere (d. June 1326), who grew up near the Thames just west of London and really was a fisherman. Esmon's son Litel Wille was a huntsman, but was not called Wille Hunt or Hunter but Litel Wille Fissher. In 1309, a London skinner was named William Spicer and was the son of Mayhew Spicer, and forty years later, Roger Carpenter worked as a spicer.[8] Thomas Carpenter, who owned houses near the conduit on Chepe and made his will in 1335, was a pepperer, and most probably his and Roger's fathers had been carpenters. Johan Chaucer, father of the poet Geoffrey, was a vintner, not a shoe-maker as per his name, and in 1320 William Taverner worked as a chaucer.[9] These men represent examples of surnames becoming fixed and hereditary rather than depending on an individual's occupation, though many others did use their own professions as their name, such as Richard Bakere, baker of Alegate, Richard Brewere, brewer of Brigge ward, and Luke Carpenter, a carpenter who fell from his ladder in 1338.

Surnames could still be rather fluid, and it often happened that people were called by more than one name. Johan Warle or Warley (fl. 1309– 33), merchant and taverner of London, was the brother of Ingelard Warle (d. 1317), keeper of Edward II's wardrobe, and was often called 'Johan Ingelard de Warle' or simply 'Johan Ingelard'. His wife (d. 1361) was named 'Alis Warlee, wife of Johan Ingelard'.[10] Godwin Hodere (d. 1313), who worked as a pheliper, was also sometimes called Godwin Pheliper, and Hodere means 'hood-maker', probably his father's profession. Godwin's grandson, his son Thomas Hodere's son, was called Estephene Godwin.[11] James St Edmunds, sheriff 1309/10, was the son of Fouke St Edmunds, sheriff 1289/90, and sometimes appears on record as James Fouke; the goldsmith Robert Denys, killed in London in December 1321, was the son of Denys of Cambridge ('Grauntebrigge'), and took his father's given name as his own second name. Johan Hamond, mayor 1343/45, was the son of a man whose given name was Hamo or Hamond.[12] Amyel (or Amiel) Honesdon, a chandler, was also known as Amyel Chaundeler, and his daughters, who died a few weeks apart in the plague year of 1349, called themselves Johane Amyel and Cristine Chaundeller. In her will of 1350, the widow of Johan Aulton called herself Katerine Estmare, and named her father as Estmare, an Old English name which had become very uncommon by the fourteenth century. Katerine's mother Isabel also used her husband's given name as her own second name.[13]

Some apprentices took the last name of their masters. Warin Page, apprentice of the butcher Maud Fattyng of Candelwikstrete in the early 1300s, also appears on record as Warin Fattyng, and William Westoye began an apprenticeship with the painter Johan Porkele in 1305 and became known as William Porkele.[14] Andrew Cros, a fishmonger who made his will in April 1349 and died *c.* July 1354, was still called Andrew Modyngham in 1327 when he was the apprentice of fishmonger William Cros (d. 1342). Hamo Chigwell, eight-times mayor of London between the late 1310s and late 1320s, was originally called Hamo or Hamond Dene, and sometime after November 1303 took the name of Richard Chigwell (d. 1307), the fishmonger who instructed him.[15] A pardon granted in 1344 to the apprentice of the Briggestrete fishmonger Robert Mas for non-payment of a fine reveals the three names by which the apprentice was known: Alban Frere, Alban Mas, and Robert Alban. Many apprentices, however, kept their own names: in 1328, the two being instructed by fishmonger Andrew Horn were Moris atte Hoke and Jordan Waltham, and *stokfisshmongere* Phelip Lucas (d. 1332) trained William atte Watere and Thomas Terel.[16]

Servants also sometimes took the name of their employer with the word 'servant' attached: two men who broke into a park in Surrey in

1325 were called Rauf Duboneye and Raufesservant Duboneye, and two timber thieves in 1319 were Johan Batesford and Johan Johanesservant Batesford. Hugh Richardesservant Swynnerton worked for Sir Richard Swynnerton, whose brother Sir Roger was constable of the Tower of London in the early 1320s, and Henry Middulmore employed a carter whose name was William Henryscartere Middulmore. The word *knave*, meaning 'boy' or 'young man', was also used in the sense of a servant, and Amice and Johan Odyngseles employed Thomas Amisservant Odyngseles and William Jonesknave Odyngseles. In 1344 William Halmedene, who worked for the abbot of Westminster, was known as *thabbotesservant of Westmynstre*, and the words *personesservant* and *personescoke* for 'parson's servant' and 'parson's cook' also appear. Master Richard Saham, parson of the church of Stebenheth in the 1340s, employed a squire called Johan Personessquyer. People who left their employment were called *sumtymservant* or 'sometime servant' of their former master.[17]

Some people were known both by their job title or their father's job title, and their place of origin. Solomon Lauvare (d. 1312), alderman, sheriff 1289/90, and cutler, was also often called Solomon Cotiller or Coteler. One of the sheriffs in 1344/45 was Geffrei Wychingham, aka Geffrei Tableter (d. 1349), and one of the sheriffs in 1347/48 was Richard Basingstoke, aka Richard Goldbetere. Geffrei Wychingham or Tableter was a mercer, but his father was perhaps a tableter; the meaning of this word is uncertain but may derive from Old French *tabletier*, 'pedlar'.[18] Great and Little Witchingham are villages in Norfolk, Basingstoke is a town in Hampshire, and Lauvare, a fairly common second name in fourteenth-century London, means the Essex villages of High, Little and Magdalen Laver. The French girdler Robert Amyas was also often called Robert Wynhelm, and 'Amyas' meant Amiens, his hometown. Roger Skirmisour or 'Fencer', who ran a fencing-school in London in 1311 (see 'Fun' below), was also known as Roger Shireburne, i.e. Sherburn in North Yorkshire, and the man who killed James 'Copin' Kyng in 1301 after a row over stolen apples (see 'Murder' above) appears in the coroners' rolls as Thomas Brewere, his profession, and in the chancery rolls as Thomas May.[19]

Richer Refham, mayor and mercer, who probably came from Reepham in Norfolk, was sometimes called Richer Botoner, and Adam Bekenesfeld (d. early 1304), a fisherman with a shop in Briggestrete, was also called Adam Fulham. Bekenesfeld in modern spelling is Beaconsfield, a town in Buckinghamshire and surely Adam's place of origin before he settled in Fulham.[20] Simond Dolshull or Dolsely (d. 1363), sheriff 1348/49, was also called Simond Farnham, a town in Surrey, and William Curteys (d. 1367), *wollemongere* and sheriff 1336/37, was also called William Brykelesworth. Brixworth, the modern spelling, is a village in Northamptonshire, and William was often called 'William Curteys of Briclesworth'. Often, however, the 'Curteys' was dropped, and in his will of 1356 he called himself 'William Brikelesworth'. He had returned from London to spend the last years of his life in his native village, and died in October 1367. If he is the 'William Cortays' who became an apprentice in London at Christmas 1310, William was about 70 when he died.[21]

Women usually took their husband's name, though some women who married twice kept their first husband's name during their second marriage, and others kept their maiden name. Beatrice Hynde of Holbourn (d. 1338) was one: her parents were Robert and Alis Hynde, while her husband was Johan Coblyngton and her son was William Coblyngton. Emme Wylekyn was married to Henry Greneford in 1306/07, and Anneis Evre was married to the cornmonger Johan Coventre in 1309/10. Aleyn Brauncastre's widow was called Anneis Stanes in 1313 and 1325, and in 1313 Margerie Lucas was named as the widow of Richard Chaam. Johane Staundon, who made her will on 9 May 1349, was the widow of Rauf Toudeby and had reverted to her maiden name, and Anneis Wynterman named herself as the widow of Johan Rasseburgh in November 1334. Isabel (d. 1349), one of the four daughters of the alderman William Leyre (d. 1322/23), married the goldsmith Johan Markynfeld, but kept her own name. Isabel Brynkele, who died in 1340, had a son named Johan Suthcote, and Katerine, widow of Richard Swote (d. 1327), kept his name through her second marriage to Richard Moton.[22]

The second name of Johane, who broke into Pandulf of Lucca's house in 1323 with her husband William Wodeford and their French accomplice Jean de Montlhéry, was Crougestere. This, clearly, was her job title and has the feminine *-stere* ending, though the meaning is uncertain, and another example of a female occupational surname with an uncertain meaning is Amice Crengestere, victim of an assault on Cornhulle in 1321.[23] A married couple, residents of Westminster in 1325, were Anneis Deye and Thomas Botiler; 'Deye' means 'dairy-maid' in medieval French and 'Botiler' means 'butler' (cup-bearer or bottle-maker), so they both used their job title as their second name.[24]

Adultery

Extramarital relations were forbidden by the Church, but often happened anyway. Alis of York was involved with two men, Wauter Anne of Hampshire and Aleyn Hacford of Norfolk, a chaplain. Alis was with Wauter at dusk on 13 February 1326 in a room he had hired in Chepe where they could meet, and Aleyn caught them together and stabbed Wauter in the stomach in a rage. Juliane Aunsel of Bisshopesgate also had a lover who was a chaplain, Esmon Brekles, and during the night of 7 June 1324 she stabbed Esmon in the stomach with the aid of an accomplice, Johan Maltone, while she was in bed with him (see 'Abjurers' above). Juliane and Johan shared a house, so were perhaps also lovers. The chaplain Richard Despenser was in a relationship in 1305 with Juliane Hoddere, called his 'concubine', and Joce Sewy and his 'concubine' Salerna lived in Faytereslanende in 1338. William Mysone, a fishmonger, rented a house from Adam Colmanbury in the parish of Seinte Katerine Coleman in Alegate ward, and was in a relationship with Isabel Heyron. In the evening of Friday, 1 November 1336, the couple were in William's home, and had a furious quarrel which resulted in Isabel stabbing her lover in the heart with a knife. He died at sunset four days later, and Isabel fled and was never caught.[1]

The criminal pairing of Johan Fuatard and his mistress Isabel (whose surname was not recorded) came to an abrupt end when they tried to rob the house of carpenter Richard Rothyng in Aldresgate ward during the night of 25/26 March 1325. Richard's servant heard them breaking in, and stabbed Johan to death with his own weapon. Johan Fuatard, or possibly his father of the same name, had himself been one of nine nightwatchmen accused of trespass in Billingesgate ward in October 1300. The nine, on being told that one Reynald the chaplain was with his mistress Isabel, wife of Estephene Fannere, in the Fanneres' home, broke in, only to find that Estephene himself was at home and that Reynald and his clerk were doing some work for him.[2] Other criminal, unmarried couples were Nichol Barbour and Anneis Houdan, two of the three persons who stabbed William Guldeford to death and robbed his body in St Swythin's Lane in January 1326, and Anneis Lavendere and Johan Bury, who, with Johan's brother Adam, attacked and killed Geffrei Berman in the high street of Bisshopesgate ward in June 1340.[3]

At twilight on Sunday, 19 November 1300, Cristine Menstre made her way home through the churchyard of Seinte Marie Wolcherchehawe. (This church was destroyed in the Great Fire of 1666, and Mansion House, the official residence of the Lord Mayor of London, now stands on the site.) William Sawiere, originally from Carshalton in Surrey, encountered her and asked her to spend the night with him. Cristine refused, and as she turned away from William, he took out a knife and stabbed her under the right shoulder-blade. The knife penetrated 6 inches and the wound proved immediately fatal. A witness raised the hue and cry, and William was pursued, captured, and sent to Neugate prison. He was hanged for murder just six days later.[4]

In 1311, Peres Taverner, found guilty of nightwalking while carrying a sword, was described as a *holer,* adulterer or fornicator. A boatman who lived in Portsokne ward in 1321, William Counte, was nicknamed *Frelove* or 'free love', and his second name, although it can mean 'count' in modern English, also meant the same thing that it signifies in Gropecountelane. This is probably not a coincidence.[5] Margarete Hontyngdone (i.e. Huntingdon), resident of Bradestrete ward, was imprisoned in the Tun on Cornhull in June 1311, on the grounds that she 'had been before driven out from the ward aforesaid as a common strumpet, and had afterwards harboured men of bad repute'. The following January, the serjeant of Bradestrete, Richard Kissere, imprisoned Margarete in the Tun again for 'being of bad character'.[6] In the 1320s, Alis Wytteney was a 'courtesan' who rented a house from Johan Assheby in Billingesgate ward, and Emme Brakkele, said to be a 'harlot', worked in Faitoreslane a few years later. In February 1339, the lorimer Geffrai Perler went there to 'lie with her'.[7] It was officially forbidden for prostitutes to reside within the city walls, but, of course, they often did.[8] One of them, at the end of the 1290s, was Cristine Gravesende. When she and 'other common prostitutes living in the city' were summoned to appear before the mayor and aldermen, she and 'a certain Robert Bonevil, her paramour' punched the mayor's serjeant Richard Peleter in the mouth.[9]

William Cok, butcher of Cokkeslane, was said to 'harbour prostitutes' in his houses (plural) in December 1300. Thomas, vicar of St Sepulchre without Newgate, and Johan Copersmyth, took matters into their own hands by breaking into the houses and tearing away eleven doors and five windows with hammers and chisels, and distributed them among William Cok's neighbours. William accused the men of trespass and criminal damage in the mayor's court, but was informed that Thomas and Johan's action was lawful. The same thing happened to Richard atte Nax in 1305: prostitutes dwelt in his house, so the prior of Holy Trinity and seven servants removed his doors and windows.[10]

In December 1310, Edward II ordered the mayor, Richer Refham, and the sheriffs, Simond Corp and Peres Blakeneye, to take measures for 'the suppression of houses of ill-fame'. Whatever measures the men took were ineffectual. William Dalton of Baynardeschastel ward was imprisoned in Neugate for over two months in 1338 for 'keeping a house of ill-fame to which married women and their paramours and other bad characters resorted'. The cordwainer Robert Stratford was accused in July 1338 of keeping a brothel where women named as Alis Donbely and Alis Tredewedowe, and unnamed others, worked, and Ellen Evesham of Fletestrete 'keeps a disorderly house and harbours thieves and prostitutes'. Sisters named Anneis and Juliane worked as prostitutes in Holbourne in the late 1330s, and in 1344 'women of ill-fame' worked in houses belonging to Sir Richard Wylughby and William Sendale in Secollane.[11] In July 1340, more 'women of ill-fame' were said to frequent a house belonging to James Sherman called *Breggehous* ('Bridge House'); Johan Catton 'keeps a common bawdy-house'; and Sarra Mareschal used the home she rented from the archdeacon of Colchester as a 'disorderly house'. The bedel of Faryngdone Without ward, Johan St Albans, was accused in 1344 of accepting bribes 'from disorderly women to protect them in their practices', and an inquisition heard that Anneis Chedyngfeld and Clarice Claterballok 'are women of ill-fame, and that a certain Sayer Valoyns, who dwells with the latter, prefers bad company to good'. Clarice's last name presumably means that she specialised in clattering her clients' *balloks*.[12]

King Edward II failed to set a good example. While holding parliament in October 1324 and staying at the Tower, he paid a man named Robyn Carter to take him over the Thames to La Rosere in Suthwerk (see 'Mansions' above), where he 'secretly took his pleasure' with an unnamed lover. The Westminster chronicle *Flores Historiarum* thundered that the king delighted in 'illicit and sinful sexual intercourse'.[13] Edward fathered an illegitimate son named Adam around 1305/10, and his legitimate son and successor Edward III (b. 1312) had a son and two daughters with his mistress Alice Perrers in the 1360s. Some London men also had illegitimate children. Henry Causton, a well-off mercer of Vinetrye ward, made his will on 13 December 1348, and died before 24 January 1350. Henry had no children with his wife Margarete, but had an illegitimate daughter named Katerine, whose mother Isabel was still alive in 1348. Henry had named his and Isabel's daughter after one of his sisters, and left Katerine 100 marks 'for her marriage'. She was still underage, and even though her mother was alive, Henry granted custody of her to his wife.[14] Simond Turnham, a fishmonger who divided his goods among his son, daughter and grandchildren in 1346, also left a tenement to his illegitimate daughter Margarete, and the mercer Thomas Worstede of St Laurence Jewry left property and money in 1345 to his legitimate children Thomas, Simond and Isabel as well as 'my bastard daughter' Alis. Wauter Schenefeld, a tanner, left bequests to his illegitimate son Johan Hadham and Johan's mother Alis Hadham in early 1347.[15] Children born out of wedlock usually, though not invariably, took their mother's name, and when men were identified as a woman's son, such as the felons Robert, son of Margerie Hedonne, Thomas, son of Sarah Bredmongestere, and Wauter, son of Beatrice Gomme, they were illegitimate.

Peres Bosenho or Bosenham, a skinner and sheriff of London 1301/02, who died *c*. June 1306, left bequests to his legitimate children Roger, Maud and Margerie and to Peres the younger, 'my son by Cristine Brawynge'. Wauter Gubbe, a *stokfisshmongere* who died *c*. April 1309, had three legitimate sons named Richard, Johan and Mayhew, and another son called Johan Bandon. He divided his tenements and shops in Thamisstrete equally among all four sons. William Newenham died in the plague year of 1349, and in his will mentioned his legitimate son William, his illegitimate daughter Anneis and her mother Anneis Dolfyn, and his illegitimate children Johan and Johane and their mother Maud Blaket of Rickmansworth, Hertfordshire. His daughter Anneis was older than her three half-siblings, and William appointed her their guardian while they were underage.[16] *Wollemongere* Johan Assheford's will of early 1329 mentions two sons and four daughters he had with two women, Johane Stodleye and Lettice Bilham, and as he did not call either woman his wife and as they were both still alive, it seems certain that the six children were born out of wedlock. Johan left all his children and the two women property, money and possessions: a brewhouse in Tourstret went to Johane Stodleye to pass eventually to their son Thomas, while £20 went to their daughters Alis and Johane, and £60 was given to Lettice Bilham and their children Johan, Katerine and Isabel. In his will of February 1348 – he did not die until *c*. March/April 1356 – Johan Assheford and Lettice Bilham's son Johan referred to his half-brother as Thomas Mordale, and Thomas was a mercer who was still alive in 1363. Johane, full sister of Thomas and half-sister of Johan, married the *haberdasshere* Johan Levynge between 21 June and 4 July 1335.[17]

Godwin Hodere, pheliper, mentioned a son called Johan Albon in his will, and the different name almost certainly means that Johan was born out of wedlock; Godwin's primary heir was his legitimate son, Thomas Hodere. Evidently Johan Albon had a good relationship with his father, as he was named in his will and, under Godwin's direction, also became a pheliper.[18] Master Richard Gloucester (d. early 1329), a parson and one of Edward II's lawyers, had a long-term relationship with London resident Katerine, daughter of Geffrei and Isabel St Alban, and left her his house in Fridaistrete for life. Richard also left property to their sons Johan and Nichol, who in October 1329 were aged 12¼ and 10 respectively when Katerine was given custody of them. In 1342, Nichol called himself 'Nichol Gloucester, son of Katerine St Alban', and in 1338 Johan, 'son of the late Master Richard Gloucester' was imprisoned in Neugate with 'other incorrigibles … to prevent their doing mischief'.[19]

Belongings

Several thousand fourteenth-century Londoners made wills to dispose of their possessions and homes, though the vast majority of city residents had no need to do so. The only belongings of Isabel Pampesworth, who hanged herself in 1321, were a blanket and a 'worn sheet' worth 6*d* and an old chest worth 3*d*, though her son was well-off enough to employ a servant. Isabel Heyron rented a house from Mabel Shereman on what is now called Threadneedle Street in the parish of Seint Benet Fink, and jurors seized her few possessions there after she killed her lover William Mysone in 1336: a small brass pot and poscenet, a bed-cover, and a small chest 'with trifling contents'. The belongings of William Grimsby of Bradstrete ward in 1322 included two 'small pigs', jointly valued at 3*s*, a broken chest and a table jointly valued at 6*d*, a pair of worn linen sheets at 4*d*, a blanket, a worn linen cloth and 'other small things' valued at 2*s* 9*d*, and the belongings of Johan Skut in Lymstrete ward in 1325 were a small pig worth 12*d*, four geese worth 12*d*, a cock and a hen worth 4*d*, a box for dice worth 6*d*, 100 flasks of ale worth 5*s*, and a quarter of brewing barley worth 4*s*.[1]

Johan Cu hired a brewhouse in the parish of All Hallows Staningechirche from Ysabel Estre for 3½ marks (560*d*) per year. Ysabel claimed in August 1305 that Johan had stolen items from her, including half a tun of ale, value 15*d*; a spade, value 8*d*; timber, value 8*d*; a sieve to clarify ale, a hammer and a basket, total value 2*s* 9*d*; a pair of handmills, value 3*s* 6*d*; and Ysabel's dog with its chain, value 20*s* 4*d*. Johan only admitted to taking the handmills, which he claimed belonged to him anyway, and stated that he thought Ysabel had freely given him the dog. He offered to give the animal back to her, as long as she promised to feed it.[2] There are very few references to pets in fourteenth-century London, and Ysabel probably kept her dog as a guard-dog; a pet was a luxury few could afford, though in the late 1200s, a London resident named Arnulph Munteny owned three greyhounds.[3]

123

Juliane Prykafeld, a *lavendere*, was stabbed to death in the Seinte Katerine hospital complex around midnight on 17 September 1337, and her killer, a skinner named Thomas Longe, stole a strong-box containing money and jewels to the value of 10 marks from her. Ten marks, 1,600*d*, seems an oddly large amount for a woman who probably earned 1*d* or 1½*d* a day to possess. On 28 August 1340, two merchants from Brabant, Godekyn and Henryk Houndesbergh, fled after committing murder. Their chattels were seized, and included a dun horse worth 160*d* and a white horse worth 120*d*, two small tunics of striped cloth, 'much worn', and an old cloak worth only 3*d*. Robert of Portsmouth, resident in Vinetrye ward, killed his wife Alis in December 1339. His confiscated possessions included an old blanket worth 20*d*; a piece of fur worth 12*d*; an old chest worth 4*d*; firewood and a barrel worth 12*d*; a surcoat (overtunic) worth 12*d*; two old coats worth 18*d*; and a woman's *curtepy* (short jacket) and coat of green cloth worth 2*s* 6*d*.[4]

At the other end of the scale, the will of the draper Richard Costantyn, dated January 1342, shows how wealthy some London merchants were. Richard inherited £40 from his father (d. 1332), also named Richard and also a draper, and left this money to his son Johan plus another 10 marks of silver, two silver goblets, a silver jug, a sapphire, a silver ring, and a horn of ivory. To his daughters Margarete and Elizabeth, Richard bequeathed 10 marks of silver and a silver goblet each, and to his wife Margarete, £60 of silver.[5] William Thorneye, the pepperer, sheriff and alderman who moved to London from Lincolnshire around 1320, also became very well-off. William came from an impoverished background: in his will he left money to his 'poor kinsfolk' in Croyland and his native village of Whaplode Drove. By January 1345, however, he was wealthy enough to be able to lend £250 (hundreds of thousands of pounds in modern values) to the abbot of Croyland.[6] The hosier Johan Holegh, though born illegitimate, also became very rich, and made a long will in 1348. He left money and possessions to relatives, apprentices and servants, including 'twelve silver spoons with *akernes*' (acorns), a black mazer, and his 'girdle with *scaloppes*' (scallops) to Thomas Taillour, and his 'entire bed' and his 'coat furred with *bevre*' (beaver) to his apprentice Johan Beauchamp.[7]

Bertelmew Deumars (d. June or July 1352), came from Southbeamflet, i.e. South Benfleet in Essex, and was one of the sheriffs of London in 1340/41. He was a corder by profession, was married firstly to Beatrice and secondly to Cecile, and had a son, Laurence Deumars. Bertelmew lived in the parish of All Hallows on the Cellar on Thamisstrete in Douuegate ward, near a wharf on the Thames which belonged to Thomas Porkele, cousin of the late mayor and alderman, Nichol Farndone. He had moved to Douuegate from Kandelwikstrate ward in 1325. Bertelmew left 100 marks of silver and his 'best bed' to his wife Cecile in his will, and twenty pounds of silver to his son, though was not convinced of Laurence's seriousness; he left his son another ten pounds of silver if his executors deemed Laurence 'willing to make good use' of it, otherwise the money was to be 'devoted to pious uses'. From 1325 onwards, Bertelmew made frequent loans of cash or advanced credit to various men, between £12 and £66.[8] Some wealthier Londoners showed compassion to those who had fallen on hard times, especially in the aftermath of the plague: in his will of September 1349, glover Hugh Robury left money to those who had 'been reduced from affluence to poverty' and were ashamed of the need to beg. Hugh also pardoned any debts owing to him if payment would cause hardship.[9]

Fun

In an age long before television, cinema, theatres as we know them, and so on, an age when the vast majority were illiterate, people took their entertainment however they could. Thomas Flete (d. 1313), a pheliper of Cornhull, was accused before the mayor's court in August 1307 of mocking the mayor (Johan Blount) and the aldermen by neighing like a horse whenever they rode past him.[1] Edward III issued a stern proclamation to children and adults in London in 1351 not to continue the game of 'taking off the hoods of people or laying hands upon them', as there was a popular trend of dashing up behind people and yanking the hoods from their heads.[2] Edward had put rather a dampener on the Christmas festivities of 1335 in London by forbidding anyone to walk the streets 'disguised with false faces', i.e. masks, and told every city resident to 'keep himself quiet and at ease within his own house'.[3] This perhaps demonstrates that the wearing of masks was a popular custom at Christmas.

Andrew Modyngham (later called Andrew Cros), apprentice of William Cros, a London fishmonger, visited the Sussex coast during the festive season of 1327. He rode a hackney horse to get there and back from the city, and spent a few days in and around Hastings and Winchelsea, 9 miles apart, with his friend Johan Roger. Hastings is 60 miles from London, so it must have taken Andrew two or three days to get there. Perhaps he regretted the effort: some provincial inhabitants could be hostile to Londoners, and four men, on hearing that Andrew came from London, 'villainously abused' him. Later, they lay in wait for him on the road home, and beat him up.[4] Hackney horses (*hakeneyes*) could be hired for travel, and Londoner William Despenser paid 12*d* to hire one for a few days in October 1319. In the late 1200s, Godfrey Belstede hired one from a man in his native village, Cheshunt in Hertfordshire, to ride into London.[5] Andrew Modyngham's experience seems to mean that Londoners sometimes went on sightseeing trips to other parts of

England or at the very least ventured out of the city to visit relatives and friends, and other city-dwellers who wished to see the countryside or escape temporarily from crowded London could hire a boat to sail them along the Thames. One Wednesday afternoon in June 1322, Johan Thorpe, his wife Anneis and their friend Johan Hegham hired William Stedeman to take them the few miles to Kyngestone in his *dongbot* (this means 'dung-boat', so can hardly have been the most fragrant mode of transport). Unfortunately, as the party passed near Potenhuth, a sudden storm blew up, and Johan Thorpe fell out of the boat and drowned.[6]

There is much evidence that people invited their friends to their home for dinner or drinks, and that groups of friends went to taverns together. Alis Pas was delighted to receive an invitation to dine with the potter Adam atte Rose (d. 1335) at his home in Bredstrate ward in May 1305, but became considerably less delighted when it transpired that Adam had ulterior motives and tried to force her to 'seal a certain document' relating to a rent she owned, which she could not read. Alis suspected Adam of trying to trick her into signing over her rents, and he was, furthermore, married.[7] Luke Havering, one of the sheriffs of London in 1300/01, invited his friend Henry Curteis to his home one Friday evening in September 1300 and plied him with alcohol (to disastrous effect), and in May 1301 Peres Huntyngdon and Andrew Prille went to the home of Wauter Vigerous to drink with him and also to wrestle, another popular activity. Gilbert Getyngtone dined at the home of his friend Ivo Percival one Friday evening in September 1323, and in February 1324 Guy and Anneis Fulberd dined with their friend Robert Holewell in his home in the parish of Seint Esmon the King.

As well as convivial evenings spent dining and drinking, many Londoners took part in physical exercise. A form of football already existed in the early fourteenth century: Edward II wrote to Mayor Nichol Farndone in 1314 complaining about the 'great noise' in London caused by 'rumpuses over large footballs' (*rageries de grosses pelotes de pee* in the French original; *rageries* literally means 'rabies' or 'madnesses'). He therefore ordered Nichol to ban football, on the grounds that 'evils' could result from playing it.[8] The sad death of young Johan atte Noke in 1337 (see 'Houses' above), who fell to the ground while attempting to recover a lost ball from a gutter, indicates that children played ball-games. A game which involved throwing 'tiles', apparently something like quoits, resulted in the death of Johan Fuatard in 1276, while playing it with his friend Johan Clerk in the churchyard of Seinte Marie Magdalene in Suthewerk. Clerk accidentally struck Fuatard on the head with a tile, and he died a few days later.[9]

Another hazardous hobby was the shooting of pigeons and other birds perched on churches or houses with stonebows, a catapult for shooting stones, and arbalests, a kind of crossbow. This was prohibited in October 1327, because the missiles wounded passersby and broke windows (a prohibition which usefully reveals the existence of a sizeable number of glass windows in fourteenth-century London). Johan Furbour of Cornhull was convicted by the mayor's court in July 1305 of practising with a stonebow 'on churches and houses in the city'.[10] Fencing also existed in the early fourteenth century, though was not valued. Master Roger Skirmisour (his name means 'fencer', though survives in modern English as 'skirmisher') from Yorkshire was imprisoned in March 1311 for keeping a fencing-school for men somewhere in London. He was accused of enticing the sons of 'respectable persons' to attend, 'so as to waste and spend the property of their fathers and mothers on bad practices; the result being that they themselves became bad men.' Oddly, a city proclamation stated that no one was allowed to keep a fencing-school by night or day, on pain of imprisonment for forty days.[11]

The fields called Elmes outside the city walls were often used for archery practice and sport. A cook named Wauter Lychefeld was killed there around dusk one day in January 1339 when someone carelessly shot an arrow in his direction, and it hit him in the stomach. The archer was never identified. Wauter's unfortunate demise shows that someone was outside practising their archery skills even in the middle of winter, though Edward III grumbled in 1337 about the 'physique' of the London archers sent to him, and demanded 'the strongest and healthiest men of the city' instead.[12] One Sunday in August 1337, *stokfisshmongere* Wauter Mordone (d. 1351) of Crokedelane in Brigge ward, sheriff 1335/36, took his whole family 'to play in the fields after dinner'. Wauter and his wife Cristine had five daughters, two sons and a grandson, and two young men remained behind to guard the house and also indulged in 'a friendly game'. The men's names were given as William Russel and Johan Paul; William's father Adam had appointed Wauter Mordone as his son's guardian in his will of 1328, and Johan was surely another young ward.[13]

Playing-cards had not yet reached England in the first half of the fourteenth century – they were invented in China around the ninth or tenth century and are believed to have arrived in Europe in the 1360s or 1370s – and although chess certainly existed, there are no examples of Londoners bequeathing any sets in the many hundreds of extant wills between 1300 and 1350. In 1321, the nobleman Hugh Despenser the Elder (1261–1326), who owned a house near the priory of St Helen at Bisshopesgate, owned three chess-sets made of crystal and others made partly of nut and partly of ginger-root.[14]

A game played with coins was cross and pile, the medieval equivalent of heads or tails, and dice games were also hugely popular. They were often played in taverns, and some men were accused of using 'false dice' in order to cheat.[15] *Hasard* or 'hazard' was a popular game, and so was *rafle*, 'raffle'. The simple objective of raffle was to roll three dice with the same number; the rules of hazard, played with two dice, were far more complicated.[16] One Sunday in late November 1321, after curfew, two men played *hasard* in a brewhouse owned by William Canefeld in Langbourne ward. They were Johan Faukes, a currier, and Michael Gaugeour, whose job involved measuring liquids for customs duties. They quarrelled, and Johan left the tavern and lay in wait for Michael. When he came out, Johan drew a falchion and stabbed Michael in the heart, and killed him.[17]

Another game was knucklebones, and in October 1339, Henry Pykard, Wauter Waldeshef and Roger Fynch were arrested, as they were addicted to playing it and led 'apprentices into gambling habits'.[18] *Quek* or *queek*, i.e. chequers, is mentioned in March 1301 when Joce of Cornwall played it on a bench with his friend Thomas of Bristol in the home of another friend, Alis Wautham, on or near Paternosterlane one Monday evening. Some people cheated by using a false *quek-bord* where the white squares were lower than the black ones, or vice versa. Anyone who played with false dice or with a false *quek-bord* was accused of *joukerie* or cheating, and was sentenced to an hour locked in the pillory either with the dice hanging round their neck or with the *quek-bord* burning beneath them. These cases reveal that games of dice and chequers were often played on painted tables, and that certain men with dubious intentions hung around in the streets asking passersby if they wished to come in and play.[19] One Monday evening just before Christmas 1323, Estephene Lenne, a taverner, played at tables for money with Arcus Rikelinge of Brabant in a tavern run by William Staneforde in Douegate ward. Arcus, losing badly, was 'moved to anger' by Estephene's gloating, and stabbed him in the belly with a knife called a *tranchour*.[20]

Most Londoners were illiterate, but a few clerks and wealthy merchants owned books. William Thorneye, alderman and sheriff 1339/40, left his book the *Proverbs of Solomon* to his 2-year-old son Johan in 1349.[21] Benet Fulsham, sheriff 1324/25, had a valuable item stolen from his home on Sunday, 8 July 1341: a breviary, i.e. a small, easily portable book containing religious texts, called a *portehors* or *portifory* in the fourteenth century. The thief was Richard Pembroke, and he appeared before the mayor, sheriffs and aldermen three days later and was sentenced to be hanged. The breviary was worth 20*s* or 240*d*.[22] The former mayor Johan Gisors bequeathed a number of religious tomes in his will of 1350: a missal in two volumes, a breviary with musical notation, and a psalter. Sir William Langeford of Clerkenewelle mentioned a *portifory* and a 'psalter with glosses' in his will of October 1346, and William Thorneye also owned a *portifory* and psalter.[23]

In December 1337, Johan Bokelond of Honilane accused Johan Writele of stealing his 'book written in English' called *Legends of the Saints*. Bokelond claimed the book was worth 40*s*; the jury who convicted Writele valued it at 30*s*.[24] Another book-owner, and evidently a man with a taste for learning, was Thomas Giles of Fletstret. In his will of early 1348, Thomas left to his and his wife Diamanda's son Thomas the younger, whom he wished to be educated as a clerk, 'all his books bound and unbound, on the canon and civil law, grammar, dialectic, theology, geometry and astronomy'. Henry Graspays, fishmonger, made his will in early December 1348, and left his son Henry his 'books of *romanse* and others' ('romance' meant any kind of fictional story, not just a love-story). A few weeks later in January 1349, the vintner Robert Felstede bequeathed 'a book called *Byble*' to Johan Heurle and 'a psalter written in Latin and English' to Johan Foxton.[25]

A jousting tournament took place at Stebbenhethe on 28 May 1309, and Sir Giles Argentein (d. 1314) was the victor and was declared 'king of the greenwood'.[26] A tournament was held in Chepe between the great cross and Sopereslane in September 1331, and the 18-year-old king, Edward III, a keen and excellent jouster, competed personally. In a procession before the tournament, each jouster was accompanied by a noble lady wearing a red tunic and white cap and led by a silver chain, and each pair rode along Chepe at Vespers to cheering crowds. The knights themselves wore masks, green tunics, cloaks lined with red, and red hoods; they were said to be 'dressed and masked like Tartars'.

Behind them came fifty squires, also masked and wearing white tunics with the right sleeve made of green fabric embroidered with golden arrows. Timber barriers were erected along Chepe for the spectators, and some kind of grandstand was built across the road for the 17-year-old queen, Philippa of Hainault, and other ladies including the king's 13-year-old sister Eleanor of Woodstock. Tragedy struck, however, when the grandstand collapsed on the first day. Queen Philippa, having fortunately escaped injury, soon recovered from the shock and rode her palfrey up and down the lists, comforting distressed and injured spectators. She later pleaded with her husband to forgive the carpenters for their shoddy and dangerous work.[27]

One of the greatest public events of the English Middle Ages took place at Westminster Abbey on Sunday, 22 May 1306: the mass knighting of Edward I's 22-year-old son the prince of Wales, and more than 250 other men. The king hired dozens of minstrels to entertain the new knights afterwards during a great banquet in Westminster Hall, and one called himself *Perle in the Eghe*, 'pearl in the eye', because he had cataracts. Others were the famous acrobat Matilda Makejoye, Januche and Gillot the trumpeters, Gillot and Adekin the harpers, Reynald the story-teller, Johan Boteler, called the 'Burning King', James 'Jaket' Cowpen, a Scottish King of Heralds who called himself King Capenny, and one named only as 'the minstrel with the bells'.[28] London minstrels of the early fourteenth century included Ivo Vala, a citole-player (the citole was a string instrument) active in the 1320s who is still well-known today in certain musical circles, and Gillot or Gillotin Sautreour, who appears on record as a court minstrel from *c.* 1298 to *c.* 1319 and whose last name means that he played the psaltery, another kind of string instrument. Ivo, who was often addressed simply as 'Vala', was with Edward II at Dover in September 1325, and his wife Annote travelled from London to see him there.[29] Gillot Sautreour, whose real name was William Grey, owned property in Thamisestrete and Ebbegate.[30]

The extant accounts of the dowager queen of England, Isabella of France, in 1357/58 reveal that there was something called a 'school of minstrelsy' in London in the middle of the fourteenth century. Isabella sent Wauter Hert, one of her vielle-players (the vielle or viol was another string instrument), to the city to learn his craft at a *scola minstralsie*.[31] Not everyone in London, however, appreciated minstrels and their music. In October 1299, Richard Davy, a baker, threw a bone at a tabor-player and broke his tabor, i.e. a small, portable snare drum, in the middle. A *menestral* (minstrel) called Thomas Somer 'came playing' to the house of Thomas Lenne in Cornhull ward one Thursday evening in May 1324, but evidently Lenne did not think much of the performance, as he took a *durbarre* (doorbar) and attacked Somer with it.[32]

The birth of Edward III, eldest child of Edward II and Isabella of France, at Windsor Castle on Monday, 13 November 1312 was the cue for heartfelt celebrations in London. Queen Isabella sent her French tailor, Jean de Falaise, the 25 miles to the city with a letter to inform the mayor and aldermen, but he dawdled and did not arrive until Tuesday, by which time the birth had already been proclaimed by one Robert Oliver. Around Vespers on Monday, the mayor, Johan Gisors, the aldermen, and an untold number of city residents gathered at the Guildhall. They sang and danced, and afterwards 'passed through the city with great glare of torches' in a spontaneous, joyful procession, playing trumpets and other instruments. Very early the next morning, before Prime, proclamation was made throughout the city that the day was a public holiday, and in fact Londoners 'rested from all work' for an entire week 'for joy at the birth' of their future king. The only unhappy person in London was Jean de Falaise. Sulking at having his thunder stolen by Robert Oliver, he ungraciously sent back a silver cup and 10 marks in cash, his gifts from the mayor for bringing the queen's letter, because 'they seemed to him to be too little'.

The following Monday, 20 November 1312, the mayor and aldermen wore their best robes and rode from the Guildhall to Westminster Abbey accompanied by the drapers, mercers and vintners of the city in costume (not described). After their return to the city, they danced, sang and celebrated for the rest of the day and most of the night. The great conduit in Chepe ran all day with free wine for the inhabitants, and more wine was made available in a pavilion for anyone who wanted some. The celebrations continued on Sunday, 4 February 1313. Queen Isabella passed through Westminster on her way to Canterbury, where she wished to give thanks at the shrine of St Thomas Becket for the birth of her son. The fishmongers of London, 'costumed very richly', fitted out a boat 'in the guise of a great ship, with all manner of tackle', and 'sailed' it through Chepe as far as Westminster, where they presented it to Isabella.[33]

Weather

The inquisition post mortem of Londoner William Kirkeby was held on 1 October 1302. He owned four acres of vineyards, a garden, twelve acres of meadow and over 100 acres of arable land in Holeburn, and his heirs were his sisters: Margarete Hotthorp, aged about 50; Alis Prilly, aged 48; Maud Houby, 46; and Mabel Grymbaud, 44. Vineyards existed in the south of England during the Medieval Warm Period, which ended *c.* 1300, and for a while afterwards; there were vineyards in the Gloucestershire village of Tewkesbury as late as 1359.[1]

The long era called the Little Ice Age is generally thought to have begun around 1300, and it does seem that the late thirteenth and early fourteenth centuries saw quite a few very cold, snowy, icy winters. The winter of 1308/09 was a harsh one, and in 1309/10, the Thames froze solidly and people walked over it to Suthewerk. A few years earlier, according to the *French Chronicle of London*, 'London Bridge was broken by the great frost'.[2] The Westminster chronicle *Flores Historiarum* states that the winter of 1282/83 saw 'such an abundance of frost, cold and snow' that even the oldest English people had never experienced before, and that five arches of London Bridge were destroyed 'by the violence of the ice'. In the winter of 1305/06, snow and ice lay on the ground from 15 December to 27 January, and from 13 February to 13 April.[3] In 1316, there was a hard frost during Christmas week, snow lay on the ground for most of the first three months of 1322, and there is a reference in the Assize of Nuisance on 6 December 1325 to the prevailing 'wintry conditions' which made outside work impossible. That month, Edward II had boats stacked with firewood taken to his palaces in London and Westminster and had himself a pair of gloves made from stag leather.[4] Nor was the freezing cold the only problem: in the winter of 1294, the Thames flooded so badly that 'it drowned a great part of the lands of Bermundeseye and of all the country round about'.[5]

Conversely, it may be that summers of the early 1300s were sometimes rather hotter than today. In 1305, the 'burning heat ... oppressed mankind', and the consequences were drought and pox, so that many children and young people were 'afflicted with freckles and spots' and died.[6] The summer of 1326 was a particularly long, boiling hot and intensely dry one, and there were droughts that year and in 1324, 1344 and 1345. Two chroniclers say that the level of the Thames in the summer of 1326 fell so low that it was overwhelmed by the sea, and people complained about the foul ale made from the salty river water. On the other hand, the summers of 1327, 1330, 1350 and 1351 were chilly and wet, as was the summer of 1348 when the Black Death arrived in England; it rained almost non-stop from mid-June until Christmas.[7] The terrible weather of the mid-1310s brought endless suffering and misery. It rained for much of 1315 and into 1316, which led directly to the Great Famine in northern Europe as crops rotted away in waterlogged fields across the country (see also 'Food' above). Two chroniclers say that it rained more or less without stopping from Pentecost (early June) 1315 until Easter (11 April) 1316, but the foul weather may have begun well before that: already in mid-August 1315, Edward II had difficulty buying sufficient bread for his household.[8]

The St Paul's annalist says that a terrific storm with much thunder and lightning took place in London on 15 July 1315, and a bolt of lightning caused a conflagration at Woburn Abbey 40 miles away. Six days later, a storm in London around midday was supposedly so bad that it swept up a boy of 14 in the parish of St Botolph without Bisshopisgate and stripped the clothes from him, but deposited him back in the same place, whereupon he excitedly related 'many wonderful things'.[9] In July 1317, another terrific thunderstorm and heavy rain caused havoc in London. People were swept away and drowned, and the rain also did great damage to the Flete and Holbourne bridges and to a number of houses and mills.[10] Something of the contemporary mentality is captured in one chronicler's magnificent description of a thunderstorm in July 1293: 'We beheld in the east a huge cloud blacker than coal, in the midst whereof we saw the lashes of an immense eye darting fierce lightning into the west ... and demons were heard yelling in the air'.[11]

Mayors

Mayors of London were elected every year on 28 October, the feast of St Simon and St Jude, by the previous mayor, the aldermen, the two sheriffs, and twelve 'good and true' men from each of the twenty-four (later twenty-five) wards, i.e. the commonalty. Sometimes a mayor held office for more than a year; Johan Blount served from 1301 to 1308, an unusually long period, and Johan Wentgrave from 1316 to 1319. Hamo Chigwell was elected no fewer than nine times between the late 1310s and late 1320s.

After his election, the new mayor was presented to the king if the latter was in London or Westminster, or to the barons of the Exchequer if not; if the king and the barons were all absent, the constable of the Tower of London was their deputy, though in all cases the mayor was presented to the king the next time he came to London or Westminster. Richer Refham, elected 28 October 1310, was presented to Edward II at the London house of the Dominican friars on 17 August 1311 after Edward finally returned to the city from a long sojourn in the north. Johan Gisors, elected 28 October 1311, was presented to Edward on 10 November. He was re-elected on Friday, 28 October 1312 and was presented to the barons of the Exchequer at Westminster the following Monday, and to the king at Westminster on 16 December by Aymer de Valence, earl of Pembroke, and Johan Sandale, acting treasurer of England. Hamo Chigwell, elected on Sunday, 28 October 1319 for the first time, was presented to the constable of the Tower the next day and was sworn into office 'outside the outer gate of the Tower'. He was presented to Edward II at Westminster on 20 February 1320, after the king returned from a stay in Yorkshire. Nichol Farndone was presented to Edward II at Westminster the day after his election on 28 October 1320.[1]

On 28 October 1309, the pepperer Thomas Romeyn was elected mayor (and was presented to Edward II on 8 December). Thomas was Italian or of Italian origin, and his wife Juliana was the sister of another pepperer, Phelip Hauteyn (d. 1304). The affluent Thomas had been alderman of

Cordewanerstrete ward since 1294, and acted as city sheriff in 1290/91. He, his wife Juliana and their daughters Rohese, Margerie, Alis and Johane lived in the parish of Aldemariecherche. Sometime before December 1312, Rohese Romeyn (b. *c.* 1286) married Johan Burford, sheriff of London in 1303/04 and briefly alderman of Vinetrye ward in 1321/22 before he died; Johan came originally from Southampton, and was a pepperer like Rohese's father and maternal uncle. Thomas Romeyn's second daughter Margerie married twice, and his other daughters Johane and Alis became nuns at Halliwell Priory in Shorisdich. He made his will in December 1312, and died not long afterwards.[2]

Johan Gisors or Gysorz was mayor three times, 1311/12, 1312/13 and 1314/15, and was the grandson of Johan Gisors (d. 1282), mayor of London 1245/46 and 1258/59. He was born *c.* 1279 to Margerie (d. 1305) and Johan (d. 1296), and was about 27 when he became alderman of Vinetrie ward in 1306 and in his early thirties during his first term as mayor. Johan had four younger brothers, Anketin, Thomas, Henry and Richard, and four sisters, Beatrice, Mabel, Johane and Isabel. When their mother Margerie died in July 1305, Richard and Isabel Gisors were underage, and Margerie appointed Thomas, her second or third son, as their guardian.[3] Anketin Gisors became alderman of Alegate, and Henry was alderman of Cornhull and sheriff of London 1329/30. Mayor Johan Gisors died in January 1351 in his early seventies, having outlived his first wife Isabel and his eldest son Thomas, who fled after killing a man named Wauter Hodesdone in Bradestrete ward in June 1326. Johan was survived by his second wife Alis, his younger sons Edward and Nichol, his daughter Juliane, and his granddaughters Margarete Picard and Felicia Gisors, Thomas's daughters. He left Felicia his house in the parish of Seinte Mildred, *Gysorshalle*, which almost certainly is the 'New Hall' mentioned in his father's will of 1296. The house was still named *Gisoreshalle* in 1429.[4] Gisors is a town in Normandy, situated between Paris and Rouen, and the family must have originated there, though Johan and his siblings were at least third-generation English. Johan was unpopular and believed to be corrupt: the *French Chronicle* complains that 'many people were imprisoned and impoverished' owing to Johan's malice.[5]

Hamo Chigwell, formerly Hamo Dene (d. 1332/33), was elected mayor for the ninth time on 28 October 1328, his rival being Benet Fulsham, sheriff 1324/25. Hamo was popular among the commonalty, who shouted 'yes!' on hearing the result, but not so much among the aldermen and sheriffs, some of whom shouted 'Chigwell!' but others 'Fulsham!' After the assembly broke up in confusion, some of the 'wiser citizens' persuaded the two candidates that to avoid commotion in the city, neither should be mayor, and Johan Grantham was chosen instead.[6] Despite being elected mayor on numerous occasions and surviving removal from office in April 1323 and November 1326 to serve again, Hamo was not universally liked. Johan Coton, alderman of Walebrok ward and sheriff 1325/26, stated sometime between July 1326 and January 1327 that Hamo 'was the worst worm that had come to London for twenty years, that there would be no peace in the city so long as he was alive, and that it would be a good thing if his head was cut off.' One Roger Bere reported his words, and Johan Coton appeared before fifteen of his fellow aldermen and Hamo Chigwell himself on 3 and 4 October 1328. He defended himself by saying that Roger Bere was ill-disposed towards him, and cleared himself by the 'sixth hand', i.e. he and five others swore an oath of his innocence.[7]

Johan Pulteneye or Poultney, mayor 1330/32, 1333/34 and 1336/37, owner of the mansion Coldharbour, was a draper by profession and was knighted in 1337. Most unusually for a merchant, he came from a noble, landowning background, and inherited property in Leicestershire.[8] Johan was old enough to act as an attorney in February 1316, so must have been born in or before the mid-1290s, and had moved to London by then.[9] He made his will on 14 November 1348, and appointed William Clinton, earl of Huntingdon (*c.* 1304– 54) and Rauf Stratford, bishop of London (d. 1354), as supervisors. Pulteneye gave Stratford 'his finest ring with a great stone called *rubie* of great value and beauty', and Clinton 'a beautiful ring with two great stones called *diamauntes*, two silver flagons enamelled, a cup, together with a certain spoon and saltcellar to match'. He died, possibly a victim of the Black Death, on 8 June 1349, leaving his son William, born between October 1340 and March 1341, as his heir to his extensive estates in seven counties and London. Sir William Pulteneye died on 20 January 1367, knighted and married but childless.[10]

Andrew Aubrey, pepperer, son of Roger and Dionise Aubrey, was one of the city sheriffs in 1331/32 and mayor from 1339 to 1341. He married Johane, widow of another pepperer named Thomas Evenefeld, who made his will on 15 October 1328 and died before 5 December that year. Evenefeld left Aubrey a tenement near Sopereslane which he held from Richard Chaucer, Richard's wife Marie, and her son Thomas Heyron, respectively the step-grandfather, grandmother, and half-uncle of the poet Geoffrey Chaucer (*c.* 1342–1400).[11] Andrew made his will on 3 October 1349, the year of the Black Death, but survived the plague and did not die until 1358. He went on pilgrimage overseas in August 1350 with his son Johan, a chaplain and a servant, and Edward III stated in November 1352 that Andrew 'has now come to old age'. Andrew was already active as a pepperer in 1321, so must have been born before 1300 and was therefore around 60 when he died. He left his wife Johane tenements in the parish of Aldermariecherche and on Milkestrete which Johan Chaucer, father of Geoffrey, had sold to him. Johane Aubrey was alive in December 1364 and dead by January 1369.[12]

Mayor Johan Oxenford or Oxford, a vintner, died in office on 17 June 1342. His eldest son, also named Johan, was born *c.* 1334, and he had younger sons William and Thomas, daughters Rohese, Katerine, Johane and Margarete and brothers Rauf and Gilbert, and named his parents in his will as Adam and Cristine. Mayor Johan left the remarkably large sum of £100 for his funeral expenses; in modern terms, this is several hundred thousand pounds. The wealthy Johan left another £100 to be distributed among the London poor on the day of his funeral, and £100 to each of his six unmarried children (his daughter Rohese was already married to Johan Preston, whose father of the same name was mayor in 1332/33). As his name indicates, Johan Oxenford came originally from Oxford or at least had close associations with the city: he bequeathed money for repairs on 'the great and little bridges at Oxford' and for the maintenance of a 'certain causeway surrounding the hospital' of Seint Bertelmew in Oxford. His eldest son Johan died in 1357 in his early twenties, and left a young son, Johan Oxenford III.[13]

On the same day as Johan Oxenford's death, the aldermen and commonalty elected Simond Fraunceys as his replacement. Simond's name means 'Frenchman', and he had been a mercer in London since at least 1327 and was sheriff in 1328/29. Simond served as mayor until October 1343, and again in 1355/56. He made his will on 19 May 1358 and died on 4 July, leaving his widow Maud, his daughter Alis, and his son Thomas Fraunceys, then about 24 or 26. Thomas (d. 1370) was Simond's heir to his two manors and a tenement in Essex, two houses and land in Bedfordshire, a manor and tenements in Kent, and three manors, arable land and tenements in Middlesex.[14] Simond held one of his manors as a gift of Elys Fraunceys, and Elys and Adam Fraunceys were Simond's executors and surely his relatives.[15] Elys was also a mercer, and Adam (d. 1375) became mayor of London in 1352.[16]

Sheriffs

There were always two sheriffs of London, elected every year in the Guildhall on *c*. 21 September, the feast of St Matthew the Evangelist, or *c*. 29 September, the feast of St Michael. One was chosen by the mayor and the other by the commonalty, i.e. the aldermen and twelve men from each ward, and as with the mayor, the sheriffs had to be presented to the king or his deputies at the first opportunity. Richard Caumpes and Luke Havering were presented to Sir Rauf Sandwich, constable of the Tower of London, by the mayor Elias Russel on 30 September 1300, and twenty-two years to the day later, Roger Ely and Johan Grantham were presented to the constable Sir Roger Swynnerton 'outside the outer gate' of the Tower, the king and the barons of the Exchequer all being away from the city on both occasions. Simond Fraunceys, elected as sheriff by Mayor Hamo Chigwell, and Henry Combemartin, elected as the other sheriff by the commonalty, both on 21 September 1328, were presented to Sir William Zouche, constable of the Tower, on 30 September.[1] The fact that there were two sheriffs indicates both the size of the population of London and its importance; the English counties had only one, and sometimes one sheriff served two counties. Unlike the mayors, the sheriffs of London served only one term and were never re-elected, and on the eve of the election every September, the outgoing sheriffs left the keys of Newegate prison and their cocket (seal) with the mayor. The court they held regularly was known as *halemot(e)* in Middle English, or 'hall-moot'.[2]

The sheriffs in 1299/1300 were Henry Fingrye, a wealthy fishmonger who died in July 1318, and Johan Armenters. Armenters died in July 1306 and was probably of French or Flemish origin, and had sons Estephene, Richard and Robert and daughter Idonea, named after his first wife. His second wife Johane survived to 1333, and lived with the pepperer William Thorneye.[3] A disaster occurred in July 1322 when dozens of men, women and children were crushed to death around the gate of the

London convent of the Blackfriars, i.e. the Dominicans. Henry Fingrye's executors had decided to distribute alms for Henry's soul on the fourth anniversary of his death, and they inadvertently brought about a tragedy. At daybreak, paupers crowded outside the gate seeking the alms, and when the friars opened the gate, a terrible, deadly crush ensued. The St Paul's annalist states that fifty-five people died, and the coroners' rolls name some of the victims: Beatrix Cole, Johane Peyntures, Alis Norice, Maud the daughter of Robert Carpenter, and twenty-two other women, and Robert Fynel, his sons Simond, Robert and William, and twenty-two other men. This comes to a total of fifty-two.[4]

Gilbert Mordon, one of the sheriffs in 1325/26, was a *stokfisshmongere* who also ran a brewhouse in Brigge ward and owned houses and shops in Thamistret, and trained Wauter Mordon, who took his name. Gilbert was married to Mabel, and although they had no children, in 1325 they were the guardians of Emme Pourte. One Sunday evening in March 1325, eighteen men attempted unsuccessfully and for unexplained reasons to abduct Emme from her guardians' brewhouse, and were chased away by neighbours. Gilbert died shortly before 23 November 1327.[5] The pepperer William Thorneye from Lincolnshire and the mercer Roger Forsham were elected sheriffs in September 1339. Roger's groom Johan Briny was killed at sunrise on 13 January 1340, during Roger's term of office, when his master's grey horse kicked him in the face in Roger's stable in the ward of Bradstrete, after Johan tried to put a halter on the horse. Roger Forsham probably came from Norfolk, as he owned property in various towns there which he left to his three nieces and two stepdaughters in 1348. Simond Corp, sheriff 1310/11, probably, like Thorneye, came from Lincolnshire, as he left 'all his tenements in the town of Seint Botolph', i.e. Boston, to his son Johan in 1329.[6]

The sheriffs of 1348/49 were the pepperer Simond Dolshull or Dolsely or Dolsali, aka Simond Farnham, and Henry Picard or Pycard, a vintner and the grandson-in-law of the mayor Johan Gisors, who was still alive and turned 70 *c.* 1349. Simond Dolshull's wife Alis was the daughter of Adam Salisbury (d. 1330), sheriff 1323/24, and the stepdaughter of Johan Hamond (d. 1349), mayor 1343/45. By September 1346, Simond and Alis had a son Thomas and daughters Anneis, Johane and Margarete. Simond died in late January 1363.[7] Henry Picard served as mayor of London in 1356/57, and in that capacity entertained and feasted John II, king of France, captured by Edward III's eldest son at the battle of

Poitiers in 1356 and held captive in England until 1364. Although Henry and his wife Margarete Gisors had no children together, Henry had an illegitimate son named Johan. Henry made his will on 3 July 1361 and died four years later; Margarete Gisors made an excellent second marriage to the nobleman Lord Burghersh (d. 1369), married thirdly Sir William Burcester, and lived until 1393.[8] Henry's last name implies that his ancestors came from Picardy, so, like the family he married into, he must have been of partly French origin.

Misteries

In the fourteenth century, the London guilds of craftsmen and tradesmen, now known as the city livery companies, were called misteries (sometimes also spelt 'mysteries', rather confusingly). On 1 December 1312, 'good men of every mistery' appeared at the Guildhall before Johan Gisors, the mayor, and put forward 'certain articles' which they wished to be observed. They complained that 'many citizens, owing to their youth, are not sufficiently instructed in the ancient laws, franchises and customs of the city', which they proposed to solve by having the statutes and ordinances regulating the various trades and handicrafts enrolled in a register and read out in public assembly once or twice a year. Written copies of the regulations should be sent to anyone who wished to have them. This of course implies that a number of Londoners in the fourteenth century were literate, though in May 1327 the *copresmethes* 'made an ordinance out of their own heads', implying that their regulations were not written down. In March 1327, Edward III gave the tailors and armourers of London the right to 'hold a gild once a year as they have been wont to do from ancient time' and to make regulations 'for the ordering of their misteries'. Those who did so confirmed that they would abide by the rules by swearing on the gospels.[1]

A useful list appears of the wardens of London misteries in December 1328: twenty-one wardens for the fishmongers; eight for the goldsmiths; six drapers; seven apothecaries; four ironmongers; fifteen saddlers; nine mercers; four girdlers; thirteen vintners; nine woolmongers; nine beaders; eight cordwainers; three haberdashers; twenty-four butchers; twelve skinners; seven cutlers; four cappers; two cofferers; five corders; six hosiers; twenty tailors and linen-armourers; six fusters; four painters; and nine cheesemongers.[2] There were, of course, far more professions than were recorded here, such as bakers, brewers, carpenters, masons, blacksmiths, weavers, dyers, fullers, fletchers, bowyers, shipwrights, gold-beaters and wire-drawers, to name but a few. It was the custom that members of a mistery were paid at the end of the quarter, 'except in cases of illness or urgent necessity' when payment might be made sooner, but paying wages in advance was not allowed.[3]

The mayor, Elias Russel, and the aldermen, working with 'good and lawful men of the craft of peltry and of the curriers' in October 1300, established prices for furs. These were: no more than 5*s* for every 1,000 *grisevere* or 'grey fur'; no more than 5*s* 6*d* for *stranglin* (fur of the squirrel around Michaelmas, 29 September) and *polan* (fur of the black squirrel); no more than 12*d* for 100 'conies of England' or 8*d* for 'conies of Spain'; no more than 3*s* 6*d* for *roskyn* (fur of the squirrel in summer); and no more than 7*d* for 100 *scrimpyns* (poor-quality fur). A set of regulations for skinners was issued in March 1327, including that a set of furs of miniver (very costly white or light grey fur made from the winter coat of the squirrel) should contain 120 bellies, and *stradlynge* (fur of the squirrel between Michaelmas and winter) should contain fifty-two beasts.[4]

The cappers lived and worked in the area around Lodgate. Edward II complained in March 1318 that some of them sold caps made of mixed wool and flocks or other wool not suitable for caps, and that they re-dyed old caps and sold them as new. He ordered the mayor and sheriffs to seize and burn any 'false caps' they found. Anneis Bury was imprisoned in November 1344 for buying 'worn-out white and light-coloured furs', giving them to the cappers to dye black, and selling them as new on Cornhull. The mayor, Johan Hamond, and the aldermen subsequently decided that 'no capper should dye any white fur, used or unused, under penalty of 40*d* for the first offence, and expulsion from the trade for the fourth offence'. Richard Byry shouted that he would continue to do so, and was imprisoned in Neugate.[5]

Potters, i.e. makers of metal pots, complained in March 1316 that many people, and especially one Aleyn Sopere, deliberately bought brass pots of bad metal and 'put them on the fire so as to resemble pots that have been used, and are of old brass'. They sold these bad pots in Westchepe on Sundays and other festival days, but when people tried to use them on a fire 'they come to nothing, and melt'. The mayor and aldermen therefore chose four trustworthy makers and four sellers of brass pots to set a standard for brass, and ordained that all workmen in the trade must abide by it. The long regulations for the mistery of spurriers issued in August 1345 declared, among much else, that no spurrier should work after the bells of curfew rang at St Sepulchre without Neugate, because many in the profession desired to work at night so that they could 'introduce false iron' and cracked iron, and put gilt on false, cracked copper. Curiously, the ordinance stated that many spurriers 'wandered about all day' without working, then became 'drunk and frantic' and disturbed the neighbourhood by working through the night.

The mistery of tapicers created a set of regulations in January 1331. Every *tapice*, a tapestry or rug of some kind, had to be 4 ells (180 inches) long and 2 ells wide, or 3 long and 1½ wide if it was of the smaller variety. If a coat of arms was embroidered onto a *tapice* or cushion, the item had to be made entirely of wool, and the wool had to come from England or Spain. The tapicers complained in 1343 that foreign tapicers sold counterfeit work in the city, with 'hair of oxen and other animals craftily woven with wool'.[6] In July 1350, the tapicer Johan Wodegate was declared 'not fit to belong to the mistery' because his apprentice Richard atte Brigge of Essex was a *pikere* and *pulfrour*, i.e. pickpocket and pilferer. Johan denied that Richard was ever his apprentice, but the mayor's court found that Richard had worked for him for ten years and was a nightwalker and evildoer who had since fled from London.[7]

The pepperers of London worked on Sopereslane. On 1 May 1316, twenty-one of them created an ordinance which stated that pepperers must not mix their goods such as putting new spices in with old ones or mixing items of different prices, and must not moisten any items such as ginger, alum, cloves or saffron to increase their weight when selling them. The group of wealthy, influential pepperers in 1316 included Richard Betoyne, mayor 1326/27; Johan Grantham, mayor 1328/29; Johan Burford, sheriff 1303/04 and son-in-law of the late pepperer Thomas Romeyn, mayor 1309/10; Rauf Balauncer, sheriff 1316/17; and Adam Salisbury, sheriff 1323/24.[8] In a tax assessment of 1332, only eleven London merchants were assessed at the highest level who had to pay £4 or more, and four were pepperers (the others were one vintner, one butcher, one draper, two woolmongers and two mercers).[9]

Twenty-seven armourers of London, five of whom used the last name Heaumer, mutually agreed a set of regulations for their profession in January 1322. These included that aketons (quilted defensive jerkins worn over a shirt and under armour) should be stuffed with new cotton cloth or cotton wool and covered with sendal (a kind of fine silk), and white aketons should be stuffed with old woven cloth or new cotton. Old bacinets (a type of helmet that first appeared *c.* 1280 as an iron skullcap and by *c.* 1330 extended down the back of the head) were being sold in the city as though they were new, 'from which great peril might arise to the king and his people, and disgraceful scandal to the armourers aforesaid'. Four armourers were appointed to view blacksmiths' work on the iron for bacinets and ensure that it was fit for purpose.[10] The London girdlers complained in March 1327 that some of their mistery failed to observe the ordinance that girdles of silk, wool, leather and linen must only be garnished with latten, copper, iron or steel. Edward III ordered all false work of lead, pewter or tin to be burnt.[11] As for the goldsmiths, they kept shop in Chepe, the goldsmiths' quarter, and hallmarked their work with a leopard's head. The wardens of the mistery of goldsmiths in the late 1320s were Thomas Berkyng, Henry More, Robert Shordich and Hugh FitzRoger. In October 1327, the goldsmiths appointed Robert Fouke to enquire into the mistery of cutlers, who were accused of 'covering tin with silver so thinly that it was not possible to separate them'.[12]

The *fruters* of London were taken to the mayor's court in 1304 for making a confederacy that 'none of them would buy the fruit of any garden within London or without' before 24 June (the Nativity of St John the Baptist) each year. This was the scheme of one Gerard Fruter, who grumbled that they were 'all poor and captives on account of their own simplicity' and could be rich and powerful if they did his bidding.[13] Many years later in October 1349, five cordwainers were accused 'of having made a confederacy' by agreeing to sell shoes at 8*d* or 9*d* a pair instead of the former price of 6*d*. The five in turn accused four curriers of selling leather at a higher price than formerly: 3*s* 6*d* for a cowhide that previously cost 2*s*, and 9*s* for an oxhide that previously cost 5*s*. The mayor, aldermen and sheriffs ordered all of them to sell their wares at the old prices. Over the next few weeks, four cordwainers were imprisoned for selling leather shoes at inflated prices; one of the victims was Isabel Rothyng, who paid 8*d* for a pair.[14] In 1350, it was the turn of the brewers, led by Adam Brewere, to organise and refuse to work except on wages of 12*d* a day. Adam was imprisoned and the attempt failed.[15]

Sometimes men of the London misteries quarrelled with each other and fought. In October 1304, eleven tailors and cordwainers were imprisoned after a night-time affray in Chepe, and bakers, taverners, millers and unspecified other misteries had to be ordered not to assault each other with 'swords, bucklers and other arms by night' in February 1320. A dispute in 1325 between the saddlers and the goldsmiths resulted in murder. After curfew on Sunday, 10 November, twelve goldsmiths lay in wait in the high street of Chepe ward for 'men of the mistery of saddlers in order to beat them'. This resulted in the death of Johan atte Vyse, saddler, after three goldsmiths beat him up, one stabbed him in the head, one nearly severed his leg with an axe, and yet another hit him repeatedly with a club after Johan fell to the ground. His friends carried him home, and he somehow lived for four days after the attack.[16]

The saddlers apparently had a talent for quarrelling, as another dispute occurred in 1326/27 between the saddlers on one side, and on the other, the joiners, painters, and lorimers (both *copresmythes* and *irensmythes*, collectively known as 'the mistery of lormerie'). On Thursday, 20 May 1326, some men on each side armed themselves and fought in Chepe and Crepelgate, so that 'the greater part of the city was in alarm, to the great disgrace and scandal of the whole city' and even the personal intervention of the mayor and sheriffs did not dissuade the men from exchanging 'serious and outrageous blows'. The joiners, painters, and lorimers complained that the saddlers owed them huge debts, but when they tried to collect the money, the saddlers only hurled offensive words at them. Furthermore, they said, the 'great lords of the realm' gave their old saddles to their servants, who sold them back to the saddlers, who deceitfully tried to sell them on as though they were new. Although Edward II met the mayor, Hamo Chigwell, the sheriffs, Gilbert Mordon and Johan Coton, and the two dozen aldermen in his chamber in the Tower on 20 June 1326 to try to resolve the issue, it was not until May 1327 that the warring parties met in the Guildhall and came to a 'final peace and accord'. In November that year, however, Edward III grumbled that the bakers, taverners, millers, cooks, poulterers, butchers, brewers and corn-chandlers of London were 'lax' in their professions and went about the city day and night armed and looking for trouble.[17]

In Easter week 1339, the skinners fought with the goldsmiths. A 'terrible affray' with weapons at the corner of Chepe and Fridaystrete in which several men were wounded necessitated the intervention of the sheriffs and the mayor, Henry Darcy, and in the complaint that 'riots in

London, which was the mirror and exemplar of the whole realm, tended to encourage the king's enemies' (i.e. the French). Two fishmongers and four goldsmiths were ordered to be arrested, but refused to give themselves up, at which point the exasperated Henry Darcy proclaimed that if they did not surrender by 1 May they 'would be taken alive or dead'. The masters, apprentices and servants of the two misteries assembled and promised to keep the peace in future, and those responsible for the fight were imprisoned.[18] Another massive argument took place in August 1340 between the fishmongers and the skinners and resulted in execution; see 'Punishment' above.

Apprentices

In December 1294, an ordinance was passed that the 'better and more discreet' of the city trades should make a register of all the names of masters, their apprentices and servants, and they should 'diligently inquire among themselves as to the conduct and behaviour of all'. It was agreed in September 1300 that the names of all apprentices should be enrolled in a 'certain schedule' and shown to the mayor and aldermen. There was a rule that apprentices' indentures, i.e. contracts, had to be enrolled during the first year of their terms, and they had to be enfranchised at the end of their terms. Extra fees were payable if indentures were not enrolled within a year and a day, and of the 294 London apprentices in the period 1309 to 1312, no fewer than 100 were registered late.[1]

The ordinance of spurriers in 1345 stated that the length of apprenticeship in the profession was seven years minimum. In 1304, Phelip Cotiller apprenticed his brother Wauter to the butcher Richard Edward for seven years and stood as surety for Wauter's 'faithful service', and the fishmongers' ordinances of 1278/79 stated that 'no-one shall take an apprentice for less than seven years' and no more than two or three apprentices each. Robert Porstok became the apprentice of the *wollemongere* Johan Hamene for seven years in 1308, and the following year Johan Lefhog completed a seven-year apprenticeship as a chandler under the instruction of Hugh Shoreham. The ordinances of lorimers, however, stated that no one should accept an apprentice for less than ten years, and in 1309 Richard, son of Elyas Brekyng, became the apprentice of the fuster Thomas Sterteford for fourteen years.[2] It was an offence against city ordinances to poach another's apprentice or journeyman. Anneis Wombe and Johane Sloghteford were accused in November 1349 of 'enticing away' Johane Whycchere from her master, Thomas Shene (in which profession is not stated), by 'flattering speeches'. They were summoned to the mayor's court. Another city regulation forbade apprentices from marrying; Adam Wytton had to leave the service of the cutler Henry Merlawe in 1299 because he married before the end of his apprenticeship.[3]

William Thorneye travelled to London from his native village of Whaplode Drove in Lincolnshire before 1323 to become an apprentice to Johan Grantham, pepperer (and mayor 1328/29).[4] Grantham is a town in Lincolnshire 35 miles from Whaplode Drove, and Johan's name implies that he himself came from there or at least that his ancestors did, and perhaps he was especially willing to teach boys from his own county. In 1310, Johan the chandler of Colmanstrete took on no fewer than five apprentices from South Mimms ('Suthmymmes') in Middlesex, which almost certainly means that it was his native village. Two were brothers, Henry and Roger, sons of Thomas Osebern.[5] Boys who became apprentices in London in the fourteenth century were generally country-born, and their names show that they came from all over England, from as far afield as Cornwall in the southwest and Northumberland in the northeast. London, as always, drew in numerous people from the rest of the country.

Groups of apprentices to the Bench (a court that always sat at Westminster, as opposed to the King's Bench which sat wherever the king happened to be) from Yorkshire and Norfolk fought each other in the streets of London in November 1325 and again in June 1326, and the St Paul's annalist called them 'northern and southern' apprentices of the law.[6] Three apprentices of the King's Bench said in November 1344 to be 'common evildoers' who mugged people at night were named as Johan of Worcester, Richard Kerdif and Johan Barri. The latter two were both Irish, despite Richard's name, which means 'Cardiff'.[7] Apprentices sometimes came from other countries as well. In 1309, the corder William Rokesle's apprentice finished his instruction after twelve years and was admitted to the freedom of the city; evidently of non-English origin, his name was Hugh of Flamma Villa. Sometime before 1309, Johan le Alemaund, son of a saddler, became an apprentice to William Flemyng, an armourer.[8] Johan's name means 'the German', and William's name means that he was a Fleming or that his ancestors were. In 1310, Geffrei Persone of Sudbury in Suffolk completed his apprenticeship with the London apothecary Richard Mountpelers (Montpellier, in southern France), and in the same year Robert Newcomen, the 'newcomer', finished a ten-year apprenticeship with Henry the Surgeon and his wife Katerine.[9]

Wauter Whyte from Chipping Lambourn in Berkshire made his son Robert a draper's apprentice in London around 29 September 1297.

As Wauter was only about 33 himself at the time, his son is unlikely to have been older than his mid-teens and was probably younger. Rauf Mymmes was 12 in 1339 when he worked as a carter's apprentice in London, Valentine Hamond was 13 when he became an apprentice skinner in Southampton in 1334, and Nichol Paumer was 12 when he began his eight-year apprenticeship with mercer William Causton in 1306.[10] Boys, and occasionally girls, therefore, became apprentices at 12 or 13 and would have finished at about 19 or 22.

London tradesmen and craftsmen were often generous and kind to the apprentices they took on. William Fullere (a fuller) left houses to his apprentice Robert in 1316, and Thomas Carpenter, a pepperer, left his apprentice Johan Clacford 40*s* in 1335. The vintner Robert Felstede left 50*s* to his apprentice, Johan Michel, in 1349, and Anneis, widow of the *stokfisshmongere* Phelip Lucas, left 40*s* in 1349 to each of her late husband's apprentices, William atte Watere and Thomas Terel.[11] Not all masters, however, looked after their apprentices well. William Beverle took the London chaucer Thomas Kydemenstre to court in January 1305, because Thomas had taken on William's son, also Thomas, as an apprentice but did not clothe, feed or instruct him. The young apprentice had lent two pairs of his master's shoes to someone and Kydemenstre beat him for it, whereupon Thomas, frightened and distressed, ran away back to his father. Thomas Kydemenstre agreed to take Thomas Beverle back and to feed and instruct him properly this time, and to give 40*d* in damages to Thomas's father, who had paid an unspecified sum of money to the chaucer for his son's apprenticeship. In February 1305, Robert Fraunceys of Maltby, Yorkshire had been apprenticed to Nichol Beaubelot (d. 1307), a spurrier in Fletestrete, for six years, but Nichol had not yet enrolled him and was therefore summoned to the mayor's court. (Judging by their names, both Robert and Nichol were of French origin.) Nichol had received 20*s* for Robert's teaching and sustenance but failed to feed or instruct him, whereupon his colleague Hugh Strubby (d. 1316) took Robert into his own service 'lest he should perish of hunger'.

The butcher Wauter atte Gate (also called Wauter Canefeld) accepted Johan Osebern as his apprentice in or before 1305 for 40*s* (480*d*), and also took on William atte Hale in 1312 for nine years. In 1303 Johan Botoner took on Thomas, son of Maud Elys of Colchester in Essex, for thirteen years on payment of 5 marks (800*d*). Botoner declared after two years that Thomas Elys was 'malicious' and caused him damage, so he returned Maud's money to her and they agreed to annul the covenant. In his will of March 1338, Johan Spray left 40*s* (480*d*) to his eldest son Elyas and ordered that the proceeds from the sale of his two shops should be used to purchase an apprenticeship for Elyas. Five marks was bequeathed to Elyas's brother Hugh to place him as an apprentice with William Shordyche, and another 100*s* (1,200*d*) to the third brother, Johan, 'that he may be taught a trade'. Johan Kemesyngg, goldsmith, left 40*s* each to his son Robert and daughter Alis in May 1341 'to put them out as apprentices to a trade'.[12]

Evidence indicates that some professions were only open to males, but sometimes girls were taken on to learn a trade: in November 1300, Johan Gildeford accepted Alis, daughter of William Thele, as his ward, and promised to 'maintain, treat and instruct' Alis (in what profession was not clarified). Alis's parents were alive, and Johan promised not to arrange a marriage for the girl without their consent.[13] Margerie and Maud, daughters of goldsmith Johan Halweford (d. *c*. January 1308), were taken on as apprentices in November 1318 by Wauter and Maud Halweford, for 10 marks. Wauter and Maud were probably the girls' grandparents, or aunt and uncle. Henry Cook of Westminster paid Roger and Amice Trugge 40*s* to take on his daughter Margarete as an apprentice in one of the cloth trades, though they took him to court in July 1318 as he still owed them 18*s*.[14] In June 1335, Alis Warle (d. 1361), widow of Phelip Taverner of Grascherche (d. 1324), asked her late husband's executors for a sum of 10½ marks which Phelip had left to their daughter Isabel to be paid out, 'for teaching her [Isabel] a trade as an apprentice'.[15] Johan Spicer, from Oxford but resident in London, left 100*s* in his will of August 1346 to his daughter Anneis 'for teaching her some craft', and in June 1340 the coteller Estephene Page bequeathed to his daughter Katerine 4 marks (640*d*) in cash as well as 'all his implements of the craft of *cotellerie* and the remaining term of Robert and John his apprentices'. Estephene also had two sons, Richard and Johan, though they were still underage, and perhaps for this reason he preferred to leave the tools of his trade and the instruction of his apprentices to his daughter.[16]

More often, girls were expected simply to marry, and were often left sums of money as 'marriage portions' or dowry, as former sheriff Adam Lucas bequeathed to his four daughters in 1347. The 1349 will of the wealthy goldsmith Johan Walpol of Bredstrete ward instructed that one of his tenements should be sold and the proceeds given partly to 'the poor members of the goldsmithery' and partly 'for marriage portions for poor girls of the same handicraft'.[17] Johan Assheford, a *wollemongere* who left generous bequests to his six illegitimate children and their two mothers in 1329, gave £20 to his daughters Alis and Johane, and in June 1335 Johane 'received all the money bequeathed to her by her father for her marriage'. She wed soon afterwards.[18] In 1339/40, the draper Johan Someresham left ten pounds of silver to each of his four sons and twenty pounds of silver to his daughter Alis, and appointed his wife Isabel as guardian of all five children 'until they are old enough to be put to a trade or marry'.[19]

The London cordwainers worked in an area called, unsurprisingly, the Cordwanerye. Eight apprentice and journeymen cordwainers, including Johan of Paris, Johan of Bristol, Johan of Kent, and Willecok Laufare, complained to the mayor's court in October 1303 that the six master cordwainers of London had lowered their wages to 1*d* for making a dozen pairs of shoes and ½*d* for a pair of ankle-boots. The court rejected their claim and told them to 'work well and faithfully' in future. Another case that came before the mayor's court in August 1306 was that of Maud Fattyng of Candelwikstrete ward, a butcher, charged with unjustly dismissing her apprentice, Warin Page (aka Warin Fattyng). She stated that Warin had beaten her, her daughter and other servants, had torn linen clothes, lent almost 70*s* of her money to other people without her permission, and, most damningly in a society where people lived hand to mouth, 'despised' her food. Warin denied the allegations, and produced witnesses that he had never torn Maud's clothes or despised her food. Even so, he was ordered to pay her 102*s*. In 1312, William Robert of Hatfield finished an eight-year apprenticeship with Maud, apparently without undue incident.[20]

The brothers Aleyn (d. 1335) and Martyn (d. 1344) Palmere were master shipwrights who worked in Petiwales next to the Tower of London. In 1326, the brothers employed four journeymen, Jack Mithe, Peres Talworth, William Stacy and Jack Stokfeld, and two apprentices, Willecok Gerard and Jack Salamon, who each earned 4*d* a day (the journeymen earned 5*d* and the Palmeres 6*d*). Another master shipwright, resident in Foleham, was Watte Talworth, and his apprentice in 1326 was his son Jack. Johan Cressyngham (d. 1339) was a master oar-maker working somewhere near the Tower, who in 1326 had two apprentices: his son Johan, known as Jankyn (d. 1364), and Aleyn Helynton.[21]

Religion

It surely goes without saying that the practice of Christianity dominated the fourteenth century in London. Edward I expelled the entire Jewish population of England in 1290, and there are fourteenth-century London records mentioning the city's former Jewish residents. In a will of 1308/09, for example, houses in Cattestrete were said to have once belonged to 'Slymina, late wife of Fictavin Fort, a Jew', and in 1348 a house in the parish of St Olave had once belonged to 'Jornin Sacrel the Jew'. The church of St Olave stood in the Elde Jurie, and its rector, Johan Brian, made his will in *c.* July 1323; he mentioned his 'houses formerly belonging to Benedict, son of Hagin the Jew' in Cattestrete, and other houses which had belonged to Roesya Duceman, also Jewish, at the corner of Milkestrate.[1]

More than 100 parish churches existed in fourteenth-century London, and in and around the city stood the houses of the Dominicans (Blackfriars), Franciscans (Greyfriars), Austin Friars, Crutched Friars or Brothers of the Cross, and the Friars of the Penance of Jesus Christ, also called the Friars of the Sack, who settled outside Aldresgate *c.* 1257 and later moved to the Elde Jurie. Sakfrerelane or 'Sack Friar Lane' is mentioned in a will of 1310.[2] There were priories at Beremundeseye, Clerkenewelle (the priory of St John of Jerusalem), Haliwelle, Smethefeld (Seint Bertelmew), Berkinge, Kelbourne, Stratford-le-Bow (the priory of St Leonard) and Holy Trinity near Alegate, often called *Cricherche* or *Cristechirch*, i.e. Christchurch.[3] Far more convents stood within a few miles of London. Edward I's brother Edmund, earl of Lancaster and Leicester (d. 1296), and his French wife Blanche of Artois, dowager queen of Navarre (d. 1302), founded a house of Minoresses or Poor Clares – Franciscan nuns – near the Tower of London in 1293. This convent was often called the Minories, and although it was closed down in 1539, the road where it stood still bears its name. In 1303, the convent was called 'Our Lady of the New Place without Alegate'.

Gilbert Asshendon complained to the Assize of Nuisance in September 1306 that the Minoresses' privy adjoined his stone wall, and in 1314, the 'abbess of St Clare', meaning the head of the London Minoresses, owned a house in the parish of St Martin Vinetrie next door to one Johan Hardel.[4] By 1338, even though it had been founded by the royal and extraordinarily wealthy Lancasters, the Minoresses' convent was not thriving, and Edward III talked of 'their depressed estate'.[5]

The largest religious building in the city was St Paul's on Lodgate Hill, now known as Old St Paul's, as the medieval church was destroyed in the Great Fire of 1666 and was subsequently rebuilt. An extension on the east side of St Paul's, begun in 1255, was finished in 1314, and in 1322 Nichol Wokyndon left 100s to 'the new work of *Seint Pool*', as St Paul's was usually spelt. In 1336, William Rokeslee ordered that after his death a third of his movables should be sold and the proceeds given to make 'some decorative work about the representation of the Annunciation of the Virgin Mary in the new work of St Paul's'. One chronicler says that some precious old relics were discovered in the belfry of St Paul's in June 1314, including bones of the 11,000 virgins, part of the True Cross, a stone from Mount Calvary, and 'a stone of the Sepulchre of Our Lord'. They were shown to the public and replaced the following month.[6]

The death in 1300 of Johan of Bristol, who sat against a pillar in St Paul's and died of *morbum caducum* (see 'Health' above), shows that many Londoners went into the church to pray – it was a Monday morning – but that, sadly, no one helped a person in need. Many people left property in their wills to be sold and the proceeds given to 'pious uses', though the nature of the evidence we have makes it impossible to know whether religious sentiments were truly heartfelt or merely dutiful. Others left money to found a chantry in a church, i.e. a priest (or several) would pray for their soul after death and the souls of others whom they chose. William Carletone, who died shortly before 5 April 1311, left money in his will for a chantry, and in 1321, Johan of Paris founded one in the church of St Martin for his parents Michael and Alis.[7] William Rothyng, one of the many thousands of Londoners who died in the plague year of 1349, left 15s annually to the church of St Magnus the Martyr for a chaplain singing *Salve Regina* (an antiphon in honour of the Virgin Mary) and keeping his obit with *Placebo et Dirige* (the opening words of Vespers and Matins sung at a funeral and on the anniversary of the person's death). Gilbert Palmere, a salter who was yet another victim of the plague, left money to purchase vestments for the priest of St Mildred's church, and also gave the church unspecified 'books and ornaments' and 'a lamp to burn before the high altar in the chancel'.[8]

Johan Holegh or Houleye or Howle, a wealthy hosier of illegitimate birth, made his will in March 1348 and died in February 1351. He requested burial with his first wife Alis in the church of St Mary le Bow, and left money for a marble stone to be placed over their tomb. Johan had no children, and most of his generous bequests were for pious purposes. These included: £20 to anyone who wished to go on pilgrimage to the Holy Sepulchre in Jerusalem and the alleged tomb of St Katherine on Mount 'Synay'; £7 for a pilgrim to travel to Santiago de Compostela in 'Galis' (Galicia); money for the 'old and new work' on St Paul's and for work on the church of St Thomas of Acre; cash to every leper and every anchorite (a religious recluse) in London, and to everyone 'going with naked feet' to the great shrine of Our Lady in Walsingham, Norfolk; and £5 to the church of St Mary le Bow to purchase a missal, another £3 to paint an image of the Virgin Mary with a crown on her head in the choir, and an unspecified sum for the ongoing work on the church belfry and for a new bell.[9] Rauf Upton and Henry Causton left money in 1341 and 1348 to all the anchorites in London, and the will of the mercer Johan Aylesham in 1345 mentions an anchorite living in the church of St Peres Cornhull and another in St Benet Fink. Rauf Upton made a donation to the 'new fabric of St Mary's chapel in St Paul's, and to the old work there', and left £10 for one or two pilgrims to travel to Santiago.[10]

An inquisition was held in February 1331 into the hermitage of St James near Cripelgate, which had been founded by King John (r. 1199 –1216) and was 16½ feet long, and was built into the city wall. There was a chapel and a house which by 1331 needed repairing, at a cost of 40 marks. Divine service was celebrated daily in the chapel, which had a missal without epistles, a gradual, two hymn-books, an 'old, useless' missal, two whole vestments 'in bad condition', an alb with stole, parure and maniple, a chalice, four towels for the altar and four candlesticks all 'in bad condition'. In September 1331, William Leycestre, warden of the hermitage, resigned, and Edward III appointed Jordan St Barbe as its keeper for life.[11] Another hermitage stood near Bisshopesgate, and in March 1322 was granted to Estephene Roo for life, as long as he 'lived as became a hermit', otherwise he would be expelled.[12]

In England in the fourteenth century, there were seventeen bishops and two archbishops, Canterbury and York (the archbishopric of Westminster was not established until 1850). London had, and still has today, its own bishop, and the office possibly existed as early as the second century and certainly by the beginning of the seventh century. At the start of the 1300s, the bishop of London was Richard Gravesend, consecrated on 11 August 1280, who died on 9 December 1303. Bishop Gravesend had held lands, marshlands, meadows, arable land and several houses in Essex, Sussex and Middlesex, and the heir to them was his brother Estephene Gravesend, whom the jurors stated to be either 'aged 40 years and more' or 'aged 50'.[13] Estephene would himself be consecrated as bishop of London on 14 January 1319 and died in April 1338, when he must have been in his late sixties or seventies. Richard Gravesend's immediate successor, however, was Rauf Baldock, who was elected on 24 February 1304 and consecrated on 30 January 1306. Baldock was responsible for the construction of the Lady Chapel at St Paul's Cathedral, then being rebuilt and enlarged.[14]

Rauf Baldock died on 24 July 1313, and his successor was Gilbert Segrave, who was a nobleman by birth, son of Nichol, Lord Segrave (d. 1295), and brother of Johan, Lord Segrave (d. 1325). Gilbert was elected on 17 August 1313, though did not have long to enjoy his position as he died on 18 December 1316. Gilbert's successor Richard Newport's reign was even shorter: elected on 27 January 1317, he died in August 1318, and his successor was the long-lived Estephene Gravesend.[15]

Tower

This massive fortification in the south-east corner of London was much strengthened by Edward I in the late thirteenth century. In the fourteenth century it did not yet have the sinister reputation it acquired in later eras, though it was already used as a prison. Edward II imprisoned a number of noblemen and knights who had taken part in a rebellion against him in 1321/22 in the Tower, though it is not certain where the prison cells were; possibly in the tower which later became known as the Beauchamp Tower. Noble prisoners were not thrown into a deep dungeon in chains, but were allowed to have at least one attendant looking after them, and received a daily allowance, usually either 3*d* or 6*d*. On 1 August 1323, Roger Mortimer, Lord of Wigmore and Ludlow, made a daring escape from the Tower by feeding his guards sedatives in their wine and letting himself down the wall by a rope ladder. Five days later, the Tower constable, Sir Stephen Segrave – nephew of the late bishop of London, Gilbert Segrave – was still seriously ill from the sedatives.[1]

The Tower was also, however, a royal residence, and the St Thomas, Wakefield and Lanthorn towers are now collectively known as the 'medieval palace'. Henry III (r. 1216 – 72) built an entry from the river which led to the king's private rooms in the Wakefield Tower, via a flight of stairs. In July 1321, Edward II's queen Isabella of France gave birth to their youngest child in the complex, and the infant, later queen of Scotland, was always known as Joan of the Tower. Edward III and Queen Philippa's second son Lionel of Antwerp, Edward II and Queen Isabella's grandson, married in the Tower of London on 15 August 1342, and the mayor, Simond Fraunceys, and the aldermen sent ten tuns of wine as a wedding gift.[2] Born on 29 November 1338, Lionel was just 3 years old when he wed, and his bride Elizabeth de Burgh, born on 10 July 1332, was 10.

Whenever the king was in residence at the Tower of London, the drawbridge was pulled up, implying that at all other times – and the king only rarely stayed in the Tower – the drawbridge was down and people could wander in and out as they pleased. A carpenter named Nichol Lightfot was murdered in his workshop within the Tower in July 1324 (Edward II was nowhere near London at the time), and the jurors noted that 'a multitude of people' were present when he died.[3] Two men, Elias Beverle and Johan Costard, drowned in 'a certain waste place within the second gate of the Tower' in separate incidents on 1 and 15 October 1321. The coroner's report stated that the drawbridge was raised as Edward II was then staying in the Tower, and that both Elias and Johan 'accidentally fell into the water', meaning the ditch, while attempting to gain entry to the fortress. Both bodies were discovered by a labourer named Robert shortly after sunrise on Saturday, 17 October, and Elias's body had been in the water for sixteen days.[4]

A letter Edward II sent on 12 December 1307 reveals the names of some of the men working in the Tower of London. William Conrad was 'master artiller of the king's crossbows' on wages of 8*d* a day, and had two journeymen on 4*d* and three apprentices on 3*d* a day each; Henry Neuwerk and three men working with him shared 9*d* a day between them, and were 'smiths working irons for the king's crossbows and quarrels'; Johan Hubert and Aleyn Fletcher, both fletchers, earned 2*d* a day each; and Master James Leuesham, smith, was on 8*d* a day.[5] In March 1326, Edward II appointed Henry of Cambridge as chief blacksmith at the Tower, and Nichol Lightfot's murder in 1324 shows that carpenters had workshops there as well. Johan Reyner, another blacksmith working in the Tower, made his will on 5 June 1317, implying that he was then very ill, though he did not die until *c.* May 1342.[6]

In 1313, the gardener of the Tower and the Palace of Westminster was Moris Grave, and Edward II ordered him to buy 'timber and peat … for the vineries and herberies in the Tower and the palace'. Edward III appointed Johan Sanderwyk as gardener of the Tower and the Palace of Westminster in 1337, and as the places stood 2.5 miles apart, the position required much to-ing and fro-ing.[7] There was also a mint in the Tower, and the Italian Lapin Lumbard was in charge of it in the 1320s, replaced by Gawan Suthorp in 1327.[8] Another, rather hair-raising, job was the 'keeper of the king's lions and leopards in the Tower'. In the 1310s this position was held by the Frenchman Pierre Fabre of Montpellier, and in 1337 the incumbent was Berenger Caudrer, who received wages of 12*d* a day (far more than most Londoners were paid) plus 2*s* 1*d* a day to buy food for the animals.[9]

Sir Johan Cromwell (d. before November 1333) was constable of the Tower for most of the period from March 1308 until July 1321.[10] During the night of 20 September 1312, there was, according to several city chroniclers, a 'great tumult' in London aimed at the unpopular Cromwell. An earthen wall which Cromwell had built opposite the outer gate of the Tower was torn down by 'armed men on horseback and on foot', who pelted city officials with mud and stones and ran around the city 'uttering a great and horrible noise'. The furious Edward II declared that he 'conceived wrath and indignation' against the city of London as a result. The row rumbled on until 1315, when the mayor, Johan Gisors, and some of the aldermen met the king in his chamber in the palace of Westminster, and 'humbly besought on their knees his grace and goodwill'. Edward remitted his indignation in exchange for 600 marks and the promise that the perpetrators would be punished.[11]

Edward II appointed Sir Roger Swynnerton of Staffordshire as constable of the Tower on 30 August 1321, replacing Guy Ferre, who had held the position only since 2 July 1321.[12] Swynnerton (*c.* 1281–1338) was about 40 at the time, and was a murderer: he killed Henry Salt in Stafford because of Salt's 'insulting language', and stabbed a forester named William Wolf to death in July 1324. Edward, however, was indulgent towards Roger Swynnerton and pardoned him in April 1325 for all murders he had committed before Christmas 1324.[13] Edward's eldest niece Eleanor, Lady Despenser (1292–1337), was imprisoned in the Tower for fifteen months following the downfall and execution of her husband Hugh in November 1326, and after her release was accused of removing cash, jewels and other high-value items from the Tower and imprisoned again.[14] Others imprisoned in the Tower in 1338 were various men of Southampton, who, an enraged Edward III declared, had been appointed to guard the coast of Hampshire from French warships but who 'basely fled' when a French fleet attacked and burnt Portsmouth and Southampton. They were therefore guilty of a 'disgraceful neglect of duty'.[15]

Bridge

London Bridge has existed for 2,000 years, since the Romans settled in the area around 43AD. The first bridge made of stone was begun in the 1170s and completed in the early 1200s, and it stood for over 600 years. In vast, twenty-first century London, over thirty bridges span the Thames, but in the fourteenth century and long afterwards, London Bridge was the only one, and as it provided the only entry and exit point from London to the south, it was always extremely busy. At the Suthewerk end stood one of the seven great gates into the city, and it had its own warden who held the key; in 1345, Johan Conduit was appointed.[1] There were always two elected wardens of the bridge itself as well, and in 1303, they were Robert the Chaplain and Johan Benere. They stated to the Assize of Nuisance that the alderman Adam Foleham had built his house on land which belonged to the Bridge in the parish of Magnus the Martyr, and that his home obscured the view of some of the houses on the Bridge as well as impeding the flow of the Thames.[2]

An extremely common bequest in wills made by Londoners in the fourteenth century was a sum of money for repairs to be carried out on London Bridge. The amounts depended on the wealth of the individual, and varied from 6*d* to 10 marks (1,600*d*). As noted in 'Sanitation' above, there was a public latrine on London Bridge, and a chapel dedicated to the London-born archbishop of Canterbury, St Thomas Becket, stood in the middle. An inventory was made of the 'books, vestments and other ornaments and goods' in the chapel in November 1350. These included three breviaries, two covered with white leather and one with red leather; two linen cloths for the altar; a silver cup for the Host; a silver vessel for incense; five candlesticks, of which three were pewter and the other two were latten; relics in a chest with an iron lock, including a ring containing a tooth of St Richard Wych of Chichester (d. 1253); and an image of Thomas Becket.[3]

In 1300/01, residents of a house on London Bridge were Simond Coteler, his wife Katerine, and their sons Johan and William. Simond and Katerine were summoned to the mayor's court by the wardens of the Bridge, William Jordan and Johan Benere, on a charge of aiding their sons to ill-treat their neighbours, and had to promise not to receive or harbour their sons 'under penalty of forfeiting their house on the Bridge'. It transpired that the couple had also assaulted several neighbours, and had threatened to 'light such a fire that it would be seen by all the dwellers in London, to the grave damage and terror of these neighbours'.[4] A fire on London Bridge certainly would terrify city-dwellers. Half a century later in 1351, the glover Thomas Gloucestre leased a shop on the bridge, between the shops of Thomas Ledrede and Johan Mucham, for life at an annual rent of 36*s* 8*d* (440*d*).[5] Despite the large number of residents, traders, pedestrians, riders, and, until 1320, ale-sellers, London Bridge was not always safe: Thomas atte Taye assaulted Alis atte Waye there on 27 November 1318, and stole the robe of *bluet* (blue woollen cloth) she wore.[6]

Rivers

In the fourteenth century, the city's main waterway was called Tames, Tamise, Thamise or Thamys, or various other spellings. Its quays, wharves and watergates included Stonwarf, Billingesgate, Oistergate, Ebbegate, Douegate, Quenehithe and Stongate, and numerous merchants owned other wharves and warehouses along the river-banks, accessed from the narrow lanes running down to the river from Thamisestrete. One stretch of the Thames along Billingesgate was (and is) called the Pool of London, usually spelt *Pole* in the fourteenth century, and ships were moored here. In 1325, a ship of Edward II's which he had named after his chamberlain and powerful co-ruler, the *Despenser*, was tied up in the '*Pole* near the Tower of London', and in 1325/26 other ships floating in the *Pole* were the *Blome*, the *Seint George* and the *Esmon* of Winchelsea, whose captain was Gerveys Whiting. In 1316, Edward II bought a ship from the London resident Simond Turgis called *La Seintecroiz*, 'The Holy Cross', and other London/Westminster ships of the era were the *Godiere* ('Goodyear'), *Margarete*, *Maudeleyne*, *James*, and *Cogge Nostre Dame* ('Cog of Our Lady').[1]

The piles and hurdles placed in the Thames in 1338 when a French invasion was feared, 'to prevent ships from passing, except one at a time', were finally removed in June 1344. The removal was intended to 'afford a free passage to vessels carrying victuals and merchandise'.[2] This removal did not, however, solve a greater problem. Edward III granted a commission to seven men in March 1348 in response to a complaint that although the 'four great rivers' of England (Thames, Severn, Ouse and Trent) 'from ancient time have been open to the passage of ships and boats for the common profit of the people', the section of the Thames between London and Henley was severely obstructed by weirs, mills, piles and palings. The result was that boats could only travel to London 'in times of excessive abundance of water'.[3] Henley-on-Thames in Oxfordshire, as the effective head of navigation on the Thames in the fourteenth century, was the place where much grain was brought and stored before transport to London. William Palmer, a blader of Newegate who died in 1349, owned a granary in Henley.[4] Obstructions of the river between Henley and London might well, therefore, negatively affect the city's food supply.

A whale which two London chroniclers both claimed to be 80 feet long swam up the Thames on or around 14 February 1309. A reference in Edward II's accounts some years later reveals that he paid three sailors (Thomas Springet, Esmon of Grenewyz and William Kempe) a pound for 'their labour in taking a whale near London Bridge', probably this one.[5] On 5 March 1309, there is a reference to a whale stranded at Stebenheth, which the bishop of London, Rauf Baldock, and the dean and chapter of St Paul's claimed should rightfully belong to them, as 'they have been accustomed to have all great fish taken in their land, except the tongue'. Two further whales were beached at Clacton and Walton-on-the-Naze on the Essex coast around the same time.[6] Something strange must have been going on with the tides in early 1309 for a number of whales to become stranded on the English coast or to swim up the Thames.

The fast-flowing, tidal Thames could be dangerous. Elena Gubbe drowned in the evening of Monday, 22 October 1324 when she went to fill two earthenware pitchers at the Lavenderebrigge, and fell into the Thames. Her father Rauf Gubbe found her body under the wharf belonging to Johan White two days later. One of the neighbours questioned was the former mayor, Johan Gisors, and another was the vintner and taverner James Beauflour. Bertelmew Deumars, future sheriff, was questioned about the death of 9-year-old Marie, daughter of Anneis of Billingesgate, on 18 April 1340. Marie was, like Elena Gubbe a few years earlier, filling an earthenware pot with river water on the wharf near Bertelmew's home, and fell into the flooded river and drowned.[7] Johan Kent, aged 12, drowned in the Thames in August 1337 when he stood on a wharf belonging to Ambrose Newburgh, and fell in. His body was later recovered under the wharf of the draper Johan Swanlond in the parish of St Andrew, Baynardeschastel ward. Richard Wrotham drowned on a wharf called Tykeneldeswharffe in the parish of Marie atte Hull in Billingesgate ward around Vespers on 3 October 1338, as the river, 'being full, flooded the said wharf'.[8]

As well as the mighty Thames, other rivers flew through fourteenth-century London: the Flete, the Walebroke, and the Tibourne.

All of them are now culverted over and run completely underground. London Bridge was the only bridge over the Thames, but the Horshobrigg stood over the Walebroke, and the Holebournebrigge and the Fletebrigge over the Flete. Ranulph, rector of the church of Seinte Margarete Lotheburi (successor of the late William, in trouble in 1300 for ordering the putrid bodies of four dead wolves from abroad) was ordered in January 1314 to remove all obstructions of the Walebrok by his house. In the same month, a cordwainer called Robert Asshe was ordered to remove firewood from the course of the Walebrok, a saddler called Johan of Paris was told to remove the beams and timber lying across it next to his house, and William Fourneis was given fifteen days to remove a privy he had built across it. Johan Laufare of the parish of Seinte Mildred Bradestrete was accused in 1309 of obstructing the course of the Walebrok by filling in with earth a section of it that ran near his house.[9]

Pestilence

On 10 August 1343, a proclamation was made throughout London that 'All men of the misteries, as well as victuallers, journeymen, labourers and servants, shall work as they used to do before the pestilence, under pain of imprisonment and fine.'[1] What this 'pestilence' was remains unknown, but evidently it had caused a shortage of labour in the city. The greatest scourge of the fourteenth century came five years later: the Black Death. The first pandemic of this terrible disease hit Europe in the late 1340s and killed a huge percentage of the population. It reached England around June 1348 and arrived in London around Christmas that year – perhaps as early as November – and raged in the city for the next few months.

In Edward III's twenty-first regnal year, which ran from 25 January 1347 to 24 January 1348, twenty-two people in London died after making their wills, and between 25 January 1348 and 24 January 1349, thirty-four Londoners made their wills then passed away. Between January 1349 and January 1350, the wills of just under 350 people were proved. Between January 1350 and January 1351, the number was fifty people, and the following year, only seventeen.[2] The 350 people who died in 1349 after making their wills represent only a small minority of the total number of Londoners who died of plague, as most people had few if any possessions to bequeath and had no reason to make a will, but this figure gives an indication of the possible death rate in the city; ten times more Londoners died in the plague year of 1349 than in 1348, sixteen times as many as in 1347, and twenty times as many as in 1351. The mortality rate among the more prosperous London residents has been estimated as at least 35 per cent and probably much higher.[3] Of the 80,000 or so residents of London, the Black Death killed many thousands, probably tens of thousands. One chronicler says that between 2 February and 12 April 1349, over 200 bodies were buried every day in a new burial ground next to Smethefeld, a number which does not include victims buried in the many dozens of city churchyards.[4]

In October 1328, there had been twenty-four wardens of the mistery of butchers; in October 1349, there were twelve.[5] Of the eight wardens of the mistery of cutlers appointed in 1344, all were dead by the end of 1349, and the same applied to all six wardens of the hatters appointed in December 1347.[6] The Assize of Nuisance did not sit at all between 26 September 1348 and 29 May 1349, and the session of 29 May was the only one which took place in the year 1349. At its next session, on 26 February 1350, five men were present rather than the usual ten or twelve.[7]

Many London children were orphaned during the Black Death, though guardians were found for them in many (one hopes all) cases. William Thorneye, pepperer, former sheriff, and alderman of Colemanestrete, died between 20 June and 27 July 1349. His wife Johane was already dead, and their son Johan was barely 2 years old when he was orphaned, though as Johan Thorneye was still alive in 1401 when he was 54, someone obviously took care of him.[8] Ten-year-old William Burdeyn lost his father Wauter in July 1349, and a guardian, Thomas atte Barnet, was appointed for him. The three sons of Hugh Plastrer – Robert, aged 12, Johan aged 9, and Thomas, aged 6 – were orphaned in April 1349 and given into the custody of William Oyldebeof, and the mercer Roger Pycot died when his sons Thomas, born March 1346, and Simond, born May 1347, were toddlers. Richard Loveye, a mercer, died before 26 March 1349, leaving a daughter, Cristine, and four sons, Thomas (b. 1339), Johan I (b. 1340), Johan II and William. Richard's fellow mercer Johan Fifhide looked after them, and happily, four of the five Loveye children survived the pestilence. Thomas was alive in 1361, and Cristine, who married the *diere* Richard Staneford, and her brother William were alive in 1371. Johan Loveye the elder lived until 1394 or later and became a mercer like his father, and served as alderman and sheriff.

Roger Peautrer, also called Roger Syward, died in the summer of 1349, leaving his 6-year-old son William, 5-year-old daughter Marie or Marion, and 1-year-old son Thomas. Roger's three other children, Johan, Custance and Johane, all died before 19 August 1349, and William Syward survived the plague but died young some years later. Marion and her baby brother Thomas were given into the custody of their uncle or grandfather Johan Syward (d. 1375), also a peautrer, and both lived into adulthood. The draper Thomas Canterbury and his wife Margerie both died before 12 March 1349, and their young sons Johan, Simond, William and Thomas were suddenly orphaned. The boys' older half-brother Thomas Kent, Margerie's son from a previous marriage, took them in. Katerine, widow of the draper Thomas Holebech, made her will on 26 March 1349 and died before 4 May. She left her children Bertelmew, William and Alis in the custody of her father Johan Pecche, but Bertelmew died before 11 May 1350. Isabel Godchep née Wolmar, who had gone before the Assize of Nuisance in 1331 to complain about the lack of light and air through a window in her home at Billyngesgate, made her will on 14 April 1349, and died before 8 June. She had outlived her daughter Lettice, her son William and her daughter-in-law Margerie, and left all her tenements to her grandson, also William. He must have been underage, as Isabel appointed guardians to look after him.

Johan Wynchelseye, baker of Algatestrete, made his will on 24 March 1349 and died before 20 July. His wife (name unknown) was already dead, and he appointed her brother Richard Walssh and his wife Margerie as guardians of his daughters Alis and Margarete. The girls also inherited their father's goods, including a silk girdle, a gold bracelet and silver cups and spoons. In his will of 8 March 1349, fishmonger William Bernes appointed Thomas Bernes (probably his brother) and William Hedrisham as the guardians of his children Benet, Roger, Albreda and Isabel, but William Hedrisham made his own will only four days later. Both men died that year, and young Roger Bernes died between 8 and 12 March 1349. The *ymaginour* Johan Mymmes of Pultrye and his wife Maud died just days or weeks apart that spring, and their daughter Alis died too; their other daughter, 8-year-old Isabel, survived and was placed in the custody of the coffrer Thomas Staundone, perhaps her maternal uncle or grandfather. Johan Mymmes specified in his will that Roger Osekyn, pepperer, should have custody of his and Maud's daughters if Maud died before they came of age, but Roger died as well in early May 1349.[9]

Thomas Maryns, chamberlain of London, made his will on 22 April 1349 and died three days later. As noted in 'Health', Thomas qualified as an apothecary after a seven-year apprenticeship in 1310, and as boys usually began their apprenticeship at 12 or 13, Thomas must have been close to 60 in 1349. At the time of his death, he was instructing an apprentice named Johan.[10] Johan Dallyng the elder, a mercer, made his will on 6 April 1349, leaving his tenement in Bassyeshawe ward to his son Johan the younger. He died before 20 May, when 'the tenement in which my father died' is mentioned in Johan the younger's will. Johan Dallyng the son died before 23 November 1349. William Haunsard, sheriff of London in 1333/34, made his will on 6 August 1349 and died before 13 October. His son William died before 9 November, and both men were buried in the church of St Dunstan by the Tower. Johan Hamond, former mayor, died before 9 February, and his stepson Adam Salisbury died before 8 June. Hamond's widow Anneis, Salisbury's mother, survived the pestilence and lived until 1361.[11]

Three members of the Shordych family of Farndone Within ward died in quick succession: Robert, warden of the goldsmiths' mistery, made his will on 24 March, and was dead by 5 April when his son Esmon made his. Esmon in turn was dead by 17 May when his mother Beatrice, Robert's widow, made her will, and she died before 25 May. Richard Shordych and his son Benet, perhaps relatives, both died before 9 March, though Richard's other children Johan and Margarete survived. The potter Johan Romeneye made his will on 23 April and died before 4 May, and his widow Anneis made her will on 9 June and died before 7 December; Thomas Fraunceys, a wax-chandler of Candelwykestrete, and his wife Anneis died just days apart in March; and cordwainer William Wynton and his wife Millicent died days apart in April. Richard Stokwell of Redcrouchestrete made his will on 4 April and his son Hugh made his on 8 April, and both men died before 4 May 1349, on which date the wills of about eighty deceased Londoners were proved. One of them was fishmonger Johan Youn, whose will of 11 April mentioned his wife Johane, daughters Johane and Margerie, son-in-law Richard, and grandson Johan. Youn's widow Johane died before 9 June; when she made her will on 11 May, she had already lost her husband, grandson, son-in-law, and daughter Margerie. Her other daughter Johane, a nun of Rusper Priory in Sussex, perhaps survived.[12]

The horror that the Black Death inflicted on Londoners, and many millions of others, is beyond imagining, and the pestilence took a tragically heavy toll on some London families. When *peyntour* Wauter Stokwell made his will in February 1349, he had four daughters and one son, Cristine, Imanya, Anneis, Alis and Laurence, and his wife Johane, his sister Isabel and his brother William were all living as well. A few months later, 7-year-old Anneis Stokwell was the only member of her family still alive; she had lost her parents, aunt and uncle, and four siblings. She was placed in the custody of Thomas Bournham, also a *peyntour* and almost certainly the 'Thomas, my apprentice' mentioned in her father's will. The skinner Adam Aspal made his will, which mentioned his wife Auncilia and their children Juliana, Johan and Richard, on 15 April. By the time Auncilia made her own will just six days later on 21 April, she had already lost her husband and two sons, and she herself died before 4 May. Adam and Auncilia's daughter Juliana Aspal survived, and her aunt and uncle, Margarete and Thomas Thame, became her guardians.[13]

Johan Acton, a *fresshfisshmongere* of Eldefisshstrete, made his will on 23 June and died before 20 July. He and his wife Cristine had an infant son named William, and Cristine was pregnant when she lost her husband. William Albon, a *felmongere* who died in or before early May 1349, had children Margarete, Margerie, Felicia, Johane, Juliane, William and Estephene, and his wife Anneis was pregnant with their eighth when he made his will on 6 December 1348; William left his 'uterine child' 10 marks. The pregnancies of at least half a dozen other London women were mentioned in their husbands' 1349 wills.[14] Not one of the hundreds of wills made and proved in 1349 mentioned the pestilence directly, though William Hanhampstede, a pepperer who died that summer, added a codicil to his will on 28 April that if his wife Anneis and all six of their children died within a year of his own death, the tenements he had left them should be sold by his executors and the proceeds given instead to 'Holy Church for the good of their souls'.[15]

Some people who made their wills that year, as a precaution in the midst of so much suffering and death, survived. One was Andrew Aubrey, the former mayor, who made his will on 3 October 1349 but did not die until sometime between late February and early May 1358. The *stokfisshmongere* and former sheriff Wauter Mordon of Crokedelane, who went out to 'play in the fields' in 1337 with his family (wife Cristine, sons Wauter and Thomas, daughters Katerine, Margarete, Avice, Johane I and Johane II, and grandson Johan Lincoln), made his will on 30 May 1349, but lived for another two years. Adam Pole, another *stokfisshmongere* who was Wauter Mordon's apprentice, made his will on 21 April 1349 and died in 1358. He left his son Wauter the huge sum of £60, plus generous bequests to numerous religious houses and hospitals. Henry atte Wode, owner of a tenement in Milkstrate which he left to his daughters Elizabeth, Alis and Katerine, made his will in early May 1349 and survived until 1357, and Margerie, widow of Johan Barat, made her will on 13 May 1349 and lived until *c.* August/October 1356. Margerie lived in Isleworth and owned tenements somewhere in London, and left two cows to her son William and her daughter Alis Wike and cloth to her underage daughter Lucy.[16] Other Londoners made nuncupative wills in 1349, that is, one made orally to witnesses, because they were too sick to make a written one or were at death's door and running out of time. One was Nichol, one of the seven children of an armourer named Peres Nayere, who died in March 1349. Nichol inherited £88 from his father and himself died before late October 1349, and in his nuncupative will left the money to be divided among his three sisters: Anneis and her husband William Glendale, Lettice and her husband Simon Beverley, and Isolda, unmarried. Peres Nayere's other three children, Johan, William and Margarete, and his wife Katerine, also died in 1349.[17]

Edward III proclaimed on 1 December 1349 that no one was allowed to leave the kingdom, which was 'much depopulated by the pestilence, and the treasury exhausted'. The king complained on 29 December that 'misdoers had flocked to the city [London] after the cessation of the pestilence'.[18] The horrendous death toll of 1349 was not the end of London's misery, and there were further outbreaks of plague in 1361 and 1369, though nowhere near as deadly. The wills of about 130 Londoners were proved after their deaths in 1361, compared to only eleven in 1358, seventeen in 1359, just under forty in 1362 and twenty in 1363 (wills from 1360 are missing). Those who died in 1361 included the goldsmith Nichol Farndone, namesake grandson of the mayor and alderman of Farndone ward (d. 1334), and another goldsmith named Robert Walcote, who bequeathed three illuminated books to friends.[19]

The Black Death, especially the first and worst outbreak, had a terrible and traumatic impact on London, and perhaps as many as half of its inhabitants died of plague in just a few months. But the city survived, and endured. In the twenty-first century, it has a population of close to 9,000,000 and is one of the most ethnically diverse cities in the world, with more than 300 languages spoken and under 45 per cent of its inhabitants identified as White British. Already in the first half of the fourteenth century, London welcomed numerous foreign residents, and its openness to the rest of the world is an enduring feature of this greatest of cities.

Appendix 1

Fourteenth-Century Given Names and Nicknames

A list of the usual spelling of given names in the fourteenth century:

Aleyn: Alan
Alianore/Alienor(e): Eleanor
Alis: Alice
Alisa(u)ndre: Alexander
Anneis/Anneys(e): Agnes
Benet/Beneit/Beneyt: Benedict
Bertelmew/Bertelmeu: Bartholomew
Custance: Constance
Dionise: Denise
Emme: Emma
Esmo(u)n: Edmund
Estephen(e): Stephen
Fouk(e): Fulk
Geffrei/Geffray: Geoffrey
Humfrai/Oumfry: Humphrey
Joce/Joice: Joseph
Johan: John
Johane/Johanne, occasionally Jone: Joan
Kateryn(e)/Katerin(e): Kathryn/Katherine
Malculin/Mauceleym: Malcolm
Margarete: Margaret
Marie: Mary
Mayhew/Mayheu: Matthew
Moris/Moryz: Maurice
Neel: Neil, Nigel
Nichol: Nicholas
Peres, occasionally Pieres or Petre: Peter

Phelip: Philip/Philippa (a unisex name; uncommon for women in England until Philippa of Hainault married Edward III in 1328)
Rauf: Ralph
Reynald: Reginald
Roese/Rohese: Rose
Simond/Symond: Simon
Stace: Eustace
Wauter: Walter

The names Adam, Edward, Gilbert, Giles, Henry, Isabel, James, Luke, Martin/Martyn, Maud(e), Robert, Roger, Richard, Thomas and William were usually spelt the same way as today, though Isabel was sometimes spelt Ysabel(l) or Yzabel(l) as well, William was sometimes spelt Wyllyam, and Richard was sometimes Ricard. The name Hugh appears in many ways, including Hugh, Hughe, Hugg, Hue and Huwe.

As there were comparatively few given names in fourteenth-century England, numerous diminutives and pet forms developed, including at least eleven for the extraordinarily common name Johan:

Adam: Adekyn, Adecok, Adinet
Alianore: Alisote, Alisour
Alis: Alison
Alisandre: Sandre
Anneis: Annote, Annet
Bertelmew: Bertelot
Eli(a)s/Ely(a)s: Eliot, Elkyn
Emme: Emmote
Esmon: Monde, Manekyn
Gilbert: Gibbe, Gibon, Gilkyn, Hille
Henry: Henriot
Hugh: Huchon, Hughelyn, Huard
Isabel: Bele, Ibote, Isode, Sibille
James: Copin
Johan: Jak/Jack/Jakke, Jakyn, Jakinet, Jaket, Jakemyn, Janyn, Jan(e) kyn, Janot, Jancok, Hancok, Hankyn
Johane: Jonet(t)e, Johanette, Jony
Katerine: Katin
Lambert: Lambyn

Malculin: Malin
Margarete: Margerie, Magote, Malle
Marie: Mariote, Marion(e)
Marmaduke: Duket
Mayhew: Maykin
Maud: Mold
Nichol: Colle, Colet, Colin
Paul: Paulin
Peres: Perot, Peryn, Petrekyn
Phelip: Phelipot
Rauf: Ravlyn
Richard: Diccun, Hick, Hichecok, Richardyn
Robert: Robyn, Robynet, Hobbe, Hobekyn, Robechon
Roger: Hogge
Simond: Syme, Simkyn, Simcok
Thomas: Thomme, Thomelyn, Thomasyn
Wauter: Watte, Wattekyn, Wauterkyn
William: Wille, Willekyn, Willecok, Willekot

Appendix 2

Fourteenth-Century London Place-Names

Abecherchelane, Abbechirchelane: Abchurch Lane

Aldermanberi/bery: Aldermanbury

Aldemariecherche, Aldermarichirche, Eldemariecherche: St Mary
  Aldermary Church

Aldrichesgate, Aldresgate, Allereddesgate: Aldersgate

Al(e)gate: Aldgate

Barbecan(e)(stret): Barbican (Street)

Basingestrete/Basingelane: now part of Cannon Street

Bassingeshawe, Bassyeshaghe etc: Bassishaw

Bat(e)richeseye: Battersea

Baynardeschastel, Bernardcastell, Chostel Baynard, Castrie Baignard:
  Castle Baynard

Belleryteryslane, Belleyettereslane: now Billiter Street

Berchenereslane: Birchin Lane

Berebyndereslane: Bearbinder Lane

Beremundeseye, Bermondeseye: Bermondsey

Berking(g)e, Berkynge: Barking

Bertelmew the Lit(t)el: St Bartholomew the Less

Bisshoppisgate, Bishoppesgate, etc: Bishopsgate

Bithewall(e): 'by the wall'

Blakehethe: Blackheath

Blemondesbiry, Bloemundesbury: Bloomsbury

Brad(e)stret(e): Broad Street

Bred(e)stret(e): Bread Street

Breggestrete, Briggestrate, Bruggestrete: Bridge Street

Brettonestrete: later called Little Britain

Brokenewerf: Broken Wharf

Candelwikstrete, Kandelwykstrete, etc: Candlewick Street

Cattestrete: Cateaton Street, later Gresham Street

Chauncellereslane: Chancery Lane
Chelchehithe, Chelchehuth, Chilchethe: Chelsea
Chep(e): Cheapside
Cherringe, Cherynge: Charing
Chesewyk: Chiswick
Chig(g)ewell(e), Chikewelle: Chigwell
Clerkenewelle, Klerkenewell: Clerkenwell
Cokkeslane: Cock Lane
Col(d)abei, Coldabey: church of St Nicholas Cole Abbey
Coldhakber, Coldhabbeye, Coldherberwe, Coldherberuy: Coldharbour
Col(e)man(e)strete: Coleman Street
Conynghoplane: Coneyhope Lane, off Poultry
Cord(e)wanerstrete: Cordwainer Street, now Bow Lane
Corn(e)hull(e): Cornhill
Crepelgate, Crepulgate: Cripplegate
Croked(e)lane: Crooked Lane
Dou(u)egate: Dowgate
Ealdefishestrate, Eldefisshstrete: Old Fish Street
Eldedeneslane, Oldedeneslane: Old Dean's Lane, now Warwick Lane
Elde Jurie, Olde Iuwerie: Old Jewry
Elmes: The Elms
Enefelde: Enfield
Estchep(e): East Cheap
Esthamme: East Ham
Estsmethefeld: East Smithfield
Fanchirche: Fenchurch
Far(y)n(g)done: Farringdon
Faitoreslane(nde): Fetter Lane (End)
Faukeshalle: Vauxhall
Fisshwarf: Fish Wharf
Flehsshameles: (Flesh) Shambles
Flete: River Fleet
Flet(e)stret(e): Fleet Street
Foleham: Fulham
Fridaystrete, Frydaiestrate, Frydeistrete: Friday Street
Fynamoureslane: now Fye Foot Lane
Fynesbery: Finsbury
Fynghislane: Finch Lane

Garlekhuth(e), Garlechethe, Garlekheth(e): Garlickhythe
Gihall, Gihale: Guildhall
Goderomlane: Gutter Lane
Graschirche(strete), Grascherche: Gracechurch Street
Grenewyche, Grenewyz: Greenwich
Guiwerie: Jewry
Hakeneye: Hackney
Haryngeye: Haringey
Heywharflane: later Campion Lane
Hoggenelane: Huggin Lane, now Goldsmith Street
Holirodewarf: Holyrood Wharf
Holeb(o)urn(e), Holleburne: Holborn
Holebournebregge: Holborn Bridge (over the Flete)
Honilane: Honey Lane
Horshobrigg, Horsshobregge: Horseshoe Bridge (over the Walebrok)
Houndeslowe: Hounslow
Hundesdich, Houndesdych: Houndsditch
Isel(e)don(e), Isyldon: Islington
Ismonger(e)lane, Ismangherelane: Ironmonger Lane
Kelbourne: Kilburn
Kentisshtoun, Kentyshtown, Kentyssheton: Kentish Town
Knyghtebregg, Knyghtesbrugge: Knightsbridge
Kyngestone: Kingston-on-Thames
Kyro(u)n(es)lane: now Maiden Lane
Lamberdeshell(e), Lambardeshull, Lamberdyshel: Lambeth Hill
Lamhethe, Lambhuthe, Lomehethe: Lambeth
Leuesham: Lewisham
Lodgate, Ludegate: Ludgate
Lotheburi, Lodingeberi: Lothbury
Loueronelane: now called Leather Lane
Lymbrennerslane: Limeburner Lane
Lymstret(e): Lime Street
Manionelane, Menchonelane, Munchenlane: Mincing Lane
Marie atte Nax(e): St Mary Axe
Marie Colcherche: St Mary Colechurch
Mart(h)elane: later Mark Lane
Medelane: Maiden Lane
Melk(e)strete/Milkestrate: Milk Street

Milesende: Mile End
Mogwellestrete, Muggewellestrete: Monkwell Street
Nedlerslane: now Pancras Lane
Neugate, Ne(u)wegate: Newgate
Oystirgate, Oystregate: a water-gate near London Bridge
Oystrehull: Oyster Hill, now Fish Street Hill
Paternostrestrete: now College Hill
Petiwales, Petygales: Petty Wales
Pole: Pool of London
Port(e)sokne, Porthesocne: Portsoken
Potenhuth: Putney
Pouleswharf, Pauliswharf: St Paul's Wharf
P(o)ultrye: Poultry
Quenhethe, Quenehithe: Queenhithe
Red(e)crouchestrate: Red Cross Street
Retheresgatelane: later Pudding Lane
Ro(u)melond(e): 'Rome Land', an area of open space near a dock; there
　was one near the Tower and another at Queenhithe
Rysselepe: Ruislip
Sacollelane, Secollane: Seacoal Lane
Seint Pool, Poul: St Paul's
Sevynglane, Sivendestret: Seething Lane
Sheterselde: Shooter's Hill
Shiteburnelane, Shitteborwelane, etc: Sherborne Lane
Sholane: Shoe Lane
Shorisdich, Shordyche: Shoreditch
Silvirstrete, Selvernestrate: Silver Street
Smethefeld: Smithfield
Soper(e)(s)lane: now Queen Street
Stebbenheth, Stebenhuthe: Stepney
Stonecrouche: Stone Cross (in Chepe)
Straund(e): Strand
Suth(e)werk: Southwark
Suthwerkbarre: Southwark Bar
Tamestrete, T(h)amis(e)strete: Thames Street
Templebarre: Temple Bar
Tibourne, Tyburne: River Tyburn
Tour: Tower

Tourhull(e): Tower Hill
Vedastlane: Foster Lane
Vinetrie, Vinetrye: Vintry
Walbroke, Walebrok: Walbrook
Wat(e)lyngstrete: Watling Street
Westchep(e): Cheapside
Westhamme: West Ham
Wodestrate: Wood Street
Wol(le)cherchehawe, Wolchirchehagh, etc, sometimes just Wollecherche: Woolchurch-Haw
Wolsiesgate: a water-gate in the Ropery
Wolwiche: Woolwich; also sometimes called Southall(e) Marreys
Woxebregg, Woxebrugg(e): Uxbridge
Wullewarf: Wool Wharf

Appendix 3

Mayors of London 1300–1350

Mayors were elected every year on 28 October, and often served more than one term.

1299/1301 Elias Russel
1301/08 Johan Blount
1308/09 Nichol Farndone
1309/10 Thomas Romeyn
1310/11 Richer Refham
1311/13 Johan Gisors
1313/14 Nichol Farndone
1314/15 Johan Gisors
1315/16 Estephene Abingdon
1316/19 Johan Wentgrave
1319/20 Hamo Chigwell
1320/21 Nichol Farndone (replaced by Sir Robert Kendale 20 February to 20 May 1321)
1321/23 Hamo Chigwell (elected 20 May 1321; removed 4 April 1323)
1323 Nichol Farndone (4 April to 7 December 1323)
1323/26 Hamo Chigwell (elected 7 December 1323; removed 15 November 1326)
1326/27 Richard Betoyne
1327/28 Hamo Chigwell
1328/29 Johan Grantham
1329/30 Simond Swanland
1330/32 Johan Pulteneye
1332/33 Johan Preston
1333/34 Johan Pulteneye
1334/36 Reynald Conduit
1336/37 Johan Pulteneye
1337/39 Henry Darcy

1339/41 Andrew Aubrey
1341/42 Johan Oxenford (died in office 17 June 1342)
1342/43 Simond Fraunceys (elected 17 June 1342)
1343/45 Johan Hamond
1345/46 Richard Lacer
1346/47 Geffrei Wychyngham
1347/48 Thomas Leggy
1348/49 Johan Lovekyn
1349/50 Wauter Turk
1350/51 Richard Kyselingbury

Abbreviations

AL	Annales Londonienses
Anon	Anonimalle Chronicle
AP	Annales Paulini
CCR	Calendar of Close Rolls
CChR	Calendar of Charter Rolls
CCW	Calendar of Chancery Warrants 1244–1326
CFR	Calendar of Fine Rolls
CIM	Calendar of Inquisitions Miscellaneous
CIPM	Calendar of Inquisitions Post Mortem
CMSL	Chronicle of the Mayors and Sheriffs of London
Coroner	Calendar of Coroners Rolls 1300–1378
CPR	Calendar of Patent Rolls
DCAD	Descriptive Catalogue of Ancient Deeds
EMCR	Calendar of Early Mayor's Court Rolls 1298–1307
LAN	London Assize of Nuisance 1301–1431
LBA	Calendar of Letter-Books of London 1275–1298; LBB: Letter-Books of London 1275–1312; LBC: Letter-Books 1291–1309; LBD: 1309–1314; LBE: 1314–1337; LBF: 1337–1352; LBG: 1352–74; LBH: 1375–1399
LPA	London Possessory Assizes: A Calendar
MLLF	Memorials of London and London Life, ed. Riley
ODNB	Oxford Dictionary of National Biography
SAL MS	Society of Antiquaries of London, manuscript
SCR	London Sheriffs Court Roll 1320
SPMR	Calendar of Select Plea and Memoranda Rolls, vol. 1, 1323–1364
TNA	The National Archives (C: Chancery; E: Exchequer; SC: Special Collections)
Wills	Calendar of Wills Proved and Enrolled, part 1, 1258–1358
Wills, part 2	Calendar of Wills, part 2, 1358–1688

Bibliography

Primary Sources

Annales Londonienses 1195–1330, in ed. W. Stubbs, *Chronicles of the Reigns of Edward and Edward II*, vol. 1 (1882)

Annales Paulini 1307–1340, in Stubbs, *Chronicles of the Reigns*, vol. 1

The Anonimalle Chronicle 1307 to 1334, From Brotherton Collection MS 29, ed. W. R. Childs and J. Taylor (1991)

Calendar of Chancery Warrants, 1 vol., 1244–1326 (1927)

Calendar of the Charter Rolls, 3 vols., 1300–1417 (1908-16)

Calendar of the Close Rolls, 15 vols., 1296–1354 (1892-1906)

Calendar of Coroners Rolls of the City of London A.D. 1300–1378, ed. R. R. Sharpe (1913)

Calendar of Documents Relating to Scotland, vol. 3, 1307–1357, ed. Joseph McBain (1887)

Calendar of Early Mayor's Court Rolls, 1298–1307, ed. A. H. Thomas (1924)

Calendar of Papal Letters, vol. 2, 1305–1341, ed. W. H. Bliss (1895)

Calendar of the Fine Rolls, 6 vols., 1272–1356 (1911–21)

Calendar of Inquisitions Miscellaneous, 3 vols., 1219–1377 (1916–37)

Calendar of Inquisitions Post Mortem, 6 vols., 1300–1352 (1913–16)

Calendar of Letter-Books of the City of London, 8 vols., 1275–1399, ed. R. R. Sharpe (1899–1904)

Calendar of the Patent Rolls, 16 vols., 1292–1354 (1895–1907)

Calendar of the Select Plea and Memoranda Rolls of the City of London, vol. 1, 1323–64, ed. A. H. Thomas (1926)

Calendar of Wills Proved and Enrolled in the Court of Husting, London, part 1, 1258–1358, and part 2, 1358–1688, ed. R. R. Sharpe (1889-90)

Calendar to the Feet of Fines for London and Middlesex, vol. 1, 1189-1485, ed. W. J. Hardy and W. Page (1892)

Chronicles of the Mayors and Sheriffs of London, ed. H. T. Riley (1863)

The Chronicle of Lanercost 1272–1346, ed. Herbert Maxwell (1913)

Croniques de London, ed. G. J. Aungier (1844)

A Descriptive Catalogue of Ancient Deeds, 6 vols., ed. H. C. Maxwell-Lyte (1890–1915)

Feet of Fines for Essex, vol. 2, 1272–1326 (1913)

Flores Historiarum, vol. 3, ed. H. R. Luard (1890)

The Flowers of History, ed. C. D. Yonge (1853)

Foedera, Conventiones, Litterae et Cujuscunque Generis Acta Publica, 4 vols., 1272– 1361 (1816–25)

The French Chronicle of London, in *Chronicles of the Mayors and Sheriffs*, ed. Riley

Issues of the Exchequer, ed. Frederick Devon (1837)

Johannis de Trokelowe et Henrici de Blaneforde Chronica et Annales, ed. H. T. Riley (1866)

Le Livere de Reis de Britanniae et le Livere de Reis de Engletere, ed. John Glover (1865)

London Assize of Nuisance, 1301–1431: A Calendar, ed. Helena M. Chew and William Kellaway (1973)

London Possessory Assizes: A Calendar, ed. Helena M. Chew (1965)

London Sheriffs Court Roll 1320, ed. Matthew Stevens (2010)

Munimenta Gildhallae Londoniensis, 3 vols., ed. H. T. Riley (1859–62)

Society of Antiquaries of London, manuscript 122 (Edward II's chamber account of 1325/26)

The National Archives records, https://discovery.nationalarchives.gov.uk/

Two Early London Subsidy Rolls, ed. Eilert Ekwall (1951)

Selected Secondary Sources

There are countless hundreds of books, articles and websites about London and its history; I have only listed those used in the text.

Barron, Caroline, *London in the Later Middle Ages: Government and People 1200– 1500* (2004)

Barron, Caroline M., and Anne F. Sutton, eds., *Medieval London Widows 1300– 1500* (1994)

Beaven, Alfred P., *The Aldermen of the City of London* (1912)

British History Online, https://www.british-history.ac.uk/

Bullock-Davies, Constance, *Menstrellorum Multitudo: Minstrels at a Royal Feast* (1978)

Butler, Sara M., *Forensic Medicine and Death Investigation in Medieval England* (2015)

Curtis, Margaret, 'The London Lay Subsidy of 1332', in ed. George Unwin, *Finance and Trade Under Edward III* (1918), 35-60

Galloway, James A. and Margaret Murphy, 'Feeding the City: Medieval London and its Agrarian Hinterland', *The London Journal*, 16 (1991), 3-14

Hamilton, J. S., 'Some Notes on 'Royal' Medicine in the Reign of Edward II', *Fourteenth Century England II*, ed. Chris Given-Wilson (2002), 33-43

Harben, Henry A., *A Dictionary of London* (1918)

The History of Parliament, https://www.historyofparliamentonline.org/

The Historic Towns Trust, 'Map of Medieval London: The City, Westminster and Southwark, 1270 to 1300'

Horrox, Rosemary, *The Black Death* (1994)

Megson, Barbara E., 'Mortality Among London Citizens in the Black Death', *Medieval Prosopography*, 19 (1998), 125-33

The Middle English Dictionary, https://quod.lib.umich.edu/m/middle-english-dictionary/dictionary

Oxford Dictionary of National Biography, https://www.oxforddnb.com/

Phillimore, W. P. W., *The London and Middlesex Notebook: A Garner of Local History and Antiquities* (1892)

Riley, H. T., ed., *Memorials of London and London Life in the 13th, 14th and 15th Centuries* (1868)

Sloane, Barney, *The Black Death in London* (2011)

Stapleton, Thomas, 'A Brief Summary of the Wardrobe Accounts of the Tenth, Eleventh and Fourteenth Years of King Edward the Second', *Archaeologia*, 26 (1836), 318-45

Summerson, Henry, 'Peacekeepers and Lawbreakers in London, 1276– 1321', *Thirteenth Century England XII*, ed. Janet Burton, Phillipp Schofield and Björn Weiler (2007), 107-21

Thornbury, Walter, *Old and New London*, 6 vols. (1878)

Thrupp, Sylvia L., *The Merchant Class of Medieval London* (1989)

Turner, Marion, *Chaucer: A European Life* (2019)

Uckelman, Sara L., *Middle English Bynames in Early Fourteenth-Century London* (2014)

Endnotes

Introduction

1. Barron, *London in the Later Middle Ages*, 4, 10.
2. *SPMR*, 107, 169.

Health

1. *EMCR*, 51. Wolves were already extinct or virtually extinct in England by 1300, except perhaps in the far north-west corner of the kingdom, the mountainous region now called the Lake District.
2. Sara M. Butler, *Forensic Medicine and Death Investigation in Medieval England*, 229.
3. *Coroner*, 22-5, 215; Butler, *Forensic Medicine*, 227.
4. *Coroner*, 5-6, 16, 177-8.
5. *Coroner*, 20-21, 63-4, 92-3, 163-5, 188-9, 205-6.
6. *Coroner*, 23-4; *CPR 1301–7*, 256. 'Robert Wynnehelme called de Amyas' made his will in December 1341 (it was proved in July 1342) and was a cousin of Juliane, wife of Étienne Fraunsard from Amiens; see 'Foreigners'. *Wills*, 458; *LBE*, 209; *LBF*, 22.
7. *Coroner*, 36-7; *CIM 1219–1307*, nos. 1136, 1296, 1375, 1384, 1422, 1767, 2202, 2220, 2261, 2276, 2279; *CPR 1292–1301*, 61, 81; *CPR 1301–7*, 458.
8. *Coroner*, 249.
9. *Coroner*, 11-12, 16, 209-10; Butler, *Forensic Medicine*, 227, 229.
10. *Coroner*, 256-7; *LBB*, 275.
11. *Coroner*, 15-16.
12. *CMSL*, 249 ('*graunt maladie des oelz*').
13. Eilart Ekwall, *Two Early London Subsidy Rolls*, available on British History Online; *LBD*, 182; *CPR 1330–34*, 230; *LAN*, no. 121; *Wills*, 234, 285, 294-5, 350, 525.

14. *LBD*, 47.
15. *LBC*, 59, 64, 191; *LBF*, 131.
16. *Coroner*, 90-91. In 1278, William Paumere fell down dead near the conduit in Chepe after excessive blood-letting the previous day: *LBB*, 272; *MLLF*, 14.
17. *SCR*, 63. A 'Johan of Cornhull, surgeon' appears on record in 1359: *CPR 1358–61*, 320. In February 1377, Richard Cheyndut was imprisoned for failing to cure Wauter Hull of 'a malady in his left leg': *SPMR*, vol. 2 (1364–81), 236.
18. *Wills*, 368.
19. *Coroner*, 37, 116-17; SAL MS 122, 75, 77.
20. Hamilton, 'Some Notes on 'Royal' Medicine', 41-3; *Calendar of Documents Relating to Scotland 1307–57*, no. 766.
21. *Wills*, 270, 410, 428, 519; *LBC*, 17; *LBD*, 125, 305; *LBE*, 25, 232, 265; *LBF*, 182.
22. *MLLF*, 273-4; *LBG*, 21.

Foreigners

1. *CPR 1301–7*, 73 (le Romeyn).
2. *Wills*, 352-4, 572; *Wills*, part 2, 23.
3. *Wills*, 192, 206, 488, 674; *CPR 1317–21*, 569; *CPR 1321–24*, 11; *LBC*, 59, 64; *LBE*, 285; *LBF*, 210.
4. *Wills*, 264-5; *LBE*, 16, 75-6; *CPR 1313–17*, 668; *CPR 1317–21*, 570.
5. *CPR 1272-81*, 125, 354, 449; *CPR 1281–92*, 318; *CPR 1307–13*, 120.
6. *CPR 1281–92*, 318, 350, 354.
7. *Coroner*, 152; *EMCR*, 9, 24, 34; *CCW*, 157; *LBE*, 144.
8. *EMCR*, 143.
9. *LBD*, 227; *SPMR*, 173.
10. *SPMR*, 246.
11. *EMCR*, 112; *CChR 1257–1300*, 202.
12. *CPR 1266–72*, 689; Thrupp, *Merchant Class of Medieval London*, 133, 366, 370; *Wills*, 267.
13. *LBE*, 120.
14. *MLLF*, 102.
15. *Coroner*, 73; *SPMR*, 218.
16. *Wills*, 458, 529-31, and see 'Health'.

17. *CPR 1317–21*, 591; *CCR 1341–43*, 24; *CPR 1346–50*, 182; *CPR 1391–96*, 302; *LBF*, 73; *Wills*, 43, 235, 428; *CIPM 1374–77*, no. 287; *CMSL*, 189, 220.
18. *Coroner*, 129-30, 265-6.
19. *LBC*, 65; *LBE*, 14; *CPR 1307–13*, 229; *CCW*, 311, 324; *SPMR*, 236, 259.
20. *CCR 1337–39*, 326; *SPMR*, 147-8.
21. *Coroner*, 232, 255-7.
22. *EMCR*, 119, 140, 182-3.
23. *Wills*, 311.
24. *EMCR*, 196; *LBA*, 199-200; *DCAD*, vol. 2, nos. A.2652-3. Other examples are German Kay of Wakefield in 1308 and 'German, son of Reynald' in 1326: *CPR 1307–13*, 165; *CPR 1324–27*, 330.
25. *CChR 1300–26*, 371; *LBC*, 41, 111, 234; *SPMR*, 151-2, 213.
26. *Wills*, 605; *LBD*, 141, 190, 241; *LBE*, 182, 189, 209, 293.
27. *Coroner*, 235-6; *LBC*, 198; *LBD*, 187.
28. *Foedera 1307–27*, 8, 17-18, 216.

Wards

1. *LBE*, 124-5; *MLLF*, xliv, xlv; *SPMR*, 116.
2. *LBF*, 20-23; *SPMR*, 221-2.
3. Turner, *Chaucer: A European Life*, 12; Barron, *Later Middle Ages*, 97.
4. *Munimenta Gildhallae Londoniensis*, vol. 1, 36-8, 337-8; *SPMR*, 109; *LBD*, 214.
5. *Wills*, 397-8. For examples of Farndone Within and Without as early as 1300/01, see *Coroner*, 8, 19, 21.
6. *Wills*, 112, 397-8, 474; *Wills*, part 2, 18-19; Thrupp, *Merchant Class*, 339; Phillimore, *London and Middlesex Notebook*, 114-15; Beaven, *Aldermen of the City of London*, 143.

Curfew

1. *Coroner*, 11-12; *MLLF*, 93; *LBE*, 142.
2. *SPMR*, 126.
3. *MLLF*, 129-30, 133, 139-41, 173, 193, 272.

4. *SPMR*, 109, 111-12.
5. *EMCR*, 57.
6. *EMCR*, 156.
7. *SPMR*, 193.
8. *Coroner*, 14-15, 70-71; *LBC*, 16; *LBD*, 263; *MLLF*, 34-5, 86-9, 91-3, 140, 143-4; *EMCR*, 74, 156, 160; *SPMR*, 154.

Sanitation

1. *MLLF*, 67-8; *Coroner*, 44-6.
2. *LAN*, no. 459.
3. *MLLF*, 223-4.
4. *Coroner*, 43, 62, 142, 221; *EMCR*, 255; *CPR 1307–13*, 38; *MLLF*, xvi, xlvi, 67, 279; *LBG*, 50.
5. *LBE*, 147.
6. *MLLF*, 34-5.
7. *SPMR*, 98, 116, 156, 192.
8. *Coroner*, 167-8.
9. *MLLF*, xvi, xlvi, 67; *Coroner*, 43, 62.
10. *SPMR*, 162.
11. *MLLF*, 214; *LBF*, 84. In return, they would give the mayor a boar's head every Christmas.
12. *EMCR*, 161-2; *SPMR*, 166.
13. *MLLF*, 240-1.
14. *Coroner*, 198-9.
15. *LBA*, 216; *LBE*, 116; *MLLF*, 20, 28, 35; *SPMR*, 158.
16. *LAN*, nos. 63, 263.
17. *Coroner*, 56-7.
18. *Coroner*, 190, 221, 256-7; *MLLF*, 260-1.

Privies

1. *LAN*, nos. 2-3.
2. *LAN*, no, 277; *EMCR*, 171.
3. *LAN*, no. 309.
4. *LAN*, no. 214.

5. *LAN*, no. 160.
6. *Wills*, 143-4, 179.
7. *LAN*, nos. 160, 325-6, 328. Andrew Aubrey was a future mayor of London; Thomas Heyron was the half-brother of John Chaucer, father of the poet Geoffrey. Johane Armenters was dead by 27 August 1333: *LAN*, no. 316; *Wills*, 389.

Privacy

1. *LBC*, 199.
2. *LAN*, nos. 14, 30, 31.
3. *LAN*, nos. 129, 359, 407, 410.
4. *LAN*, nos. 361-6; *Wills*, 253, 349.
5. *LAN*, nos. 355, 381; *Wills,* 30, 397-8.
6. *LAN*, no. 312; *Wills,* 251, 581.
7. *LAN*, nos. 351, 369-71.
8. *LAN*, no. 12.

Houses

1. *LAN*, p. xxii, nos. 97, 131, 334.
2. *MLLF*, 65-6; *LBC*, 165; *Wills*, 237.
3. *Wills*, 242; *LBE*, 21.
4. *LBC*, 239; *LBE*, 8.
5. *LBE*, 8.
6. *Wills*, 175.
7. *LBE*, 144.
8. *LBF*, 82; *EMCR*, 127.
9. *LAN*, no. 359; *Coroner*, 142.
10. *Wills*, 86, 189, 269.
11. *Wills*, 227, 363, 450.
12. *Coroner*, 41.
13. *EMCR*, 110, 249.
14. *Wills*, 676.
15. *Wills*, 53, 122, 332, 405, 478.
16. *LBF*, 85; *Wills*, 563-5. Thomas Hodesdone died in Estephene's home in April 1325; see 'Hospitals'.

17. *LBB*, 265-6; *MLLF*, 11-13.
18. *LAN*, nos. 204, 212, 323, 325-6, 328, 403.
19. *LAN*, nos. 222, 378, 500-01.
20. *LAN*, nos. 54, 71, 104, 154.
21. *Coroner*, 185, 191.
22. *LAN*, no. 219; *Wills*, 86.
23. *LAN*, no. 183; *Wills*, 489; *LBE*, 114. Francis Vilers was murdered in August 1324: *Coroner*, 91-2.
24. *LAN*, no. 399; *Wills*, 155.
25. *EMCR*, 120.
26. *LAN*, nos. 340-1, 362.
27. *LAN*, nos. 352, 358.
28. *LAN*, nos. 32, 66, 93, 217-18, 276, 278-9, 288, 293, 307, 380, 416, 496, 595.
29. *LAN*, nos. 331-2, 352, 408; *Wills*, 557-8, 579.
30. *Wills*, 125, 212, 223, 240, 273, 293, 323, 338, 354, 367, 404, 472, 498, 530, 566-7, 579, 672, 674; *Wills*, part 2, 29; *LBF*, 177; *CIPM 1374–77*, no. 287.

Hostels

1. *MLLF*, 323; *Wills*, 427; *SPMR*, 233.
2. *SPMR*, 220-21.
3. TNA E 101/380/4; *MLLF*, 323.
4. *SPMR*, 17, 156, 164, 189.
5. *EMCR*, 213; *Wills*, 185, 222.
6. *SPMR*, 169.
7. *MLLF*, 323.
8. *LBE*, 206-7; *CPR 1324–27*, 145-6.
9. *MLLF*, 64; *LBC*, 155, 158.

Mansions

1. *EMCR*, 261; *LBE*, 108.
2. *LBF*, 158; *Wills*, 609-10; *LPA*, no. 117.
3. *LAN*, nos. 375-6; *Wills*, 246.
4. TNA E 101/380/4, fos. 25v-29r; SAL MS 122, 67-8; TNA SC 8/11/513.

5. *CIPM 1300–07*, no. 434; *CIPM 1307–17*, no. 62; *CIPM 1336–46*, no. 185; *CIPM 1352–60*, no. 523; *CIPM 1405–13*, no. 850; *CIPM 1432–37*, no. 500; *Wills*, 539.

6. *CPR 1292–1301*, 30; *CIPM 1327–36*, no. 82; *CPR 1334–38*, 206.

Gardens

1. The 'Map of Medieval London: The City, Westminster and Southwark, 1270 to 1300'; Sloane, *Black Death in London*, 18.
2. *LBC*, 237; *Wills*, 152, 183-4, 270.
3. *LBE*, 118, 193; *LBF*, 86; *LAN*, no. 30; *Wills*, 227.
4. *Wills*, 280, 358-9, 451, 620, 699; *LAN*, no. 188; *LBF*, 35, 70. *Roumelond* or 'Romeland' was an open space near a dock; see Appendix 2.
5. *LAN*, nos. 266, 276.
6. *LAN*, nos. 307, 310-11.
7. *LAN*, no. 34; *Coroner*, 113-14.
8. *LBF*, 186, and see 'Adultery'.
9. *LAN*, nos. 66, 218.
10. *MLLF*, 228-9.

Hospitals

1. *CPR 1317–21*, 127.
2. *Calendar of Papal Letters 1305–41*, 318, 411-12.
3. *Coroner*, 92-3, 114-17, 132-4, 140-41, 166-7, 250-51.
4. *Coroner*, 43.
5. *Wills*, 648-9, and see also Johan Triple's will on p. 311 of *Wills*.
6. *CPR 1343–45*, 84.
7. *Coroner*, 102-3.
8. *CCR 1323–27*, 603.
9. *Coroner*, 197-8.
10. It was called 'the new hospital' in 1242, 1279 and 1324: CPR *1232–47*, 283; *CPR 1272–81*, 352; *CPR 1321–24*, 359.
11. *CPR 1324–27*, 98, 150; *LAN*, no. 369; *LBC,* 238; 'The Priory of St. Mary Spital' in *Survey of London: Volume 27, Spitalfields and Mile End New Town*, ed. F. H. W. Sheppard (1957), 21-23, and 'Hospitals: St Mary without Bishopsgate', *A History of the County of London:*

Volume 1, London Within the Bars, Westminster and Southwark, ed. William Page (1909), 530-35, both available on British History Online.

12. *Coroner*, 250-1; *CPR 1317–21*, 587, 399; *CPR 1324–27*, 153.
13. *CPR 1313–17*, 293; *Calendar of Papal Letters 1305–41*, 203-4, 208, 473.
14. *CPR 1321–24*, 234.
15. *Wills*, 595.
16. *Wills*, 362, 562, 684; *CPR 1330–34*, 49, 173; *CPR 1340–43*, 415-16.
17. *Wills*, 364.
18. *Wills*, 694; *Wills,* part 2, 3, 24-5, 45.
19. *MLLF*, 230-1.

Roads

1. *Wills*, 581.
2. *Wills*, 147, 162, 171, 528.
3. *LBD*, 291; *MLLF*, 98-100.
4. *LAN*, nos. 97, 327, 396, 577.
5. *MLLF*, 95-6.
6. *LAN*, nos. 140, 188, 222, 266, 277, 292, 358, 375, 572, 577, 618; *EMCR*, 113; *LBF*, 184.
7. *LBF*, 103; *SPMR*, 208-9, 220.
8. *CPR 1281-92*, 10.
9. *LBA*, 217.
10. *LBC*, 130, 240.
11. *Wills*, 616-17.
12. *LAN*, nos. 140-2, 186, 300, 369.
13. *MLLF*, 35; *LAN*, p. xxviii, nos. 234, 547-8, 574; *LBA*, 217.

Trading

1. *SPMR*, 2; *LBE*, 156-7.
2. *LBB*, 236; *LBD*, 229; *LBE*, vii; *MLLF*, 33, 75.
3. *CPR 1321–24*, 425-6; *CPR 1364–67*, 5; *LBD*, 281-2; *LBE*, 179-80; *MLLF*, 179-80, 222-3, 226.
4. *LBB*, 217; *LBD*, 58; *LBE*, 56-7, 167; *MLLF*, 36-7; *EMCR*, 102-3.
5. *MLLF*, 216-19.

6. *LAN*, no. 206.
7. *LBF*, 95. Johan was the son of Richer's son Johan, a fishmonger: *Wills*, 339; *Wills*, part 2, 10-11.
8. *LAN*, nos. 233-4; *LBF*, 187; *Wills*, 627.
9. *Wills*, 62, 192, 213, 275, 313, 681; *LBC*, 87; *LBE*, 85; *CCR 1354-60*, 207; Barron and Sutton, *Medieval London Widows*, 11-13.
10. *Wills*, 30, 74, 155, 236-7, 319-20, 620.

Food

1. *MLLF*, 90.
2. *EMCR*, 66-7; *MLLF*, 119-20; *SPMR*, 5; *LBE*, 8.
3. *MLLF*, 71, 80.
4. *LBA*, 213, 216; *SPMR*, 23.
5. *MLLF*, 133.
6. *LBF*, 208.
7. *SPMR*, 251; *LBF*, 227; *MLLF*, 266.
8. *MLLF*, 141-2.
9. *Coroner*, 127-8.
10. *Anon*, 90.
11. *Foedera 1307–27*, 263, 266; *Anon*, 88-90.
12. Summerson, 'Peacekeepers and Lawbreakers in London, 1276–1321', 111.
13. *LBC*, 156; *LBE*, 43; *SPMR*, 145, 165, 203, 219, 232, 241.
14. TNA E 101/380/4, fo. 19r; SAL MS 122, 87.
15. *MLLF*, 83-4; *Wills*, 345, 552.
16. *LBB*, 261; *CIPM 1327–36*, no. 82; *CPR 1334–38*, 206.
17. *MLLF*, 228-9; Galloway and Murphy, 'Feeding the City: Medieval London and its Agrarian Hinterland', 8.
18. *Coroner*, 14-15, 169-70, and see 'Murder'.

Drink

1. *AP*, 267.
2. As well as running *Drinkewaterestaverne*, James Beauflour (d. October 1328) was the collector of customs in London. *Coroner*, 100, 140-41; *CCR 1318–23*, 700; *CCR 1323–7*, 613-3, 648; *CCR*

1327–30, 177-8; *CCR 1333–7*, 532; *CPR 1324–7*, 194; *LBE*, 38; *Wills*, 336-7, 505; *MLLF*, 131-2.

3. *CPR 1321–24*, 1; *Wills*, 241, 445, 699; *Wills*, part 2, 217, 245, 515, 521, 536; *CIPM 1365–69*, no. 282; *DCAD*, vol. 2, no. B.2124; *Coroner*, 50; *SPMR*, 43; *MLLF*, 264; and see also tenement names in 'Houses'.

4. Harben, *Dictionary of London*, 307; *SPMR*, 109; *LBH*, 12.

5. *SPMR*, 235.

6. *SPMR*, 45, 164, 235; *LBF*, 77-8, 246; *CPR 1327–30*, 184-5.

7. *LBD*, 242; *MLLF*, 81-3.

8. *EMCR*, 253.

9. *MLLF*, 181; *SPMR*, 120, 204, 219; *LBF*, 83, 246; *LBG*, 4, 137.

10. *MLLF*, 181-3.

11. *CPR 1321–24*, 8-9; *Wills*, 269, 394, 450; *CIPM 1365–69*, no. 275.

12. *LBA*, 216; *LBG*, 4; *MLLF*, 264; *SPMR*, 125.

13. *LBD*, 240; *LBE*, 71, 131; *LBF*, 27; *MLLF*, 78, 137.

14. *MLLF*, 265; *LBG*, 6.

15. SAL MS 122, 75.

16. *MLLF*, 225.

17. *MLLF*, 77-8, 107, 148-9; *LBD*, 236-7, 299.

18. *LBF*, 28; *SPMR*, 144.

19. *MLLF*, 200-01; *SPMR*, 143.

20. *MLLF*, 264-5.

21. *LAN*, nos. 219, 307, 395; *Coroner*, 94-5, 115-16, 270-1.

Drunkenness

1. *EMCR*, 239.

2. *Coroner*, 2, 12-13.

3. *Coroner*, 194-5, 231-4.

4. *Coroner*, 28-30; *CPR 1301–7,* 21. Elena Scot may be the woman of this name who fell down her stairs in 1321; see 'Houses'. *Trede* means 'tread' or 'trample' and *keile* meant a skittle; *hurlen keiles* meant to hurl abuse at someone. See the Middle English Dictionary at https://quod.lib.umich.edu/m/middle-english-dictionary/dictionary, accessed 30 September 2020.

5. *Coroner*, 177, 244-5.

Misadventure

1. *Coroner*, 4-5.
2. *Coroner*, 2, 12-13, 36-7, 82, 139-40, 256.
3. *Coroner*, 30-31, 34-5. Olive's husband Robert made his will in *c.* July 1319; they had a son Johan and a daughter Johane, and owned a tavern in the parish of St Botolph Billingsgate. *Wills*, 284. Their name sometimes appears as Soroweles or Soreweles, and means 'sorrow-less'. The earl of Arundel was the son of Alesia di Saluzzo (d. 1292).
4. *Coroner*, 100.
5. *Coroner*, 94-5, 270-1.

Murder

1. https://www.medievalists.net/2018/11/digital-map-reveals-medieval-londons-homicide-hot-spots/, accessed 27 August 2020.
2. Summerson, 'Peacekeepers and Lawbreakers', 108-10.
3. *SPMR*, 164.
4. *Coroner*, xxiii, 19, 62, 112, 118, etc.
5. *Coroner*, 114-16, 232-3.
6. *Coroner*, 14-15; *CPR 1301–7*, 114. 'Copin' was probably a diminutive of Iacobus, the Latin form of 'James'.
7. *Coroner*, 119-20; *CPR 1324–27*, 200; *LAN*, no. 288.
8. *Coroner*, 54-6; *CCR 1318–23*, 607.
9. *Coroner*, 169-70; *CPR 1324–27*, 329; *LBF*, 39.
10. *Coroner*, 52-3.
11. *Coroner*, 65-6; *CCR 1318–23*, 636.
12. *EMCR*, 125-6.
13. *Coroner*, 66-7.
14. Summerson, 'Peacekeepers and Lawbreakers', 107, 120.

Theft

1. *SPMR*, 50.
2. *LBE*, 276-8; *LBF*, 264; *SPMR*, 49, 109.

3. *Coroner*, 204-5.
4. *Coroner*, 191.
5. *Coroner*, 182-3, 187. Johan's death was originally blamed on his fellow cutpurse Geffrai Herdwych.
6. *SPMR*, 137.

Assault

1. *Coroner*, 3-4.
2. *Coroner*, 20-21, 166-7; *SPMR*, 253.
3. *EMCR*, 115-17; *CIM 1219–1307*, no. 1865; *Coroner*, 26; *CFR 1272–1307*, 447; *CCR 1296–1302*, 546.
4. *SCR*, 12, 13, 58, 90, 92.
5. *EMCR*, 61.
6. *EMCR*, 239, 254.
7. *SPMR*, 110, 137-8, 192, 216.
8. *SPMR*, 154-5, 206-7; *LBF*, 234; *Wills*, 685.

Disturbance

1. *LBD*, 215; *MLLF*, 80; *SPMR*, xxiii; *AL*, 175-6; *AP*, 321.
2. *EMCR*, 23-4, 74.
3. *EMCR*, 124-5.
4. *Coroner*, 46-7. 'Grimsby' is spelt in four different ways in this entry: Grymysby, Grymyby, Grymisby, Grymesby.
5. *SPMR*, 189.
6. *LBD*, 242, 263-7.
7. *LBD*, 263-7; *MLLF*, 86-9; *EMCR*, 189-90; *Coroner*, 147-8.
8. *SPMR*, 109-12, 124-6, 188.
9. *LBD*, 264-6.

Punishment

1. *EMCR*, 124.
2. *AL*, 139-42; *EMCR*, 220.

3. *AP*, 303; *CPR 1321-24*, 148.

4. *Anon*, 131; *AP*, 322.

5. *SPMR*, 122-9; *Coroner*, 266-9; *CPR 1340-43*, 226-7.

6. *Coroner,* 53-4, 67.

7. *CPR 1317–21*, 292, 307, 386.

8. *CPR 1313–17*, 237.

9. *CPR 1330–34*, 442-3.

10. *CPR 1313–17*, 270.

11. *CCR 1327–30*, 146, 549; *CFR 1327–37*, 169-70.

12. *Coroner*, 121-3; *CMSL*, 259.

13. *CPR 1324–27*, 86; *CPR 1327–30*, 20; *Coroner*, 130-1.

14. *MLLF*, 129-30, 133, 139-41.

15. *CIM 1308–48*, no. 77.

16. TNA SC 8/176/8753, SC 8/59/2947; *CPR 1330–34*, 404.

17. *Wills*, part 2, 3.

18. *CCR 1337–39*, 156-7; *SPMR*, 183; *LBG*, 49-50.

19. *CIPM 1327–36*, no. 467; *CIPM 1336–46*, no. 214; *CIPM 1347–52*, no. 383; *CPR 1350–54*, 9; *CPR 1361–64*, 96, 184; *SPMR*, 186.

20. *MLLF*, 129; *Wills*, 74; *SPMR*, 251. See also http://www. ladydespensersscribery.com/2018/03/15/punishment-of-the-pillory/, accessed 23 September 2020.

21. *LBD*, 242; *MLLF*, 79-80, 139-40, 240-1, 266; *SPMR*, 251, 256.

22. *MLLF*, 319, 324, 367-8, 375; *LBH*, 10, 272, 363.

23. *EMCR*, 66-7.

24. *MLLF*, 119-23.

Abjurers

1. *CPR 1334–38*, 486.

2. *Coroner*, 87-90.

3. *Coroner*, 84-5, 124, 130-1; *CPR 1338–40*, 423.

Defence

1. *MLLF*, 86-9, 91-3, 102-4, 140, 143-4; *LBC*, 154, 158-60; *LBD*, 214; *LBF*, 15.

2. *SPMR*, 102 note 1, 128, 167, 176-7; *LBF*, 20-23; *CPR 1338-40*, 172.
3. *SPMR*, 102, 167; *CPR 1338-40*, 172.
4. *Coroner*, 202-3.

Fire

1. *Coroner*, 73; *Wills*, 263.
2. *MLLF*, 46-7.
3. *LBE*, 39; *MLLF*, 116.
4. *MLLF*, 227.
5. *LAN*, no. 77.
6. *EMCR*, 139.
7. *LBD*, 291; *MLLF*, 98-100.
8. *Coroner*, 51-2.
9. *Coroner*, 170-1.
10. *Coroner*, 183-4.

Children

1. *Coroner*, 219-20. I have been unable to discover what happened to Rauf after he fled.
2. *EMCR*, 167.
3. *Coroner*, 222-3, 254-5, 260-1.
4. *Coroner*, 83.
5. *Coroner*, 25.
6. *Wills*, 233-4, 403-4, 435-6, 669-70.
7. SAL MS 122, 62.
8. *Wills*, 237-8; *LBE*, 17-19.
9. *LBE*, 52, 136; *MLLF*, 117-18; *Wills*, 261, 344-5.
10. *Wills*, 241; *LBE*, 57.
11. *EMCR*, 77; *SPMR*, 205; *LBD*, 224; *LBF*, 104; *Wills*, 427, 677.
12. *Wills*, 134-5; *LBC*, 92.
13. *Wills*, 182, 211, 242; *LBD*, 183-4, 224; *LBE*, 21-22.
14. *Wills*, 175-6, 379, 680-1; *EMCR*, 239; *LBB*, 22; *LBC*, 167, 200-01, 216.

15. *LBD*, 183-4, 224; *LBF*, 42-3, 56; *Wills*, 211, 423, 353, 438-9, 561; *SPMR*, 163.
16. *Wills*, 182, 186, 261, 311, 462-3.
17. *Wills*, 313; *LBE*, 199, 205.
18. *Wills*, 467-8, 625-6; *Wills*, part 2, 77, 174, 388-9; *MLLF*, 248-9, 310; *LBF*, 203; *LBG*, 141.
19. *Wills*, 332; *LBE*, 47, 229, 266-7; *SPMR*, 205-6.
20. *LBE*, 47-8. Simond's first wife was Elena Juvenal: *Wills*, 277.
21. *LBE*, 208, 293-5; *Wills*, 317. Paulin Turk's will of 1325 mentions his children Johan, Peres, Elena and Cristine; by early 1335, only Johan and Elena were still alive. For Mordon, see 'Fun' and 'Plague'.

Women

1. *Wills*, 189, 266-7, 289-91, 458-9, 474, 495, 557-8, 575, 603, 649-51. William Thorneye was not, as stated in Sloane's *Black Death in London*, a half-brother of Geoffrey Chaucer's father John; he left his son a shop which he had acquired from John's half-brother Thomas Heyron.
2. *Wills*, 149-55, 189-99, 295-303, 392-401.
3. *Wills*, 105, 188.
4. *EMCR*, 230; *LBB*, 168; *Wills*, 76, 148.
5. *Wills*, 473.
6. *LBD*, 47, 109-10, 114, 149, 159.
7. *Wills*, 558, 576.
8. *EMCR*, 148-9, 246-7; *LBC*, 123; *LBD*, 47, 175. See also 'Misteries' and 'Apprentices' below.
9. *Wills*, 401-2, 475.
10. Stapleton, 'Brief Summary of the Wardrobe Accounts', 322; *CCR 1323–27*, 336; TNA SC 8/178/8894.
11. SAL MS 122.

Families

1. *Wills*, 271-2, 399-400, 458-9, 521-2, 573, 614.
2. *Wills*, 248; *LBE*, 32.
3. *Wills*, 371; *LBE*, 268-9.

4. *Wills*, 243; *LBE*, 23.
5. *Wills*, 373, 498, 517, 523; *LBF*, 6, 22, 49.
6. *Wills*, 192, 403-4, 588-9.
7. *CIPM 1347–52*, no. 245. For other examples, see my *Living in Medieval England: The Turbulent Year of 1326* (2020), 147-8, and for Pulteneye, Thorneye and Aubrey, see chapters 'Mayors' and 'Pestilence' below.
8. See the chapters Mayors, Names, Plague, Houses, Health, Children and Apprentices.
9. *Wills*, 238; *CIPM 1317–27*, no. 696.
10. *Wills*, 185, 221-2.
11. *Wills*, 241; *LBE*, 91, 99.
12. *Wills*, 323; *LBD*, 184-6.
13. *Wills*, 455-6; *LPA*, no. 13; *CPR 1358–61*, 101; Feet of Fines, Oxfordshire, CP 25/1/190/21, no. 40, available on medievalgenealogy.org.uk.
14. TNA E 101/380/4, fos. 20v, 24r; *Wills*, 412.
15. *Wills*, 412, 434, 474, 600, 602.
16. *Wills*, 263, 268-9, 506, 515-16, 518, 634.
17. *LPA*, nos. 28, 30; *Wills*, 353, 378; and see 'Children'.
18. *Wills*, 186-7, 285; *LBD*, 181-2, 187, 223-4, 230.

Names

1. *Wills*, 60, 68, 73, 116, 119, 151, 159, 172, 212, 216, 226, 253, 275, 283, 300, 305, 311, 360, 363, 457, 519, 521, 526, 547, 608, 692, 695; *Coroner*, 12-13; *LAN*, no. 38; *LBE*, 111-12.
2. *Wills*, 423-4; *Wills*, part 2, 2-3.
3. *EMCR*, 10, 100.
4. *Coroner*, 10-11, 27-8; see also *LBB*, 266, for Johan *Navereathom*.
5. *LBD*, 93, 150; *Wills*, 154; SAL MS 122, 19. Richard Bokeskyn or Bukkeskyn appears in the coroners' rolls in 1325: *Coroner*, 118-19, 149-51.
6. *LBC*, 111; *Coroner*, 111, 267.
7. *SPMR*, 161.
8. *LBD*, 216; *LBF*, 200.
9. *Wills*, 411, 532; *SCR*, 25.
10. *LBD*, 55; *LBE*, 189, 192-3, 200; *CPR 1307–13*, 204; *CPR 1317–21*, 37.

11. *LBA*, 18, 30, 200; *SPMR*, 227.
12. *Coroner*, 41-2; *Wills*, 516.
13. *Wills*, 463, 514, 519, 642-3; *LBF*, 175; *London Subsidy Rolls*.
14. *LBC*, 123; *LBD*, 122; *LBE*, 234. For Maud, see 'Apprentices' and 'Women'.
15. *Wills*, 382-3, 465, 679; *SPMR*, 54-5; *Feet of Fines for Essex*, vol. 2, no. 740, p. 98.
16. *CPR 1343–45*, 238; *Wills*, 354-5, 517.
17. *CPR 1317–21*, 363; *CPR 1324–27*, 72; *CPR 1330–34*, 497, 500; *CPR 1334–38*, 389; *CPR 1343–45*, 408; *CPR 1354–58*, 63, 386-7; *CPR 1361–64*, 541.
18. *Wills*, 586; *London Subsidy Rolls*, Appendix. Uckelman, *Middle English Bynames*, 66, suggests a maker of chess or draught boards.
19. *Coroner*, 23-4; *Wills*, 458; *LBD*, 229; *LBE*, 209; *LBF*, 22. For Robert Amyas, see 'Health' and 'Foreigners'.
20. *LBD*, 208, 212-13; *Wills*, 162.
21. *CCR 1327–30*, 518; *CCR 1337–39*, 536; *Wills*, part 2, 104-5, 119-20; *LBD*, 143; *LBG*, 286.
22. *Wills*, 188, 216, 242, 244-5, 300, 403, 427, 438, 570; *Wills*, part 2, 9; *LBD*, 109; *LBE*, 198, 224.
23. *Coroner*, 73; *SCR*, 28.
24. SAL MS 122, 40.

Adultery

1. *Coroner*, 87-9, 147-8, 173-4; *EMCR*, 184; *SPMR*, 188.
2. *Coroner*, 113-14; *EMCR*, 70.
3. *Coroner*, 143-4, 257-8.
4. *Coroner*, 7-8.
5. *MLLF,* 87; *Coroner*, 39.
6. *MLLF*, 89; *LBD*, 277.
7. *Coroner*, 86, 208-9.
8. *LBA*, 218.
9. *EMCR*, 14.
10. *EMCR*, 211, 218-19.
11. *LBD*, 242; *SPMR*, 167, 173, 188. For Robert Stratford, see also 'Gardens'.

12. *SPMR*, 124-6, 212-13.
13. TNA E 101/380/4, fo. 19r; *Flores Historiarum*, vol. 3, 229.
14. *Wills*, 637-8; *CIPM 1370–73*, no. 174.
15. *Wills*, 489, 495, 556.
16. *Wills*, 177, 205, 593; *LBA*, 195; *LBC*, 182-3.
17. *Wills*, 354-5, 689; *CCR 1354–60*, 43; *CCR 1360–64*, 525; *LBE*, 250, 256.
18. *Wills*, 241; *LBE*, 137, 145, 176; *CIPM 1365–69*, no. 282; *SPMR*, 227.
19. *Wills*, 342; *CIPM 1327–36*, no. 223; *LBE*, 239, 250; *LBF*, 75; *SPMR*, 168; *CPR 1324–27*, 1; *CFR 1327–37*, 119; *Feet of Fines for London and Middlesex*, vol. 1, Edward II, no. 333.

Belongings

1. *Coroner*, 36-7, 46-7, 108-9, 173-4.
2. *EMCR*, 217.
3. *LBB*, 267; *MLLF*, 10-11.
4. *Coroner*, 197-8, 246-7, 265-6.
5. *Wills*, 374, 482, 584.
6. *CCR 1343–45*, 490; *Wills*, 603, 649-51.
7. *Wills*, 657-9, and see 'Religion'.
8. *Wills*, 662; *Coroner,* 119-21, 252-3; TNA C 241/109/104-107, C 241/130/126, C 241/103/243, etc.
9. *Wills*, 641.

Fun

1. *EMCR*, 261; *Wills*, 241. Each alderman was given three horses during his term of office; *LBC*, 154.
2. *MLLF*, 269.
3. *MLLF*, 193; *LBG*, 3.
4. *SPMR*, 54-5.
5. *SCR*, 50; *MLLF*, 19.
6. *Coroner*, 58.
7. *EMCR*, 176; *LAN*, nos. 28, 81; *Wills*, 407.

8. *Munimenta Gildhallae Londoniensis*, vol. 3, 439-41. Edward II himself, however, often played or watched an unspecified ball game, perhaps football; in September 1325, he paid twenty-two men for 'playing at ball' for his entertainment, which sounds like two teams of eleven players. SAL MS 122, 21-2.

9. *MLLF*, 3-4.

10. *SPMR*, 36; *ECMR*, 205.

11. *MLLF*, 88; *LBC*, 16; *LBD*, 266; *Munimenta*, vol. 3, 440. Roger Skirmisour or Shireburne was a tenant of Elena Scot and one of the men she sent to attack Johan Melkesham in 1301; see 'Drunkenness'.

12. *Coroner*, 213; *LBF*, 10.

13. *Coroner*, 196-7; *Wills*, 338, 653-4; *Wills*, part 2, 3-4.

14. TNA E 42/95; *CCR 1318–23*, 544.

15. *MLLF*, 86.

16. See http://www.diceagegame.com/hazard/, accessed 21 August 2020.

17. *Coroner*, 38-9.

18. *SPMR*, 113. Henry Pykard was presumably the man of this name who served as mayor in 1356/57.

19. *Coroner*, 17-18; *MLLF*, 395-6, 455-7.

20. *Coroner*, 77-8.

21. *Wills*, 649-51.

22. *LBF*, 255.

23. *Wills*, 489, 643-4, 649-51.

24. *SPMR*, 145.

25. *Wills*, 557, 627, 636.

26. *AP*, 267.

27. *Anon*, 145-6 (Philippa stayed with Nichol Farndone on Wodestrete during the tournament); W.M. Ormrod, *Edward III* (2011), 130.

28. Constance Bullock-Davies, *Menstrellorum Multitudo*.

29. SAL MS 122, 25.

30. *LBC*, 213, 244; *CIM 1308–48*, no. 186; *CCR 1302–7*, 108; *CPR 1301–7*, 420; *CPR 1307–13*, 41; *CCR 1313–18*, 311-12; *CCW*, 206, 314; *LAN*, no. 110.

31. E.A. Bond, 'Notice of the Last Days of Isabella, Queen of Edward the Second, drawn from an Account of the Expenses of her Household', *Archaeologia*, 35 (1854).

32. *EMCR*, 66-7; *Coroner*, 85-6.

33. *CIPM* 1327–36, no. 542; *MLLF*, 105-7.

Weather

1. *CIPM 1300–07*, no. 91; *CIPM 1352–60*, no. 523.
2. *CMSL*, 240, 249.
3. *Flowers of History*, vol. 2, 476, 582.
4. *CMSL*, 208; *LAN*, no. 281; SAL MS 122, 44.
5. *CMSL*, 243.
6. *Flowers of History*, vol. 2, 582.
7. SAL MS 122, 66; *CPR 1324–27*, 295; *AP*, 312-13; John M. Stratton, *Agricultural Records A.D. 220-1977* (1978), 27-30.
8. *Anon*, 90; *Livere de Reis*, 332-3; *Johannis de Trokelowe*, 92.
9. *AP*, 278.
10. *CMSL*, 252.
11. *Chronicle of Lanercost*, 103.

Mayors

1. *LBC*, 173-80; *LBD*, 16-31.
2. *Wills*, 238; *CIPM 1317–27*, no. 696.
3. *CIPM 1300–07*, no. 266; *Wills*, 57, 128, 171, 378.
4. *Wills*, 128, 643-4; *Wills*, part 2, 453; *Coroner,* 163-5.
5. *CMSL*, 252.
6. *SPMR*, 72-3. Hamo made his will on 16 June 1332 and it was proved on 22 February 1333: *Wills*, 382. His parents were Thomas and Cecile.
7. *SPMR*, 69-70; *EMCR*, xxx-xxxvii.
8. *AP*, 366; *ODNB*; Thrupp, *Merchant Class*, 361.
9. *CPR 1313–17*, 382.
10. *Wills*, 609-10; *CIPM 1347–52*, no. 183; *CIPM 1365–69*, no. 162; *CIPM 1374–77*, no. 172; *CCR 1349–54*, 249; *CCR 1360–64*, 318-19, 394-6; *CCR 1374–77*, 107-8, 201-2, 411.
11. *CPR 1350–54*, 416; *Wills*, 340-41.
12. *Wills*, 544, 590-1; *Wills*, part 2, 1-2, 222; *CPR 1346–50*, 561; *CPR 1350–54*, 361; *CCR 1364–68*, 92-3, 488, 500; *ODNB*.
13. *MLLF*, 212-13; *LBE*, 224; *Wills*, 460-1, 699; *CIPM 1336–46*, no. 366.
14. *Wills*, part 2, 5; *CIPM 1352–60*, no. 439; *LBG*, 273.

15. TNA C 241/139/87; *CCR 1354–60*, 519. 'Simond Francis de Ponfreit', i.e from Pontefract, apprenticed his son Johan with the mercer Simond of Paris in July 1311 (*LBD*, 150), and is identified as Mayor Simond by the *ODNB*. As Simond's son and heir Thomas was born in the 1330s and he himself lived until 1358, this is surely another man of the same name; a man old enough to apprentice his son in 1311 cannot have been born later than *c.* 1280.

16. TNA C 241/113/55, C 131/10/24; *CIPM 1374–77*, no. 131.

Sheriffs

1. *LBC*, 79, 173-80; *LBD*, 31; *SPMR*, 69.
2. *LBC*, 110; *SPMR*, 23.
3. *Wills*, 143-4, 179, 389; *EMCR*, 250-1; *LAN*, no. 316.
4. *Coroner*, 61-2; *AP*, 304; *Wills*, 278.
5. *Coroner*, 114-16; *Wills*, 324.
6. *Coroner*, 248; *Wills*, 253, 349, 377, 477, 506, 688.
7. *Wills*, 361, 515-16; *Wills*, part 2, 75.
8. *DCAD*, vol. 2, no. B.2000; *Wills*, part 2, 89; *CCR 1374–77*, 415-16; Thornbury, *Old and New London*, vol. 1, 398; https://www.historyofparliamentonline.org/volume/1386-1421/member/burcester-sir-william-1407, accessed 5 October 2020.

Misteries

1. *LBE*, 13-14; *MLLF*, 159; *CPR 1327-30*, 29; *EMCR*, 51.
2. *LBE*, 232.
3. *SPMR*, 225.
4. *LBC*, 79-80; *LBE*, 232-4; *MLLF*, 153-4.
5. *LBE*, 87; *SPMR*, 213-14.
6. *MLLF*, 118-19, 178-9, 226-8; *CPR 1343–45*, 93, 278.
7. *SPMR*, 237.
8. *MLLF*, 120.
9. Curtis, 'London Lay Subsidy of 1332', 58.
10. *MLLF*, 145-6.
11. *CPR 1327–30*, 40 (*latoun, baterie, fer et asser* in the French original).

12. *CPR 1327–30*, 42-3, 323, 448; *LBE*, 232.
13. *EMCR*, 157-8. Possibly Gerard Fruter was the man of this name stabbed to death in October 1324: *Coroner*, 97-8.
14. *SPMR*, 229-30, 233.
15. *SPMR*, 235.
16. *MLLF*, 54; *LBE*, 116; *Coroner*, 132-4.
17. *MLLF*, 156-62; *Coroner*, 209; *CCR 1323–27*, 562-3; *CPR 1327–30*, 185.
18. *SPMR*, 103-7.

Apprentices

1. *LBB*, 241; *LBC*, 84; *SPMR*, xxxiii, 237.
2. *MLLF*, 227; *EMCR*, 158; *Munimenta*, vol. 3, 254; *SPMR*, xxxi; *LBD*, 97ff.
3. *SPMR*, 231; *EMCR*, 47-8.
4. *Wills*, 650; *SPMR*, 4.
5. *LBD*, 119. South Mimms is now in Hertfordshire.
6. *Coroner*, 134-5, 156-7, 226; *AP*, 313.
7. *SPMR*, 213.
8. *SPMR*, xxxiv; *LBD*, 97, 103.
9. *LBD*, 47, 107, 176.
10. *CIPM 1317–27*, no. 191; *Coroner*, 219-20; *CIPM 1352–60*, no. 330; and see 'Children' above.
11. *Wills*, 261, 411, 495, 517, 576, 636.
12. *EMCR*, 52, 166, 169-71, 190-2; *LBD*, 167; *Wills*, 194-5, 431, 445.
13. *LBC*, 81.
14. *LBE*, 8-9; *Wills*, 203; *SCR*, 28.
15. *LBE*, 200, 205; *Wills*, part 2, 57, 63. Isabel Taverner had brothers William and Thomas and sisters Alis and Johane; Alis, the eldest daughter, was born in 1317.
16. *Wills*, 439-40, 498.
17. *Wills*, 563-5.
18. *Wills*, 354; *LBE*, 250, 256.
19. *Wills*, 441.
20. *EMCR*, 148-9, 246-7; *LBD*, 175.
21. SAL MS 122, 17, 60, 87; *Wills*, 412, 434; *Wills*, part 2, 85.

Religion

1. *Wills*, 203, 303, 531.
2. *LBC*, 61; *LBD*, 248; *CPR 1301–7*, 47, 316; *Wills*, 214.
3. *SPMR*, 101 and *LBE*, 8, for Christchurch.
4. *LAN*, nos. 45, 80, 102, 211.
5. *CPR 1338–40*, 86; *CPR 1343–45*, 434.
6. *Wills*, 290, 416; *CMSL*, 251.
7. *LBD*, 254, 268; *Wills*, 221, 289.
8. *Wills*, 595, 616-17.
9. *Wills*, 657-9; *CPR 1350–54*, 242; *CIPM 1347–52*, no. 5. Johan inherited tenements in Gropecountelane from Thomas Burton, his second wife Isabel's uncle; see 'Roads'.
10. *Wills*, 453-4, 483-4, 637-8.
11. *CIM 1308–48*, nos. 1238, 1401; *CPR 1281–92*, 401-2; *CPR 1330–34*, 169.
12. *LBE*, 165.
13. *CIPM 1300–07*, no. 207.
14. *ODNB*.
15. *CIPM 1336–46*, no. 176, is Gravesend's IPM; Newport's will of 1315 is in *Wills*, 281.

Tower

1. *CCR 1323–27*, 13, 132; *CPR 1321–24*, 335, 425; *CMSL*, 258.
2. *SPMR*, 153.
3. *Coroner*, 34, 90-1.
4. *Coroner*, 33-4.
5. *CCW*, 268-9.
6. SAL MS 122, 56; *Coroner*, 90-1; *Wills*, 456-7.
7. *CPR 1307–13*, 557; *CPR 1334–38*, 472.
8. *CPR 1327–30*, 25; *CFR 1327–27*, 18.
9. *CCR 1313–18*, 4, 60, 124, 163; *CCR 1337–39*, 67.
10. *CFR 1307–19*, 18, 80.
11. *CMSL*, 250; *AP*, 272; *CCR 1313–18*, 308; *CPR 1313–17*, 410-11.
12. *CFR 1319–27*, 63, 70.
13. 'Plea Rolls for Staffordshire' on British History Online.

14. *CPR 1327–30*, 492; *CCR 1327–30*, 590; *CCR 1330–33*, 182.
15. *CPR 1338-40*, 180-81.

Bridge

1. *LBF*, 138.
2. *LAN*, no. 52.
3. *LBF*, 228; *MLLF*, 263-4.
4. *LBC*, 76; *EMCR*, 110.
5. *LBF*, 244.
6. *SCR*, 78.

Rivers

1. *EMCR*, 168; SAL MS 122, 7, 29, 54, 68; *CPR 1313–17,* 442; *CPR 1324–27*, 7, 116, 272, 300.
2. *LBF*, 108.
3. *CPR 1346–50*, 76.
4. Galloway and Murphy, 'Feeding the City', 6; *Wills*, 538.
5. *Issues of the Exchequer*, ed. Devon, 126; *AL*, 157; *AP*, 267.
6. *CIM 1308-48*, no. 57; see also *CPR 1324–27*, 283, 290.
7. *Coroner*, 100, 252-3.
8. *Coroner*, 194, 201.
9. *LAN*, nos. 109, 198-200.

Pestilence

1. *SPMR*, 164.
2. *Wills*, 492-656.
3. Megson, 'Mortality Among London Citizens', 125-33, using *LBF*, 143, and see Sloane's analysis in Chapter 3 of his *Black Death in London*.
4. Cited in Horrox, *The Black Death*, 65.
5. *LBE*, 232; *SPMR*, 228.
6. *MLLF*, 219, 240.

7. *LAN*, nos. 418-19.
8. *Wills*, 603, 649-51; *LBG*, 129, 146, 228; *CCR 1399–1402*, 419; TNA C 241/183/9.
9. *LBF*, 189-91, 193-4, 202-4, 211, 216; *LBG*, 8, 145, 219; *Wills*, 251, 312, 485, 543-4, 558, 560-1, 576, 581, 596, 611, 613-14; *Wills,* part 2, 183, 320; *LAN*, no. 625.
10. *LBF*, 191-2; *Wills*, 568-9.
11. *Wills*, 515-16, 594, 599, 612, 615, 618-19, 634; *Wills*, part 2, 65, 76.
12. *Wills*, 425, 531-2, 540, 542-3, 555-6, 573, 576, 580, 582, 622.
13. *Wills*, 543, 563, 640; *LBF*, 211, 229.
14. *Wills*, 542, 552, 569, 573, 576, 582, 616-17.
15. *Wills*, 598.
16. *Wills*, 423-4, 653-4, 692-3, 699-700; *Wills*, part 2, 1-3.
17. *Wills*, 535; *LBF*, 207.
18. *LBF*, 199, 207, 210, 222; *CPR 1346–50*, 459; *MLLF*, 253-8.
19. *Wills*, part 2, 1-82.